DRAFTING TO WIN

THE ULTIMATE GUIDE TO FANTASY FOOTBALL

ROBERT ZARZYCKI

authorHOUSE™

1663 LIBERTY DRIVE, SUITE 200
BLOOMINGTON, INDIANA 47403
(800) 839-8640
WWW.AUTHORHOUSE.COM

First published by AuthorHouse 06/10/05

ISBN: 1-4208-5919-6 (sc)

Printed in the United States of America
Bloomington, Indiana

This book is printed on acid-free paper.

Author: Robert Zarzycki

Copy Editor: Nicole Cicoria

Content Editors: Robert Giovine and Peter Loibl

Cover Design by Jeremy Truppi

For information visit DraftingToWin.com.

*For Mom, Dad, and Sis, for encouraging me
to follow my dreams.*

CONTENTS

ACKNOWLEDGEMENTS

Thanks to Emil Kadlec and Lenny Pappano for the World Championship of Fantasy Football. An extra thanks to Emil for supporting me when I told him about this book idea. Thanks to Bob Harris for taking me under his wings as well as editing many portions of this book. I'd like to thank Mark St. Amant for his advice on being a first-time author. Thanks to Brian Vermeulen and Bob Weaver for inviting me to play in their Hoboken Premier League which was the first fantasy football league I ever played in – life obviously has never been the same since. Thanks to my sister Cheryl who co-owned a restaurant with me years ago. It was her extra hard work that allowed me the free time to devise many of the strategies laid out in this book while preparing for the very first World Championship of Fantasy Football. Thanks to Joe Bryant and David Dodds for speeding up my learning curve in this fascinating hobby. Thanks to Rudy Brunetti and Sean Murphy for putting the TV "spotlight" on me and this book. I'd like to say thank you to Roger Craig for his support. A special thanks must also go out to Mary Ann and Linda Brunetti for their hospitality during my TV debut. Thanks to Nicole Cicoria for her tremendous job in copy editing. Thanks to Bert Giovine and Pete Loibl for making my material much more entertaining, enjoyable, and readable. Thanks to Jeremy Truppi for his outstanding cover design as well as his assistance in laying out all charts/graphs in this book. Thanks to Kevin Clegg for use of his camera on taking pictures of the trophy for the cover. Thanks to Anthony Gilardi for building DraftingToWin.com. Thanks to the AuthorHouse team, especially Author Services Representative April LeVay, Design Consultant Gina Paris and Book Designer Lori Fender, for doing a terrific job in helping me publish this book in a professional manner. And finally, the biggest of thanks to my parents, Terry and Chet. Without their support there's no way you would be reading this. I also should mention that my Dad, who knew next to nothing about fantasy football, helped proofread every word to make sure it was understandable for beginners.

THE AUTHOR'S STORY IN BRIEF

If you observe the types of casino games people play to win money and concentrate on those forms that involve any bit of skill such as single-deck blackjack, sports betting, and of course we cannot ignore poker in this day and age, you'll find that in each area there is a minority of disciplined individuals who actually make their living playing these games. They play utilizing their skills, making smart and consistent decisions in order to thrive on long-term, positive results. Well, consider Robert Zarzycki as one of those individuals who found such a niche in fantasy football.

Zarzycki's career in fantasy football blossomed after he realized it is a game that involves a lot of skill and plenty of people playing it for money. It is so widespread you can practically find it played in every corner of the United States, from Las Vegas to the common household to the local tavern to the corporate office. Fantasy football offers great profitability because most of the folks that play do it mostly for fun and hardly analyze the part of the game that requires skill. So Zarzycki made it a goal of his to study the hobby and figure out a way to win at it consistently. His results have been so successful you can consider him to be the first publicly known "professional fantasy footballer."

Zarzycki began playing fantasy sports in 1991, although he didn't start playing fantasy football until 1997 after joining a local league, competing against his high school and college buddies. Not knowing much about the game, he finished dead last that year yet, amazingly, he was hooked to the hobby forever. He couldn't believe how much fun it could be to "own" NFL football players. Thus, his passion for fantasy football was born.

After losing his second season Zarzycki's competitive side soon realized that fantasy football was really a game that could be won with the use of math, statistics and probability – areas in which he was well versed after receiving a Bachelor's of Science in Mechanical Engineering and a Master's of Business Administration from Rutgers University. He instantaneously advanced his level of competition to the point where he found himself in the fantasy playoffs every single year, and he eventually made it to the league's championship game in 2001.

Then life was really about to take a turn. Near the end of the 2001 season Zarzycki received an e-mail from Footballguys. com promoting the inception of the World Championship of Fantasy Football. The WCOFF is basically a high-stakes fantasy football competition held in Las Vegas pitting anyone who has the skill, guts, and money to contest for a $200,000 grand prize. (See "About the WCOFF" in next section).

Zarzycki was immediately fascinated about the idea of taking his proven skills, strategies and theories from the local level and testing them on the national stage. Unfortunately, he didn't have a whole lot of money at the time and the cost to enter the WCOFF was roughly $1,350 plus travel and hotel expenses. So he began to ask a few of his buddies to see if any of them wanted to co-own a WCOFF team in order to split the costs (and the rewards too). There were no takers.

That wasn't going to stop Zarzycki. Equipped with the knowledge and confidence to compete, he was willing to take a chance. He went ahead and financed his own entry fee and travel expenses via credit card. Risk quickly turned into reward as he grossed $22,000 in prize money that year after finishing in 2nd place among the 552 fantasy teams in the 2002 WCOFF competition. Ironically, this finish might be considered a disappointment because the eventual co-winners, Chris and Melissa Schussman, surpassed Zarzycki in total fantasy points during the very last Sunday night game to snatch the WCOFF title and $200,000 away.

One year wonder? Absolutely not. Zarzycki parlayed his earnings into another $15,000 in prize money the next year by taking 3rd place among 600 teams in the 2003 WCOFF. To put this two-year accomplishment into perspective, the odds of winning the WCOFF in 2002 as the Schussmans did in 2002 was 551:1; the odds of finishing 2nd and 3rd overall as Zarzycki did in 2002 and 2003 was 55,199:1. That's not a typo folks.

In 2004, Zarzycki was invited to play in four high-stakes-high-profile leagues including two WCOFF leagues, the first annual Fantasy Football Masters competition (fantasyfootballmasters.com), and the second annual Kentucky State Championship of Fantasy Football (champchamp.com). Not surprisingly, he finished all four leagues with a winning record. He tied for the best record in the Fantasy Football Master's League with a 7-4 record and collected a chunk of prize money after walloping his opponent in the playoffs. In the Kentucky State Championship season, he closed the season with the second-best record (7-4) in the Purple League.

Zarzycki's proudest 2004 moment may be from the WCOFF's first annual Hall of Fame League. WCOFF co-founders, Emil Kadlec and Lenny Pappano, were generous enough to put up $5,000 of their own money for this winner-take-all, invite-only event that pitted the twelve most successful and proven WCOFF'ers against each other to ultimately determine who's who in fantasy football. Zarzycki took revenge on those who denied him the grand prize in 2002 and 2003 by whipping Schussman's Point Mongerers (2002 WCOFF champ) in a head-to-head match-up in Week 2 and pummeling Hayden and Michaelson's *Meat Helmets* (2003 WCOFF champ) in Week 5. Zarzycki was one of only four teams to reach the Hall of Fame playoffs but unfortunately fell short to Jon and Ian Millman (FFChamps.com) who were very deserving of their Hall of Fame victory.

Aside from playing fantasy football Zarzycki is very involved in the industry, on the Web and in magazines. He was hired by Footballguys.com in 2003 for his expert analysis on player profiles, projections, and rankings. In 2004 Zarzycki signed on as a senior strategist at Footballdiehards.com. His work there involves weekly columns including the popular *Sleepers and Stay Aways.* He is also actively involved on the Diehards message board all year long assisting fantasy footballers with drafting, trading, and starting lineup inquiries. In 2005, Zarzycki joined as a member of the Fantasy Sports Trade Association (FSTA.org), a non-profit trade organization founded for the betterment of the fantasy sports industry and to encourage participation in Fantasy Sports Leagues.

During the fantasy football "off-season" (January through June) Zarzycki spends his time writing for various fantasy football publications such as *Fantasy Football Cheatsheets*, Fantasy Footballdiehards.com, *Fantasy Football Draftbook*, and *Fantasy Pro Forecast*. In fact, he was featured on the cover of the 2004 issue of *Fantasy Pro Forecast* for his article, "Projecting Statistics Using AVT," focusing on the Average Value Theory (revised and published in this book).

Zarzycki is not shy to the television either. In November of 2004, he was featured on Comcast SportsNet's *SPOTLIGHT: Fantasy Football* for his unsurpassed success in the World Championship of Fantasy Football. The show aired nationwide via DirecTV and locally in the greater Philadelphia area.

Robert Zarzycki (left) and 2002 WCOFF
Champ Chris Schussman (right) hang at
ESPN Zone Las Vegas

ABOUT THE WCOFF

Two industry veterans, Emil Kadlec of Footballdiehards. com and Lenny Pappano of Draftsharks.com, have created the fantasy football event of the year known as the World Championship of Fantasy Football (wcoff.com). This league has been so successful that many are trying to emulate the idea, but no one has succeeded yet.

The WCOFF main event involves hundreds of fantasy footballers buying in for approximately $1,450 for the chance to compete for a grand prize of $200,000 and the coveted position of being named World Champion of Fantasy Football. Each year the event's draft is held at a major hotel and casino in Las Vegas. The MGM Grand hosted the first annual WCOFF. In 2003 it was the Rio, and the Hilton Las Vegas played its part in 2004 and 2005.

According to Pappano, the WCOFF's creation came not from watching a sporting event, but from Pappano and Kadlec watching the World Series of Poker held at Binion's Horseshoe Hotel and Casino in Las Vegas. So it's no wonder that the WCOFF shows a very strong parallel to the WSOP. Both are held in Vegas annually, both are considered the biggest event in their respective industries, and both offer higher payouts than any other competition available in their respective industries.

Similarly, the WCOFF and the WSOP both offer a series of smaller events leading up to the main event. For example, there's an auction WCOFF league that costs around $650 to enter, and its draft is usually held the day before the main event. This not only creates an atmosphere of excitement and anticipation for those fantasy football fanatics waiting for the main event, but it also allows some of them the opportunity to enter multiple WCOFF leagues. The WCOFF festivities culminate in a fabulous sports fan party at the ESPN Zone in the New York New York Hotel and Casino in Las Vegas. All these activities combined truly make the WCOFF the fantasy football event of the year.

Of course, it's the WCOFF main event that gets most of the attention because it attracts a significant majority of the entrants, and its winner pockets a cool $200,000. It's also the main event in which Robert Zarzycki has succeeded to get his recognition as being one of the best fantasy football managers in the world. So, from this point forward "WCOFF" shall refer to just the main event.

The WCOFF keeps growing each year. The event consisted of 552 teams during its inaugural season in 2002, then it grew to 600 teams in 2003, and they saw an astonishing 672 teams enter the WCOFF in 2004.

Since most WCOFF teams are co-owned – two people per team are allowed to attend the event, manage a fantasy team, and share the costs/prizes – you are looking at well over 1000 individuals participating in the main event each year. Imagine hundreds of fantasy football fanatics shouting and drafting NFL players in a single room simultaneously. What makes the WCOFF such an electric experience is that it is such an incredible, exciting, and enjoyable event. WCOFF'ers look forward to it every year, and with a little more exposure, who knows how big this thing will get in the future!

The true beauty of the entire WCOFF might be how Kadlec and Pappano have done a marvelous job in setting up the rules, scoring, and prize distribution to satisfy the needs of most fantasy footballers. For something so big it could not be more organized than it already is. They were extremely wise in giving everyone the realistic chance to win a ton of money while maintaining the feel and atmosphere of playing in a local league – which is what most people are used to playing. The trick was dividing all the fantasy teams into random leagues of twelve teams per league, and then to let each of those leagues draft players and play a season of fantasy football independent of one another as if each were its own "local league." For example, the 672 fantasy teams in the 2004 WCOFF were divided into 56 separate leagues. Each league had its own web-site where owners can manage their teams, view the standings, analyze player statistics, and even talk trash in a message board forum. The fact that each WCOFF league develops its own unique camaraderie and level of competition is what makes the league extraordinary.

The winner of each league is finally determined during NFL week 12, after playing an 11-game regular season. The week 12 championship game pits the league's best record against the league's highest fantasy point scorer to see who ultimately goes on to advance to the WCOFF playoffs. Actually, some fantasy teams that lose this championship game still go on to advance to the playoffs if their overall standings during the regular season are good enough.

Furthermore, the competition gets truly exciting in the WCOFF playoffs. The format consists of all the league winners battling it out for the top prize money during NFL weeks 13-16 in an all-out war based on who can accumulate the most points during this four-week span. Of course, the winner of this playoff is awarded $200,000, but there is much more at stake. The WCOFF champ also receives an all-expense paid trip to the NFL city hosting the Super Bowl. Here is where the $200,000 check will be presented in a glorious fashion at an exclusive pre-Super Bowl party. As an added bonus, the winner has the opportunity to rub elbows with and bump into many television personalities, celebrities and ex-NFL greats during the festivities. To give you an idea, in 2002 and 2003 the WCOFF check was presented by ESPN's Suzy Kolber. The 2003 champs, Alex and Jed, got the chance to meet Kansas City Chiefs superstar RB Priest Holmes during their trip to Houston, TX.

If that's not enough, the WCOFF champ also receives an exquisite customized crystal trophy worth approximately $5,000. This WCOFF crystal trophy is created by Crystal Signatures, which also designed and created the MVP trophy of the NHL All-Star Game.

It's important to point out that not just the World Champ gets paid good money. Each WCOFF league winner wins $5,000, each league runner-up wins $1,500, and each league's third place finisher receives $500, according to 2004's prize distribution. That's not bad considering there are only twelve teams per league. Furthermore, the WCOFF pays thousands of dollars to other top finishers in the playoff rounds. For example, in 2004, the 2nd place finisher overall received a nice lump sum of $45,000. See the chart below for a complete view of all prizes paid out in 2004:

2004 PRIZES

WCOFF Place	Prize
WCOFF Champion	$200,000
Customized Crystal Trophy	$5,000
Trip to Jacksonville, FL on the weekend of Super Bowl XXXIX (no tickets)	$2,500
2nd Place	$45,000
3rd Place	$22,500
4th Place	$13,500
5th Place	$9,000
6th Place	$7,200
7th Place	$6,300
8th Place	$5,000
9th & 10th	2005 Events Free
56 League Champs	$5,000 Each
2nd place in each league	$1,500 Each
3nd place in each league	$500 Each
Consolation Bowl Winner	$3,000
2nd	$2,500
3rd	$2,000
4th	$1,600
5th	$1,200
6th	$1,000
7th	$700
8th	$500
9th & 10th	2005 Events Free

BEST LEAGUE PRIZE:
THE LEAGUE WITH THE MOST TOTAL FANTASY POINTS
(WEEKS 1-11) WILL BE AWARDED $1,000 PER TEAM
FROM THE SECOND PLACE TEAM TO THE TWELFTH PLACE
TEAM. TOTAL OF $11,000 FOR THE ENTIRE LEAGUE.

Finally, if you are curious about the WCOFF scoring rules, they are in Appendix A.

Robert Zarzycki (left) and WCOFF co-founder
Emil Kadlec (right) pose after 2004 WCOFF
Draft

Robert Zarzycki (left), Chet Zarzycki (middle), and
2002 WCOFF Champ Chris Schussman (right)
enjoy themselves at the WCOFF draft party at the
ESPN Zone, Las Vegas

ABOUT THE NFFC AND FANTASY FOOTBALL MASTERS

With the advent and success of the WCOFF, and coinciding with the United States philosophy of being the "land of opportunity," we are witnessing many other fantasy football entrepreneurs offer their own high-stakes versions of the WCOFF. Leagues such as the Fantasy Football Tournament of Champions, Million Dollar Fantasy League, the National Fantasy Football Championship, Fantasy VIPs, Kahuna Frenzy, and the World Fantasy Tour all came about within a few years of the inaugural season of the WCOFF. Nevertheless, fantasy football fanatics are constantly lurking and searching for that next big league that offers a good game, mucho credibility, and a great deal of prize money. Two that demand much attention are the Fantasy Football Masters and the National Fantasy Football Championship.

Fantasy Football Masters (FF Masters) (fantasyfootballmasters. com) seems to be the most prestigious and up-and-coming high-stakes internet league. Adding much to its credibility is that this league is also owned and operated by Kadlec and Pappano, the co-founders of the WCOFF. In its inaugural season of 2004, Fantasy Football Masters paid nearly $100,000 in total prize money including a top prize of $30,000 and a trip to

Jacksonville for the Super Bowl. The entry fee was $500, and all the scoring and league rules are similar to the WCOFF. A large number of fantasy football experts entered to play in this extraordinary league. Chris Schussman (2002 WCOFF champ), Alex Hayden (2003 WCOFF Champ), Greg Kellogg (FantasyAsylum.com), and Stacie The Sports Chick (Maxim Girl) all competed. All in all, the prize structure was terrific, the competition was friendly, (and hot in some instances), the online draft and regular season were managed very well, XpertLeagues.com did a tremendous job in managing the online commissioner software, and most importantly, this author made the FFMasters playoffs and won several hundred dollars!

The National Fantasy Football Championship (fantasyfoot ballchampionship.com), also known as the NFFC, is a high-stakes league that shows similarities to both the WCOFF and FF Masters, and it is lead by the expertise and experience of Greg Ambrosius and the staff at Krause Publications. Like the FF Masters, the NFFC was started in 2004. However, the NFFC offers a much higher payout than the FF Masters including a whopping $100,000 to its first place winner. Like the WCOFF, the NFFC conducts a live draft with a buy-in of around $1,250, and the fantasy scoring and league rules are very similar with a few exceptions such as NFFC leagues are comprised of 14 teams as opposed to 12-team leagues in the WCOFF. One attractive feature of the NFFC is that it hosts drafts in three major cities (Las Vegas, Chicago, New York) with plans to eventually expand to every NFL city. This way more people can participate in the huge buy-in event without having to worry about inconvenient travel plans and expenses.

There is no guarantee that any high-stakes leagues will be around in the long run, but with Emil Kadlec, Lenny Pappano, and Greg Ambrosius in control, you should feel very comfortable entering any league these gentlemen host. These reputable fantasy footballers take exceptional care of their leagues and pay close attention to their participants. Most importantly, all their winners are treated like gold!

LOCAL LEAGUES

Over 90 percent of you who buy this book most likely will have no intention of entering a high-stakes league such as the WCOFF or NFFC. Rather, your intention will be to rule your own local league and create dynasty havoc year after year against friends, families, and personal foes. That's great news actually. Although this book may revolve around the WCOFF, these same concepts originated from experience gained playing in a local league -- the Hoboken Premier League (now called the CrackerSlaps League). Therefore, you can apply all of the concepts and formulas listed in this book to almost any fantasy football league. In fact, the concepts will be especially strong if you applied them in homegrown and local fantasy leagues considering the competition will be blindsided by how hard you are going to hit them. So, enjoy the book, win lots of money, and take down the trophy no matter what league you play in!

FOREWORD

By

Emil Kadlec

In the fall of 1962, in the old Manhattan Hotel, a unique man got together with two friends during an Oakland Raider east coast road trip and laid down the framework for what is now a billion dollar a year industry. It would be fascinating to get his impression of how his hobby has grown. Unfortunately, Wilfred Winkenbach passed away in 1993.

He left us with his creation, and now fantasy football has turned into a monster. Millions of people play. Some play for fun, and some play for the ultimate prestige: to become the World Champion of Fantasy Football.

In 2002, the World Championship of Fantasy Football (WCOFF) exploded on the scene, giving the elite fantasy football players a platform to test their skills against each other. The beauty about an open contest of such magnitude is that great fantasy football players come in all shapes and sizes. Yes, there are dozens of industry types who proclaim their brilliance, and a few have actually done very well in the WCOFF. However, the best of the best have been a unique and rare breed. One of these standouts is Rob Zarzycki.

Rob did what many believed could not be done. In the WCOFF's inaugural season, he finished 2nd overall. But that wasn't enough for him; he followed it up with a 3rd place finish the very next year! A top three repeat is phenomenal. No one else has even come close.

So what is Rob's secret? Is he just lucky? The more I get to know him, the more I realize how unique his talent is. Not only does he have a truly modern and well thought out drafting strategy, he also has a real knack for understanding the ins and outs of drafting and managing his fantasy team throughout the year.

For me, this book is a must for all levels of fantasy football players. If Mr. Winkenbach could only see how far his hobby has come, how detailed and competitive the drafts are, I think he would be proud of where we are now. And because of this ever-increasing competitiveness, Rob Zarzycki's concepts are critical for fantasy football players to understand to reach the top and stay there.

Knowledge is the key. Don't be left out.

CHAPTER 1 – INTRODUCTION TO FANTASY FOOTBALL

My buddy Tom loathes Peyton Manning with a passion. Ever since Manning was a freshman at Tennessee, Tom couldn't stand how the experts praised him as a great college football quarterback who would win multiple Heisman Trophies. He couldn't stand how these experts claimed this when Manning could not beat Florida, never mind win a national championship.

His intense hatred for Manning grew even more in the professional ranks where experts portrayed Manning as the league's best player even though he couldn't win a playoff game until his sixth season. Tom's hatred of Manning increased following the QB's dream individual season where Manning topped Dan Marino's touchdown record, but he could not muster up one single score for his team against New England in the playoffs—when it counted. Furthermore, Tom couldn't stand Manning's golden boy image, his pedigree or how he pointed at the defense at the line of scrimmage to communicate to his teammates. My buddy literally foamed at the mouth when someone would even mention his name.

Now, despite all of this hatred, who do you think Tom chose for his first draft choice when he had the first pick of his

2004 fantasy football league draft? Could it have been Priest Holmes? Randy Moss, perhaps? Gus Frerotte?

Nope! It was none other than...Drum roll, please...You guessed it, Peyton Manning. Now to make a long story short, Tom won his league single handedly because of Peyton Manning.

Not surprisingly, Tom's criticizing of Manning completely stopped all of a sudden. There were no quips about his lack of mobility, no complaints about his won-lost record, and no insults about his mother. Manning became the greatest player in the world to Tom.

While I'm not personally a big fan of drafting a QB in the first round, the point here is that this little tale epitomizes the craze of what fantasy football has become to millions of fans around the globe. Fantasy football has become immensely popular because it affords the opportunity for the average Joe to live vicariously through NFL players and owners, and fans get to realize what it takes to manage a football team. Fantasy football is also such a growing sensation because it enables fans to forget about the personal feelings they may have towards a player and cause them to worry about what truly counts: performance.

In other words, fantasy football offers NFL fans the otherwise unattainable ability to "get in" on their favorite sport by requiring them to assume all the responsibilities associated with operating real NFL franchises.

By asking participants to serve as owner, general manager, and head coach, anybody from the casual observer to the most ardent fan is afforded the unique opportunity to greatly increase the level of fun and excitement they already draw from NFL games as a "normal" fan to exhilarating new heights.

Now, aside from a date with Pamela Anderson: What could possibly beat that?

The short answer, of course, is darned little.

Apparently, millions of "you" already realize the excitement. According to a Bob Harris Interactive Poll in 2003, nearly 30 million Americans are on the Fantasy bandwagon, a number that grows exponentially with the start of each new season. That same poll tells us the average fantasy football manager spends $110 a year on the hobby. Add the fact that many companies and fantasy football entrepreneurs – such as Emil Kadlec, Lenny Pappano, and Ryan Houston – are successfully operating high-stakes "professional" leagues, it's a no-brainer that the industry is skyrocketing. The World Championship of Fantasy Football itself, co-founded by Kadlec and Pappano, pays out over half a million dollars in prize money with the champ receiving a cool $200,000. Folks, fantasy football is a multi-billion dollar industry.

This brings us to what actually might be cooler than the exhilaration of playing fantasy football, and that is the exhilaration of winning lots of money at playing fantasy football. Not many reach these heights, which makes it even more thrilling when you find yourself on top of the fantasy football world. For all those people who haven't succeeded yet, never before have the famous words from the heralded Green Bay Packer Coach Vince Lombardi, "Winning isn't everything, it's the only thing," probably meant so much.

This is exactly why I have written – and most likely you have purchased – this book: so you can achieve the exhilaration of winning. However, one must wonder, if winning is "the only thing" and so many people are gunning for it, does this make it more difficult to achieve? Surprisingly, winning is not that difficult.

Similar to the average schmuck at a poker table who is just there to have fun, the good fantasy football player knows that this is a game of skill. Therefore, the wise and disciplined fantasy football player can easily beat that other player when he applies his skill. Furthermore, an astute fantasy football player can drastically increase his odds of winning by managing his fantasy football team like a tight and aggressive poker player.

I'll emphasize this again: fantasy football is a game of skill! Yes, I have won a great deal of money because of this concept. This means the studious can win quite often. Fantasy football offers great profitability because, as I estimate, about 75 percent of the people who play do it for the fun of it without much regard for its skill aspect. These people may snag the occasional playoff spot or championship title, but they unknowingly rely on lady luck to get there. As they say in the poker world, these people are "dead money."

Inevitably, whenever skill and money intertwine, you can expect the shark fins to appear. For even if lady luck strikes in favor of the unskilled hobbyists, fantasy football often has plenty of leftovers for the sharks to devour. I know because I've made a living "feasting" off of fantasy football. The truth remains, a skilled fantasy football participant can take advantage of opponents in a variety of ways, and none are more significant than having draft-day savvy which is what this book is all about teaching.

With the advent of several high-stakes leagues, I imagine many people will make a nice profit in fantasy football for years to come. I have no doubt many of you will study this book and achieve long-term profitability in fantasy football whether it's a league in your hometown, online against strangers, or in the Las Vegas glamour. But before you get to that point, it's a prerequisite that you understand the basics of fantasy football including its participants, components, and terminology. You can then learn to strategize from this understanding. Here are the basics:

MANAGER

Here is where you get to pretend you are Bob Kraft or Jimmy Jones. The manager is essentially the owner of the team. As the manager, you are responsible for duties such as paying team costs (entry fees), drafting players, submitting weekly starting lineups, making trades, adding/dropping players, and much more. These are duties similar to that of a NFL team manager, coach, and general manager combined.

CO-MANAGER

It is common for two or more people to co-manage a fantasy football team and share the responsibilities of being a manager. There are many reasons why participants would want to become co-managers:

1)   The entry fee is too expensive for one person.

2)   One person does not have enough time to manage the team alone.

3)   One person wants to learn from another, especially during the draft.

4)   It can be more fun with a partner.

Having a co-manager can be like having a double-edged sword. Although it can be advantageous to combine two heads into one, it can turn counter-productive if both are not on the same page. If you are considering a co-manager, then make sure you understand each other's goals, strategies, responsibilities, and rewards (rights to profits) before committing. When things are done right, it can be a marvelous and exhilarating year for all. But if the fantasy team starts losing, then co-managers tend to blame each other, especially when there's money at stake.

LEAGUE COMMISSIONER

Like Paul Tagliabue on a small scale, the commissioner is the person, or company in the case of the WCOFF, responsible for creating and governing the fantasy football league. Specific duties of the commissioner include finding managers, collecting entry fees, establishing rules and scoring, setting a draft date and location, determining draft positions, keeping track of the draft, logging team rosters, supervising league activity, and ultimately awarding prizes.

ONLINE COMMISSIONER SERVICES

Also known as "league hosts," these are online services that handle all the activities involved in a fantasy league from drafting players to keeping track of team rosters to calculating a team's score at the end of the day. A good site will operate in real-time so you can keep track of your fantasy score, as well as your opponents, exactly as the action is happening on TV!

Most services charge an annual fee of around $50-100 per league, but from my experience it is well worth the investment. Some of my favorite commissioner services include CBS Sportsline.com, Total Quality Stats.com, and Xpertleagues. com. The World Championship of Fantasy Football is commissioned by TQStats.com, and Fantasy Football Masters uses Xpertleagues.com. Both provide excellent services.

THE DRAFT

The draft occurs when fantasy managers get to pick up players to fill the fantasy roster, which is generally around 20 players max. Once someone drafts a player, no one else can. The earlier a manager gets to pick, the better because then there are more NFL players available.

Fantasy drafts can sometimes be as easy as choosing sides for kickball in gym class to as difficult as the actual NFL draft held during the third Saturday in April. Fantasy drafts can last anywhere from a few hours to several days, depending on the number of rounds and the length of time allowed per pick. The number of rounds is equivalent to the size of the roster. If your team can have up to 20 players then the draft would be 20 rounds long. This makes perfect sense. The length of time a manager has to make a pick can range from a minute to several hours. Most live drafts (i.e., everyone is physically in the same room) allow about one minute per pick, which translates into approximately a four-hour draft. However, some online drafts, where managers are apt to be on very different schedules as well as different time zones, may allow managers several hours per pick for convenience. This can translate into a draft extending over several days.

THE DRAFT ORDER

The draft order decides who gets to pick first, second, etc. It is the commissioner's responsibility to give each manager a random draft position. "Draft position" is the spot, or slot, when a manager gets to pick. For instance, if you were given the No. 4 spot, then you would be the fourth manager to pick.

Each manager gets one pick per round. It used to be that each manager always picked in the same draft position each round known as a "straight draft." To be in the No. 4 spot meant to always be the fourth manager to pick in each round. After a while, many fantasy participants felt this was an unfair drafting system because certain managers always picked before others in every round. Consequently, a new drafting style was developed known as "serpentine drafting." A serpentine system has managers picking from lowest-to-highest draft positions in the odd rounds and highest-to-lowest draft positions in the even rounds. If you were the No. 4 draft position in a 12-team league you would be the fourth team to pick in rounds 1, 3, 5, etc. However, you would be the ninth team to pick in rounds 2, 4, 6, etc. This style is popular because it negates the advantage managers have by drafting early in one round because they are forced to draft later in the next.

"ON THE CLOCK"

A manager is "on the clock" when it's time to draft a player. Managers have a pre-specified time limit to make a pick. Once a manager drafts a player, the next manager in the draft order is immediately put on a new clock so the draft can proceed in a timely fashion. If a manager misses a pick (the clock runs down to zero), then the next manager in the drafting order gets to choose, and the manager who let the time run down to zero cannot pick again until the next manager in line makes a pick. Once that happens the manager who passed is given another window of time, sometimes just a few seconds, to pick a player. If this window is passed up again the draft continues to the next manager waiting in the draft order, and the process repeats itself until the manager who keeps passing finally drafts a player. I've actually passed on my pick in several occasions for strategy purposes. This will be covered later in the book.

THE CHEAT SHEET

Do you know that card of hits and sticks that you are supposed to keep with you at the blackjack table? Do you remember that one time when you should have doubled down and it cost you a fortune because you didn't pay attention to the small details? Well, just like that blackjack card, the cheat sheet is the single most important tool a person can have at the draft. It's basically a sheet of paper that contains mostly fantasy player rankings and projections. Player rankings tell the fantasy manager which NFL players are more valuable within each of the fantasy positions. So when the manager decides he wants to draft a QB it's a simple matter of taking the highest available ranked QB listed on the cheat sheet. Player projections tell the fantasy manager how many fantasy points each player is projected to score that season. These projections become important in determining which position to draft from each round. I will explain in much more detail how to create your own successful cheat sheet as you read through the chapters of this book.

STARTING LINEUPS

During the season fantasy managers are required to submit weekly starting lineups in order to compete against the other fantasy teams. For instance, the required starting lineup in the WCOFF is 1 QB, 2 RBs, 3 WRs, 1 TE, 1 K, 1 D/ST, and 1 Flex (RB/WR/TE).

The deadline for submitting the starting lineup is usually around 12 noon or 1pm on Sunday, which is just prior to the first NFL game kicking-off. If no lineup is submitted in a given week then it is assumed (by the commissioner and commissioner service) that the team's starting lineup is the same as the prior week.

Unlike real sports, the fantasy starting lineup cannot be altered once the games begin, even if a player is injured on the first play of the NFL game. In other words, there are no substitutes allowed in fantasy football while the NFL games are being played. This allows fantasy managers to just kick back, relax, and enjoy all the action without having to worry about who to sit and who to start.

Of course, this locked-in lineup also means only the starting lineup can score fantasy points for your team in a given week. The remaining players on a fantasy roster not in the starting lineup, known as bench players, do not contribute any fantasy points even if you watch them score three touchdowns and play a great game in the NFL. This makes it all the more important when deciding who to start and who to bench.

Fantasy starting lineups have both offensive and defensive positions, although most leagues heavily favor the offense because that's what generates the most attention.

OFFENSIVE FANTASY POSITIONS

With all proper respect to offensive lineman, the "glamour positions" are what counts in fantasy football. The main offensive positions in fantasy football are the quarterback (QB), running back (RB), wide receiver (WR), tight end (TE), and kicker (K). One note I'd like to make is that the RB position in fantasy football includes both NFL RBs and NFL FBs (fullbacks). Also, some commissioners do not separate the WR and TE positions making all NFL TEs to be considered fantasy WRs. My apologies to you, Orlando Pace!

Another offensive position that has recently become very popular in fantasy football is known as the flex starter, or flex position. This position can be labeled such as "RB/WR/TE" which means the manager has a choice to start a RB, WR, or TE as the flex starter. More and more leagues are turning into "flex leagues" which require a flex starter. The WCOFF and Fantasy Football Masters use a flex position.

DEFENSIVE FANTASY POSITIONS

Not to ignore those who believe in the maxim that "defense wins championships," the vast majority of fantasy leagues also require their managers to start a single defensive/special teams position abbreviated as D/ST. Although D/ST is a single fantasy position or "player" it is actually comprised of an entire unit of NFL players. For example, if you drafted the Miami Dolphins as your D/ST then all the defensive and special teams players on the Miami Dolphins work towards getting fantasy points for that position. D/ST includes a NFL team's defense, kickoff unit, kickoff return unit, punting unit, and punting return unit. Field goal units are not considered as part of a fantasy team's D/ST because the kicker is usually a separate offensive position. However, the defensive side of a field goal unit is considered part of a D/ST because it is part of a NFL team's defense. Again, all the stats and fantasy points accumulated by all the NFL players involved with the D/ST are credited to a fantasy team's score.

Some fantasy football leagues do not involve a D/ST rather they allow owners to draft and start individual defensive players, also known as IDPs. IDP leagues generally include the following defensive fantasy positions: defensive lineman (DL), linebacker (LB), and defensive back (DB).

Although this book refers mostly to drafting offensive fantasy positions and D/STs, it's important to note that the same concepts can be applied to drafting IDPs.

FANTASY SCORING

Prior to draft day and the season starting, there has to be a set of rules that let the managers know what fantasy points will be scored according to an NFL player's statistics. This is known as fantasy scoring. There are two general types of fantasy scoring leagues: basic scoring and performance leagues. Basic scoring awards fantasy points solely for touchdowns. For example, six points may be awarded for each touchdown your fantasy player scores, and there are no other scoring possibilities. Basic scoring used to be prevalent years ago, but nowadays the vast majority of leagues are performance-based, including the WCOFF.

Performance leagues typically offer fantasy points for the following offensive NFL achievements: passing TDs, passing yards, receiving/rushing TDs, receiving/rushing yards, receptions, two-point conversions, extra points, and field goals. Sometimes bonus points are awarded for extra-long field goals and/or TDs. Defensive and special teams' NFL achievements can include sacks, interceptions, fumbles recovered, safeties, blocked field goals, blocked punts, and returned TDs. The league commissioner is responsible for ultimately determining how many fantasy points are awarded for each of these various NFL achievements. Today's standard in scoring seems to be that of the WCOFF, provided in Appendix A.

There are three reasons for the movement from basic to performance scoring. First, managers play fantasy football for the excitement and action. Performance leagues satisfy this need by awarding fantasy points for almost every single NFL play. Second, basic scoring relies on too much luck. TDs in the NFL can be sporadic, and they are prone to be few and far between. Good NFL players could easily hit a TD drought while mediocre players can hit a lucky streak of getting into the end zone. Remember Jerome "The Bus" Bettis' touchdown streak in the Pittsburgh Steeler's first game against the Oakland Raiders in 2004? He scored three TDs after rushing for just one yard (yeah, figure that one out) while starting RB Duce Staley rushed for 91 yards and zero TDs. So, to be a winning fantasy manager in a basic scoring league usually means to be very lucky. Third, basic scoring leagues were deemed unfair. Many managers complained because their fantasy players gained a lot of yards for zero fantasy points only to watch other fantasy players get easy short-yard TDs and lots of fantasy points. Fantasy managers felt this was unjustified. Such a problem is obviously removed in performance leagues. Therefore, this book focuses on drafting players in performance leagues.

THE FANTASY FOOTBALL SEASON

The fantasy season is comprised of a regular season and playoffs. The fantasy regular season, like the NFL, pits teams against one another in head-to-head weekly match-ups. The manager that sets his/her starting lineup to score the most fantasy points wins the match-up.

The goal of fantasy managers in the regular season is to qualify for the fantasy playoffs. The usual requirement to qualify for the playoffs is to have one of the best records, if not the best record. Another playoff qualification method that has recently become popular in certain fantasy football leagues is having the most fantasy points scored during the regular season. The WCOFF, for example, qualifies two teams for its playoffs – the team with the most wins and the team with the most fantasy points scored.

Whether it's the fantasy regular season or playoffs, fantasy games can only be played during the NFL regular season and not during the NFL playoffs. The NFL playoffs are incompatible with fantasy football because most NFL players, also fantasy players, are no longer playing football since their respective NFL teams were eliminated from playoff contention. This makes it unfeasible for fantasy managers to set a complete starting lineup. If actual playoffs counted in the standings, then guys like Joey Harrington or Jake Plummer would be useless for your team.

In addition, commissioners should make sure the fantasy season does not extend itself into the last week of the NFL season (Week 17). Like the NFL playoffs Week 17 is troublesome for fantasy leaguers because many starting NFL players who are important fantasy players are subject to sit out or see minimal playing time in Week 17. There are two scenarios that make this possible. The first is when a NFL team is eliminated from the playoffs (usually many teams are eliminated by NFL week 17). Here the NFL coach may decide to play second and third string players because his team isn't "playing for anything" anymore, and he now is afforded the opportunity to play his bench players to see what potential they have in the future. The second situation is when a NFL team already clinched a playoff berth (many NFL teams clinch a berth before the last week). Again, these teams are considered to be "playing for nothing" since they already clinched. Here the coach will often bench his starters in order to minimize risk of injury prior to when the games really count. Could you imagine the horror of turning on the television to see Dave Speewack starting over Michael Vick or Hands Maguilicutty playing instead of Terrell Owens because their coaches wanted to rest the star players for the playoffs? This would be disastrous to your team's point earning potential. In either case, NFL week 17 is disastrous for fantasy football, so most commissioners will steer clear of it.

FREE AGENCY "ADD/DROP"

From "duds to studs," free agents are NFL players not on anyone's fantasy roster. NFL players that are not drafted become free agents. The term "add/drop" was coined because whenever you add (or pick up) a free agent player, you must drop a player from your roster so as not to exceed maximum roster limits.

Managers may look to pick up a free agent player under any of the following circumstances:

1) One or more fantasy players on the roster are injured and need replacement.

2) A "fill-in player" is needed to cover during a fantasy starter's bye week.

3) A potential fantasy star is on the rise and no one drafted or picked him up yet.

4) A free agent becomes more valuable than a player currently on the roster.

Many times, several managers will chase the same free agent at the same time. Therefore, there are several ways a commissioner can govern and supervise the free agency market. One method is the "first come, first served" system. Whoever picks up the free agent first, gets him.

Known as the waiver wire system, another method is to allow the teams with the worst record first dibs on free agents. This system encourages league parity by giving worse teams a better chance to improve by picking up the top prospects.

The World Championship of Fantasy Football uses yet another method known as a blind bidding process. This system gives each manager an annual budget of funny money. Throughout the season managers can bid on free agent players but such bids must be made without knowing who the other managers are bidding on. Hence the term "blind bidding." The highest weekly bidder gets the free agent. If a manager spends the entire budget before the bidding season comes to an end, many times this "end" occurs before the fantasy playoffs begin; then, no more bids are allowed by that manager.

TRADING

Do you remember how much fun you had as a kid trading your Topps All Pro Joe Montana and Art Monk cards for a Dan Marino rookie card? Well, trading players during the fantasy football season is no different. Trading is when managers swap players and/or draft picks. Many find this aspect of fantasy football to be the most enjoyable part. Managers will spend hours a day concocting trade offers and counter-offers just so they can talk fantasy football with their buddies. As a manager you should jump into the fray, or at least observe what is going on since you may find some great players available from trade offers.

Although fantasy footballers are not on the same level as Microsoft, you should pay attention for collusion. Some managers purposely make lopsided trades in order to strengthen a certain team. If you find such shenanigans, present them to your league commissioner for review. If you tend to be a skeptic filled with paranoia on every trade, have no fear. There are many leagues available, including the WCOFF, that do not allow trading for the very reason that collusion is possible. If you join such a league you sacrifice one of the most enjoyable aspects of fantasy football, but at least you can be rest assured it's collusion-free. In maintaining the credibility of this great hobby, I should mention I have yet to personally witness collusion. Even so, I still enjoy the peace of mind of no trading in high-stakes leagues.

Chapter 2 – Finding and Choosing a Fantasy Football League

Do you buy jeans that are two sizes too big or wear shirts that are so tight that it looks like you are trying to squeeze into your fifth grade little league jersey? Of course not! You always want to buy the clothes that fit. Similarly, you must know what league to choose that best fits the goals you have for your team. So, before we get into the nitty-gritty of how to win in fantasy football let's cover the variety of fantasy football leagues that you can choose from. There are so many options involved in choosing a league, and each variation entails a unique strategy. Some cater to the skilled manager, others favor the lucky, and some favor those who have a lot of time on their hands, etc. Bottom line, it makes no sense to join a league if it doesn't fit your mold, especially if your fantasy football knowledge and strategies cannot be applied to their full extent.

This brings us to the first step in strategizing to win and that is: selecting the right league. The following material describes the various options that are made available when choosing or creating fantasy football leagues. I recommend reading this chapter twice – once now and once after you've learned all the strategic concepts in this book – for then you can better grasp which leagues are right for you based on your likes, dislikes, expertise, and knowledge.

PLAY VS. MONEY

Do you play poker for match sticks? I didn't think so. Then, considering you purchased this book I can only guess you are serious about playing fantasy football for money. You're not alone. While bragging rights are extremely important, most fantasy footballers compete to ultimately win money. The entry fees for money leagues can vary significantly. Some cost a few bucks, others – like the WCOFF experts league – can run as high as $5,000. According to a 2003 Bob Harris Interactive Poll, the average money spent in fantasy football is $110 per team per year. That's a lot of money to be flying around. Since someone has to catch it might as well be you!

If you are new to fantasy football I recommend getting your feet wet in a free or low-stakes league first unless you have a very experienced and qualified co-manager to show you the ropes (and share the costs) in a high-stakes contest.

For those of you who aren't interested in the money as much as playing for fun, your best bet is to search for a free online league at sites such as Yahoo.com or, better yet, start a league with friends and family. Again, most fantasy footballers play for money so it'll be tough to find an already existing league that doesn't have an entry fee. You might even want to take a small collection from everyone in order to buy and reward the winner a league championship trophy. This makes it that much more exciting to compete for the title!

RE-DRAFT VS. KEEPER/DYNASTY

Most fantasy leagues are re-draft leagues. These are one-year leagues that terminate at the end of the season. In other words, managers draft an entirely new team each year, hence the term "re-draft." Sorry, no New England Patriots type of dynasties exists in this league. If you enjoy participating in drafts, as I do, then re-draft leagues are just for you Another cool thing about re-draft leagues is that you can wipe the slate clean each year. So if your team was horrible one year, then you can leave it all behind and start over the next season.

Keeper and dynasty leagues are types of continuous leagues that play for many years. In these leagues managers get to keep players on their roster from year to year. Keeper leagues allow a limited number of players to be carried over by managers, usually two to four players per manager. Dynasty leagues allow most or all players to be carried over. The term "dynasty league" comes from the idea that a manager can build a dynasty team, comprised of the same stud players, that dominates the league for consecutive years.

I recommend that only hardcore fantasy footballers enter continuous leagues because they demand a lot of time, concentration, and good judgment. Preparing for draft day is crucial because the players you take may be stuck on your team for years to come if they are plagued by injuries or bad performances. Imagine drafting Fred Taylor his rookie season only to be constantly disappointed by his "annual" injuries. Furthermore, understanding how to make trades is a key part in building a strong fantasy team, and keep in mind trades can occur all year long even after the football season is over. Imagine being fed up with Taylor's injuries, trading him away, and watching him turn into a stud for the next three to five years only to benefit your opponent's squad. Mistakes like these could prevent you from winning a fantasy championship not only for one season but many.

Of course, continuous leagues can be very fun and attractive if you play your cards right. The single most attractive part about continuous leagues is that you can build a team to be a lot stronger than you could in a re-draft. Such a dominant team becomes very lucrative if you can put together a string of league championships over several years. This is kind of like the fantasy football version of the aforementioned New England Patriots.

Many of my friends love playing in a keeper league because they thrive on the prospect of building a championship fantasy squad over many years. If that's something you think you'd like, then by all means go ahead and give it a try. Keep in mind, however, many of these leagues require all managers to make a deposit into an account that is collectively kept on the side, sometimes in a savings account or CD. Any manager who drops out of the league loses his share of the savings deposit. This gives everyone incentive to stay in the league to keep it running.

BASIC VS. PERFORMANCE

There are two general types of fantasy scoring leagues: basic scoring and performance leagues. Basic scoring awards fantasy points solely for touchdowns. Performance leagues offer fantasy points for touchdowns, yardage, and sometimes more.

Although most leagues today are performance-based you may occasionally find a basic scoring league. I strongly urge that you do not enter a basic scoring league if you want to put your fantasy football skills to maximum use. Like a roulette player hoping to see his 21 hit with a big bet, basic scoring forces the managers to rely on too much luck. TDs in the NFL can be sporadic, and they are prone to be few and far between. Good NFL players could easily hit a TD drought while mediocre players can hit a lucky streak of getting into the end zone. So to be a winning fantasy manager in a basic scoring league usually means to be very lucky.

Basic scoring leagues also seem unfair. Many managers complain because their fantasy players gain a lot of yards for nothing (zero fantasy points) only to watch other fantasy players get easy short-yard TDs (lots of fantasy points). Can I get a Jerome Bettis, anyone? Such a problem is obviously removed in performance leagues. More importantly about performance leagues is that they offer a lot more for the skilled owner to exploit and take advantage of, especially on draft day. As you'll soon find out, most of the concepts and strategies in this book are best applied in performance leagues.

Straight vs. Serpentine

In a straight draft, managers always get to pick in the same draft position every round. So if you are given the No. 1 spot, then that means you always get to pick first in every round of the draft. Not too shabby, huh?

Yet, even if draft slots are determined at random you still want to avoid participating in a draft that follows a straight order. There is just too much of an advantage given to the managers who get to draft early each round over those unlucky souls picking near the end, which very well could be you.

I recommend playing in a league that utilizes a serpentine draft. This method is just like the method your gym teacher ordered you to do when you picked teams for dodgeball in the seventh grade. This method has managers picking from lowest-to-highest draft positions in the odd rounds and highest-to-lowest draft positions in the even rounds. If you were the No. 4 draft position in a 12-team league, you would be the fourth team to pick in rounds 1, 3, 5, etc. However, you would be the ninth team to pick in rounds 2, 4, 6, etc. This style is popular because it negates the advantage managers have by drafting early in one round because those same managers are forced to draft later in the next. However, if you were to draw the No. 12 draft position in that same league, you would be the last to pick in the first round, but you would be the first to pick in the next; therefore, you would have consecutive turns.

D/ST vs. IDP

The vast majority of fantasy football leagues play a D/ST rather than IDPs. However, IDP leagues are more advantageous to the skilled and knowledgeable fantasy manager for two reasons. The first is that they offer more fantasy positions to draft from and more players and positions to analyze. Anytime there is more analysis involved it favors the prepared and studious. For instance, if you know that John Runyan is on the doubtful list and the second stringer is a rookie who just knocked up his girlfriend, then wouldn't you expect Michael Strahan to dominate this match up? Of course, you would want to activate Strahan that week for your team. The second reason that IDP leagues favor the experts is that people generally pay most of their attention to offensive players and statistics. Thus, experts can use their defensive knowledge of the NFL to reap huge rewards by knowing which IDPs to draft and when they are worth drafting relative to the offensive players. If you wish to play in an IDP I strongly recommend you check out Ryan Houston's FantasyAsylum.com. This site specializes in providing excellent information and rankings on IDPs.

Unfortunately, for those who favor IDPs, there are not many IDP leagues available. That's the nature of supply and demand. Americans concentrate on the offense. Until people starting showing more of an interest in defensive players, fantasy football will continue to be a offensive-based game. And I don't see our culture changing in the near future. Until then, Champ Baily and Warren Sapp will have to keep preaching to the choir.

ONLINE vs. LIVE DRAFT

Strategically, there is not much difference between drafting players online or in a live draft room where all the managers are physically present. It's not like a poker game where you can look at your opponents and get a physical read off of them in order to take advantage of it.

Socially, there is a huge difference. Many people enjoy a live draft because it's a huge social event, everyone is in the same room, there's a lot of joking, laughing, eating, drinking, etc. If you are one of these people that derive pleasure from the social aspect then you should obviously enter a league that has a live draft. However, as you'll learn later in this book, it's very important to take the draft more seriously than your opposition if you want to maximize your chances of winning. It's kind of like how I won 500 bucks from some drunk at a poker game last summer.   He obviously didn't take the game serious enough to be sober. So, this presents the thought, "Maybe *it is* strategically to one's advantage in a live draft if everyone else's attention and concentration is distracted by the event itself." So be sure to bring a six pack of Schlitz for your buddies at the next draft!

SMALL VS. LARGE

Who says size doesn't matter?   Well, whether you are the fantasy football equivalent of Arnold Schwarzenegger or Danny Devito, then you can find a league of fantasy football that is played on both a large and small scale. Small-scale leagues involve a limited number of managers ranging between 10-12 managers, but sometimes they involve as little as eight managers or as many as sixteen. Large-scale leagues typically involve hundreds or thousands of managers competing for a single title.

Small-scale leagues are much more common than large-scale leagues, and anytime friends, co-workers, and/or family get together to form their own fantasy league, it is of the small-scale variety.

I like small-scale leagues because they have a draft day. This is where I really start to strategize and out-think my opponents. Obviously, most of the information, concepts, and strategies offered in this book apply to drafting in the small-scale arena.

For beginner fantasy footballers, I recommend starting in an eight or ten-team league. With so few fantasy managers drafting, and so many great fantasy football players to draft, just about everyone is able to land a good team. Moreover, the free agent pool after the draft is full of additional talent making roster management that much easier as the season progresses. All of this results in a very competitive league from top to bottom. Parity favors the beginner, of course, because it's anybody's game to win.

After you garner some experience and skill, I recommend tackling a league that has 12-16 teams. Here, the skill aspect becomes more of a factor favoring those who have skill and experience. I particularly enjoy 12 and 14-team leagues because they do not fully dilute the free agent pool of fantasy players. This allows managers some flexibility in managing their roster throughout the season and doing a lot of add/drops. A 16-team league, however, tends to dilute the free agent pool making it difficult to patch up any holes left after draft day. In such a league, it's vital to enter draft day with a solid game plan and complete understanding of how to draft. Fortunately, this book teaches you just that.

Large-scale leagues are very different than small-scale leagues in many aspects. First, they have hundreds, sometimes thousands, of managers competing against each other in a single league. Second, there is no draft. Instead, managers acquire their players usually with a pre-specified budget. They buy players to fill their roster. The commissioner service hosting the large-scale league (e.g., Yahoo, ESPN) will place a price on each NFL player. Managers can purchase any combination of players as long as they stay within the budget (salary cap). Quite often, the best NFL players are found on multiple fantasy teams. Third, large-scale leagues usually do not involve head-to-head competition since there are way too many people competing. The league champ is determined by which team scores the most fantasy points during the season.

I'm not a big fan of large-scale leagues because they require a ton of luck. The key to winning large-scale leagues is finding that rare combination of fantasy players that outscores every other combination. It's almost like trying to win the lottery. But the one advantage to large-scale leagues is that it offers bigger prize money, sometimes in the thousands of dollars.

In 2002, Emil Kadlec and Lenny Pappano ingeniously created the WCOFF, a hybrid league combining the best of the small and large-scale variety. The WCOFF begins the season like a small-scale league where each WCOFF league is limited to 12 participants with its own draft, regular season, head-to-head competition, champion, and prize pool. Then, in NFL weeks 13-16, the WCOFF transforms into large-scale competition by pitting all the small-scale winners against each other for grand prize money, with the winner receiving $200,000. This hybrid has been so successful for Kadlec and Pappano that many other fantasy football entrepreneurs are following suit creating additional hybrid leagues such as the Fantasy Football Masters and National Fantasy Football Championship.

WAIVER WIRE: WORST TO FIRST VS. FIRST COME FIRST SERVED VS. BLIND BIDDING

A waiver wire system regulates and governs how managers are able to pick up free agents. The three most common systems are worst-to-first, first-come-first-served, and blind bidding. Each offers distinctive advantages and disadvantages to the skilled and unskilled.

Worst-to-first allows managers who have poor records first dibs on picking up free agents. While this is good for league parity, it is horrible to skilled fantasy owners. Ever lose at poker with a full house because some chump limped in the pot with 2/3 suited and scored a straight flush on the river? Well, this is why I have never liked playing in worst-to-first leagues. Like clockwork, I usually build a lead in the fantasy standings only to watch the weaker teams get stronger and catch up because they have the right to pick up the best free agents before I can. Therefore, my recommendation is to avoid these leagues, assuming you are a skilled fantasy owner. On the other hand, if you are new to the game and still have a lot to learn, then worst-to-first is perfect for your transition into the world of fantasy football. Should you have a bad draft and start losing some games right off the bat, you'll still have a great chance to patch up any holes in free agency.

First-come-first-served states that whoever is the first manager to claim a free agent player, gets him. I'm not a big fan of this system either because I feel like I have to stay glued to the internet 24/7 so I don't miss any good opportunities. This system favors those who don't have a date on a Saturday night and can see the Vikings general manager on television announce to the world that Randy Moss can't play on Sunday's game. Furthermore, this system puts those people who have other matters besides fantasy football on their mind at a disadvantage. Basically, if you are not at the computer when big NFL news is reported, especially involving injuries or lineup changes, then you won't be the lucky manager who gets to pick up the stud free agent. Of course, if you are the type to always be at a computer and have the time to keep an eye on NFL news, then you can take advantage of your opponents by always beating them to the punch. So these are some things to consider before you should join a league that uses a first-come-first-served method for acquiring free agents.

My favorite type of free agency system is blind bidding. This process gives all owners a fixed budget of funny money to be used to bid on free agents each week of the fantasy regular season. Usually the bidding time frame is from Tuesday to Friday, and all managers bid on players blindly. In other words, no one knows whom anyone is going to bid on and for how much.

Blind bidding is great because it doesn't treat anyone unfairly. You are not punished for having a good record or going on a date with a super model (hence, being away from the computer). I also like it because it involves more strategizing. I like to sit and analyze how much I should bid on a player. There's a lot of psychology in this aspect of the game because the goal is to bid as low as possible on a player without losing him to someone else. Keep in mind, if someone bids $500 on Player A, and no one else bids more than $150 on that same player the person who bid $500 still has to ante up all that money even though he could have purchased him for just $151.

Blind bidding has been successfully implemented by the WCOFF, NFFC, and Fantasy Football Masters competitions.

TRADES VS. NO TRADES

If you join a local fantasy league with co-workers, friends, and/ or family, then you probably want to promote as much trading as possible. It's a lot of fun to talk trades and discuss fantasy football over a lunch break or via the internet when you get home from work. And when a blockbuster deal goes down, it's an incredible adrenaline rush as you wait in anticipation to see who's going to benefit the most from the trade.

This is going to sound odd, especially considering that trading is one of fantasy football's most enjoyable aspects, but I prefer playing in leagues that do not allow trading. There are four reasons for my opinion. The first, which is probably my least concern, is the possibility for collusion. I don't think there is much collusion going on in fantasy football, and I've never seen it in any of the leagues that I participated in. However, most of the leagues I now play in are against strangers so I feel more comfortable when no trading is allowed.

The second reason why I don't like playing in leagues that allow trades is that I found most managers, including myself, tend to overvalue their own players. As a result, many otherwise fair trade offers are quickly turned down only because managers become attached to their own fantasy players. In the end, a vast majority of trade offers go for naught.

The third reason is that I've witnessed too many managers bickering and fighting over little stuff. For some reason or another certain fantasy managers turn sensitive when another manager makes a "ridiculous" trade offer. All of a sudden tempers flare and what once was a happy-go-lucky league turns into a bitter atmosphere. Always remember, trading should be enjoyed by all. If someone makes an unfair offer, then the other manager should simply say "no thanks," or better yet, make a counter-offer. Hey, unless Rodney King is your commissioner, then it is difficult for us all to get along. So, keep in mind, people shouldn't be offended by trade offers because that will only lead to bitterness.

The fourth, and maybe the biggest, reason why I prefer to stay away from trading is that I tend to get too involved, almost to the point where I'm counter-productive. I have such a competitive nature that I would sit at the computer for hours a day staring at all my opponents' line-ups looking for possible trade offers that I felt would help both my squad and theirs. Yes, I'm a fantasy football psycho. While I had fun doing this, I ended up committing so much time I never seemed to do anything else. The biggest downer would be when my trade offer was declined, quite possibly because of the tendency of managers to attach themselves to their own players.

Don't get me wrong here. I think trading is a great facet of fantasy football, especially for those who are skilled at analyzing players and knowing how to make great trade offers. If you feel you have the time and the capability to wheel and deal then by all means join a league where you can do it. Besides winning, nothing is more thrilling than making a blockbuster trade (Okay, maybe that date with Pamela Anderson).

AUCTION VS. STANDARD DRAFT

Chances are you will be in a league that hosts a standard draft. Such a draft has each manager picking one player at a time in a certain draft order. Almost all leagues follow a standard draft, and that is what this whole book revolves around.

There is another kind of draft known as an "auction league." These leagues involve an entirely different drafting method. Actually, managers don't exactly draft players but rather bid on players. Think Happy Gilmore bidding on his grandmother's house. Each manager starts with a predetermined bankroll with which to finance the bidding process. Players are bid on one at a time with managers verbally declaring their bid in front of all the other managers. The highest bidder receives the player and the bidding process moves on to another player. This process is continued until all fantasy rosters are full. It's not unusual to see one manager fill a roster well before another.

Many fantasy football enthusiasts believe auction leagues are the purest form of fantasy football. These leagues require considerable planning and strategizing; significantly more than any other kind of fantasy league. Of course, this makes it very favorable to those who are very competent. This book, however, does not cover concepts regarding auction leagues for two reasons. First, auction leagues are very rare and, therefore, there is less demand for such information. Second, if I ever decide to write about auction leagues I will most likely dedicate an entire book to the subject since there is so much to write about. In the meantime, this book's focus will be on the standard draft.

PRIVATE VS. PUBLIC

Most fantasy football leagues are organized, supervised, and commissioned among friends, family, and/or co-workers. These leagues are known as private leagues because you need to know someone in order to participate in them. I'd bet dollars to donuts you already know one or more people playing in a private league. Ask around, you'll see. When you do find someone playing in a league ask that person about the league: the rules, the entry fee, and the prizes. Also ask who plays, who's the commissioner, do they enjoy it, and maybe the most important question of them all: Do they have room for one more!

Private leagues are filled with passion and exhilaration because friends are competing against friends, and there is the usual boost of money at stake. If you can't find a private league, then a public league is a great alternative. Public leagues are readily available and open for anyone to join. These leagues are organized, supervised, and commissioned by a professional service or company. Unlike private leagues, public leagues involve mostly strangers. Most public league commissioners will not allow trades to eliminate potential collusion. So if you love the trading aspect, then you may have to revert back to a private league that allows such activities. Also, keep in mind that there is usually an additional fee in public leagues due to the services of the professional service or company hosting the league. Nevertheless, I find most public leagues to be well worth the fee.

You can find public leagues by sifting through magazine ads, such as the Fantasy Football Pro Forecast, or searching on the internet. I recommend checking out the following companies (they all have web-sites and fantasy football leagues available): WCOFF, Yahoo, Sandbox, ESPN, Antsports, MockDraftCentral, NFL, Fantasy Football Masters and CBS SportsLine.

Some ancient words of wisdom state that man cannot discover new oceans if he is afraid to lose sight of the shore. With this in mind, if you can't find a league that you like, then feel free to start your own private league. Starting your own league has three big advantages. The first is that you can customize the rules and scoring to your own liking. This includes entry fees (if any), fantasy scoring, playoff formats, team roster requirements, starting positions -- the whole works! The second is that you can be selective as to who gets to play in your league. You can invite friends, family, co-workers, stupid people, etc. Fantasy football has become so popular you shouldn't have a problem finding enough managers. The third advantage is that today's online commissioner services make it so easy for anyone to start up and commission a fantasy football league, even for those who don't have any experience. Take a free tour on some of the online sites I already mentioned and see for yourself.

Chapter 3 – Player Projections: Average Value Theory (AVT)

If you were dangling from a bridge and I lent you my hand, then would you take it? Of course you would. You would be a fool to refuse it. So, take my advice on this concept: fantasy football is a strategic game of math and statistics. I'll say this many times over. Consider the situation faced when analyzing which fantasy players to draft. We know each player is going to score a certain number of fantasy points. So, the ultimate goal is to draft the right combination of players and positions that will score the most fantasy points possible. It's a numbers game, and the manager who accomplishes this goal most efficiently is likely to win the league championship. There's one problem: no one yet knows exactly how many fantasy points each player is going to score in the upcoming season. So what's a manager to do?

The answer is simple: managers must face the task of projecting how many fantasy points are going to be scored by each player in each fantasy position.

Of course, the answer is simple, but is the process?

I guess it depends on your method of choice. Conventional projection methods involve analyzing each player individually and projecting stats in every NFL statistical category that would result in fantasy points. Let's say we wanted to do a projection on a particular WR in preparation for the WCOFF. This would require analyzing that player's past performances, as well as his current situation, and then using that information to make the best possible educated guess on how many receiving yards, receptions, and receiving TDs he's going to get this season. We might even want to project him to rush for a number of yards if the WR has been known to run on a lot of end arounds. Once all the pertinent projections are made, they can be converted into fantasy points and added up to get his total fantasy point projection for the upcoming season.

Ever sit down in a chair on your porch in front of your lawn and watch the grass grow, or hang out in front of your freshly painted fence and watch the paint dry? Well, if you have never accomplished these exciting feats, then let me tell you that they are boring, slow and painstaking. Now although making projections in fantasy football is not boring, the process is definitely slow and painstaking. Most fantasy football experts who have done projections in this manner, including me, will agree with this statement. Projections must not only be carefully made in multiple statistical categories but also for every NFL player that is potentially draft worthy, which could very well run over 200 players. The worst part about this method is that the work never ends until the draft begins. Projections need to be continuously tweaked until the very minute of the fantasy football draft. Why? Because the NFL constantly throws us player news, team notes and new injury conditions, all of which ultimately cause our projections to change. Suppose the Minnesota Vikings No. 1 receiver badly sprains his ankle in Wednesday's practice and is reported to miss two to four weeks into the NFL regular season. Under this scenario, you would need to reduce his projections by two to four weeks' worth of statistics. You also should increase the projected stats of the other Vikings receivers since they are expected to get more playing time. Remember, one's loss is usually another's gain in fantasy football. Getting even more ticklish, you may have to lower the projections on the Vikings quarterback because he just lost his best wide receiver. How much to adjust everyone's projections is a whole other issue in and of itself. So as you can see, conventional methods require lots of work, careful analysis, much discretion and, most importantly, plenty of time.

Consequently, nearly all fantasy managers will stay away from doing projections as if it were the Ebola virus, and understandably so. This is a shame because projecting is one of the biggest aspects of preparing for a fantasy football draft, and more importantly, it is one of the best ways to out-smart your opponent. The only option left is to pay, and defer judgment to, an expert fantasy football service for a set of player projections. I should say this was the only other option … until now.

Have you ever spent days on end trying to do your own taxes when it is much easier to put your trust in an accountant and get the job done in an hour rather than an eternity? Well, if you have endured that agony before, then put your trust in my methods for making a shorter alternative to projecting fantasy points. Here is an amazing alternative for doing just that. It's a method that you can do in just a day's work, and no tweaking is necessary thereafter. Best of all, the results have proven to be better than the hard-working experts who spend weeks and months churning the conventional methods.

Does it sound too good to be true? It does, doesn't it? Nonetheless, that is what I thought until I started winning fantasy leagues using such a method. It's a little-known concept called the Average Value Theory (AVT). AVT is a statistical method that projects fantasy points solely according to historical results.

One of the nuances of the AVT system that makes it relatively simple is that fantasy points are projected on generic rankings and positions rather than actual NFL players. By doing this, you eliminate the constant manicure required on the projections of actual players as NFL news comes in.

I think the best way to describe the unique AVT process is by example. Suppose you want to project the fantasy points for this year's crop of running backs. To keep the example short and simple, let's focus our attention on the top ten ranked RBs. According to AVT, you would need to observe the fantasy points scored by the top ten fantasy RBs in recent years. The names of the players need not be observed, just their positions and ranks. You would then log all the data into a chart or spreadsheet in order to calculate an average value for each position and rank. Such average value then becomes this year's projection. Take a look at Figure 1 to see how it's done.

FIGURE 1: 3 YEAR AVT CHART (FANTASY POINTS SCORED)					
POSITION & RANK	3 YEARS AGO	2 YEARS AGO	LAST YEAR	TOTAL POINTS	THIS YEARS PROJECTION
RB1	456	426	443	1325	442
RB2	401	339	386	1126	375
RB3	342	327	371	1040	347
RB4	324	306	347	977	326
RB5	312	301	333	946	315
RB6	307	279	331	917	306
RB7	303	278	322	903	301
RB8	297	266	317	880	293
RB9	284	241	302	827	276
RB10	283	232	289	804	268

The projection in the right column is the average result, or average value, of the three-year history. Take a look at RB1 for example. His three-year history includes fantasy points of 456, 426, and 443. Adding these values gives us 1325 fantasy points. Dividing by three gives us a 442-point average. So, this year's projection for RB1 should be 442 fantasy points.

When implementing the AVT methodology keep in mind that you don't have to limit yourself to three years' worth of data as shown in Figure 1. You are free to use two years' or four years' worth, or however many years you want to use for that matter. I recommend implementing a *three-year AVT* – meaning an AVT that uses three years' worth of data – because of its proven track record. I'll get into this subject a little bit later in the chapter. For now, just try to grasp the general concept of how AVT works. In this case, projections are determined by taking the average results of the past.

You also need to take the time to understand the concept and use of the *generic positions and ranks* I alluded to earlier. In helping you do this I'll start by briefly clarifying the terms listed in the left column of figure 1 entitled "Position and Rank," then I'm going to describe how I found the three years' worth of historical data listed in the middle columns. If you haven't realized yet, this is actual data used for the 2003 WCOFF draft. So "3 Years Ago" really means the year 2000, "2 Years Ago" means 2001, "Last Year" means 2002, and finally "This Year's Projection" was for 2003. And lastly, I'm going to show you how I applied the projection results in the right column to my 2003 WCOFF draft cheat sheet. Once you understand these three processes, then you should have a complete understanding of how the Average Value Theory works.

To begin, let's start by clarifying the left column of Figure 1 labeled "Position and Rank." This column indicates the generic names given to fantasy football players. RB1 refers to the best fantasy running back, RB2 refers to the second best running back, etc. Each fantasy season provides us with its own set of positions and ranks.

Now, let's get into how I found the three years' worth of data for the generic positions and ranks. The second, third and fourth columns of Figure 1 list how many fantasy points were scored by the top ten RBs in each of the prior three years. It was important that these results be based on the same fantasy scoring rules as used in the 2003 WCOFF, otherwise it would send me in the wrong direction. I was fortunate enough to already have the 2002 results on hand because I kept a record of the fantasy points scored by all of the players and positions after playing in the 2002 WCOFF. So I could easily see that Priest Holmes was 2002's highest scoring fantasy running back with 443 fantasy points, LaDainian Tomlinson was second with 386 fantasy points, and so on. All I had to do was take these results and plug them into the column labeled "Last Year." Holmes' stats fit into RB1, Tomlinson's fit into RB2, etc. This step essentially transfers the fantasy points from an actual player's name to a generic position and rank.

I was still faced with the tricky task of getting the fantasy results for the 2000 and 2001 seasons. Since the WCOFF hadn't been formed until 2002 I had no data on record. I could look up the NFL statistics of all the players in those years and calculate the fantasy results by hand or spreadsheet, but this would take much too long to do. After searching for another alternative I was fortunate enough to find Emil Kadlec's *Stat Ledger* at Footballdiehards.com. This is an all-encompassing program that is user friendly and versatile. Simply plug in the fantasy scoring criteria and out comes the historical data you need going back as far as 1996. It can be customized to fit almost any fantasy league scoring, so I had no trouble getting the WCOFF data for the 2000 and 2001 seasons.

After inserting this data into the second and third columns of Figure 1, it was a simple matter of calculating the average values for each generic rank and position. I added up the three-year totals for each generic position and rank, then divided by three. The results are listed in the right column of Figure 1 labeled "This Year's Projection."

Lastly, I want to show you how I applied these projection results. There was nothing left to calculate using the AVT methodology so the next task was to rank the NFL players for the 2003 fantasy season. This would allow the AVT projections to be transferred from a generic position and name back to an actual player's name. By the way, ranking players is an entirely separate process from AVT and will be extensively covered in the next chapter. For simplicity sake, let's just jump to the point where I already had a set of player rankings in hand so I can explain to you how I applied the projections. Let's focus on my top three ranked running backs: LaDainian Tomlinson, Marshall Faulk, and Priest Holmes. This meant Tomlinson was projected to be RB1, Faulk to be RB2, and Holmes to be RB3 by the end of the 2003 season. After applying the results in Figure 1, Tomlinson should be projected to score 442 fantasy points, Faulk to score 375 fantasy points, and Holmes to score 347 fantasy points. That's all there was to it. I followed this same process for all other ranked running backs.

Now that you've seen how I applied the methodology, here is a step-by-step guide so you can apply your own three-year AVT:

Step 1) Determine the number of projections needed per position.

In the prior example I determined ten projections in the RB position. Realistically, a lot more projections are needed than that. You'll need a projection for each player you plan on ranking on the cheat sheet. So, it's a matter of figuring out how many players you plan on ranking in each position. As boy scouts are "always prepared," here's the general rule of thumb in determining how many players to rank for each position (also detailed in the next chapter):

Rank twice the maximum number of players that can be started among the entire league.

Suppose you played in a 12-team league that required each manager to start two RBs. This would mean 24 RBs would be started among the entire league. Twice that is 48 RBs. Therefore I would rank and project 48 RBs.

Now suppose this same league added a flex starter (RB/WR/ TE). In this case, managers would be required to start two RBs, but they also have the option to start a third RB as the flex starter. This means as many as 36 RBs could be started within the entire league. Therefore, I would rank and project 72 RBs.

The World Championship of Fantasy Football has twelve teams per league, and the starting lineup is 1 QB, 2 RBs, 3 WRs, 1 TE, 1 K, 1 D/ST & 1 FLEX (RB/WR/TE). So the maximum number of players that can be started in each position per team is 1 QB, 3 RBs, 4 WRs, 2 TEs, 1 K, & 1 D/ST when factoring in the flex. After running the numbers the WCOFF cheat sheet should have approximately 24 QBs, 72 RBs, 96 WRs, 48 TEs, 24 Ks, and 24 D/STs ranked and projected.

Step 2) Obtain historical fantasy results.

You need to apply your league scoring rules to each of the last three NFL seasons in order to obtain the fantasy points scored by the top players in each position per season. Again, the number of players you need to observe per position is determined in the prior step. I recommend Emil Kadlec's *Stat Ledger* at Footballdiehards.com for finding historical fantasy results if you don't already have the information on record. This will save you a great deal of time instead of doing the calculations by hand.

Step 3) Apply generic rank and position.

By now you should have a list of actual player names and their fantasy points scored per fantasy position per season. Now is the time to replace all the player names with the appropriate generic positions and ranks. For instance, if you see Torry Holt finished the 2003 season as the second best WR, then go ahead and replace his name with WR2. Do this for every player, position and rank in all three years.

Step 4) Log data into AVT chart or spreadsheet.

You'll need to log all the data into a chart or spreadsheet similar to that of Figure 1. Log a separate chart for each fantasy position. Each chart should have one column for generic position and rank, three columns for the three years' worth of fantasy points scored (assuming three-year AVT), one column for the total points, and another column for this year's projection.

Step 5) Calculate Projections.

Use the chart or spreadsheet to calculate each generic rank and position's projection. The calculations are pretty simple. Add up the total fantasy points scored by a particular rank and position over three years and divide that value by three. This will give you this year's projection, also known as the average value.

Step 6) Rank players.

The projections as determined in Step 5 cannot be applied until after you have a complete list of ranked players in each position. I remind you, this step is a separate process that will be detailed in full in the next chapter.

Step 7) Apply AVT projections.

Once you have a complete list of ranked players, you can apply the AVT projections by assigning the projections to the players accordingly. For example, if you rank Randy Moss to be this year's sixth ranked wide receiver, then you would assign WR6's average value to being his projection.

That's every step involved with the AVT system. I am largely in favor of this system for two reasons. First, it requires little work and less analysis – something I savor these days – especially relative to the time-consuming conventional methods. The AVT projections are essentially pre-determined. It's just a matter of running the numbers. There is no guessing, no tweaking, and no worrying about day-to-day NFL news changing the projections.

The second, and more important, reason is that AVT projections have proven to be significantly more accurate than the experts and their conventional ways. Let's take a closer look at this one.

For the past several years I have received much better projections with AVT than what the leading fantasy football experts have offered. The system has been a huge contributor to my WCOFF successes and, for obvious reasons, I've been very secretive about it until this book. While I have always felt and experienced the success of the system, I still wanted concrete evidence to assure myself it wasn't a mirage. So, in 2004, I did a study to see exactly how my AVT projections stacked up against two well-known experts in the 2003 WCOFF. Let's call them "Expert1" and "Expert2". Although the experts will remain anonymous, I should note that they are two of the most well-respected and successful providers of fantasy football knowledge. Chances are, you or someone you know, have paid money to one of them for a set of their expert projections.

The objective of the study was to find concrete evidence revealing how much more accurate one set of projections is over the others, if there was such evidence. All the data required by this study is listed in Figure 2. You'll find my 2003 WCOFF projections for the top 69 RBs according to a three-year AVT, labeled under AVT. Also listed are the projections of Expert1 and Expert2. I determined their WCOFF projections by taking the NFL statistical projections on their own top 69 ranked fantasy backs and converting this data into WCOFF fantasy points. The last column lists the actual 2003 results of the top 69 RBs.

Before continuing with the study, we need to touch base again with the use and purpose of generic names. As you can see in Figure 2, there are no actual player names listed. Only generic positions and ranks are listed in the left column. In doing this I had to replace the names of the players ranked by the experts with generic names RB1, RB2, etc. The reason for this step is because the actual names of the players are irrelevant to the study. I am concerned only with how accurate the positions and ranks were projected, not how well the real-life players themselves were ranked or projected.

To make this point clear, suppose it was Marshall Faulk that Expert1 projected to score the highest with 414 fantasy points.

FIGURE 2: AVT, EXPERT 1, EXPERT 2 AND ACTUAL RESULTS

POSITION & RANK	AVT	EXPERT 1	EXPERT 2	ACTUAL RESULTS
RB1	441	414	377	447
RB2	375	405	363	444
RB3	347	377	338	395
RB4	326	374	334	337
RB5	316	364	328	333
RB6	306	354	322	315
RB7	301	350	322	311
RB8	293	342	314	284
RB9	276	339	311	282
RB10	268	331	305	272
RB11	262	330	297	257
RB12	254	325	296	252
RB13	250	314	289	245
RB14	246	291	271	233
RB15	238	264	257	222
RB16	231	251	251	222
RB17	227	249	236	222
RB18	222	248	234	211
RB19	217	238	234	210
RB20	213	236	229	198
RB21	205	232	228	185
RB22	202	232	221	179
RB23	199	228	214	171
RB24	190	211	213	168
RB25	178	203	203	167
RB26	173	202	192	166
RB27	169	197	188	164
RB28	159	196	187	163
RB29	151	176	186	156
RB30	149	170	184	154
RB31	145	168	182	151
RB32	139	158	165	147
RB33	137	141	151	147
RB34	134	141	130	132
RB35	125	140	125	131
RB36	121	140	123	126
RB37	120	138	115	123
RB38	115	137	113	118
RB39	111	128	106	116
RB40	109	124	96	115
RB41	103	122	90	105
RB42	99	97	86	102
RB43	96	97	85	101

Figure 2 continued on next page

The study interprets this as Expert1 projecting the best fantasy RB, or RB1, to score 414 points. Strange as it sounds, how many points Faulk finishes the season with really doesn't matter to anyone. What is important is how many points RB1 – the guy is who scores the most points during the season, whomever that may be – scores at season's end. Let's say Priest Holmes ends up being the season's top scoring RB, coincidentally scoring

FIGURE 2: AVT, EXPERT 1, EXPERT 2 AND ACTUAL RESULTS				
POSITION & RANK	AVT	EXPERT 1	EXPERT 2	ACTUAL RESULTS
RB44	95	93	84	97
RB45	91	92	76	89
RB46	88	90	72	84
RB47	87	90	68	82
RB48	82	86	68	80
RB49	81	83	68	77
RB50	80	74	65	76
RB51	77	73	65	75
RB52	75	66	63	74
RB53	74	63	57	73
RB54	73	58	55	73
RB55	71	58	54	72
RB56	69	56	54	71
RB57	68	52	53	70
RB58	67	51	53	69
RB59	65	46	52	69
RB60	63	46	52	67
RB61	60	40	51	66
RB62	58	40	51	65
RB63	57	39	51	65
RB64	56	32	49	64
RB65	55	30	49	64
RB66	53	26	49	64
RB67	52	25	48	63
RB68	52	20	46	62
RB69	51	19	46	62

414 fantasy points. This would mean that Expert1 was perfect in projecting the fantasy points of RB1 while simultaneously wrong in ranking Faulk and Holmes in the correct spots. Changing things up a bit: what if Marshall Faulk did in fact finish the season as the highest scoring RB with, say, 460 fantasy points? In this particular instance Expert1's No. 1 ranking of Faulk may be right on, but the projection of RB1 would be 46 points off target.

We've just witnessed two scenarios. The first had a perfect projection but imperfect ranking, and the second had a perfect ranking but imperfect projection. So what's more important, having a better projection or a better ranking? The answer is that both are equally important when it comes to winning your fantasy league. Nevertheless, this chapter is about player projections so the study will focus on the accuracy of the projections of AVT, Expert1 and Expert2. How well the actual players might have been ranked by the experts will be ignored. Keep in mind, having a good set of player rankings will be given top priority in the next chapter.

Getting back to the study, we need to determine the set of projections in Figure 2 that best represents, or is closest to, the actual results. This set can then be considered the most accurate in the RB position. Since mere eyesight of Figure 2 isn't good enough to take to the bank, then we'll need to apply a statistics formula that objectively measures the accuracy of each set of projections. I decided to implement a measure of variability similar to what is known by statisticians as the *standard deviation*. The standard deviation measures how far a set of data deviates from a central point or mean. Since I didn't exactly have a "central point," my study measured how far the set of projections deviated from the actual results. Consequently, since I didn't want to turn this book into a lesson on statistics, I listed the formula breakdown in Appendix B if anyone wants to have fun. All you need to understand is that the lower the standard deviation is, then the better the projection will be (because it doesn't deviate far from actual results); and the higher the standard deviation is, then the worse the projection will be (because it deviates far from actual results).

After running several calculations as recorded in Appendix B, the standard deviations for the three sets of player projections are shown in Figure 3.

FIG 3: STANDARD DEVIATIONS FOR RB 2003 PROJECTIONS			
	AVT	EXPERT 1	EXPERT 2
STANDARD DEVIATION	13.58	33.21	26.97

These results clearly indicate AVT was more accurate than the experts in 2003, at least in projecting the RB position. Most impressive is that AVT's results look to be twice as accurate or more than the experts. This is owing to the fact that the AVT's deviation is about half as much as Expert2 and less than half as much as Expert1. Indeed, we now have numerical and empirical evidence in favor of AVT.

Moreover, how did AVT's projections fare against the experts in the other fantasy positions?

Following the same process, I went ahead and calculated standard deviations for AVT, Expert1, and Expert2 in all WCOFF fantasy positions for the 2003 season. While I spare this book the data and calculations (you are just going to have to trust me), the results are shown in Figure 4.

FIG 4: 3 YEAR AVT IS MORE ACCURATE IN EVERY POSITION (2003 DATA)			
	AVT	EXPERT 1	EXPERT 2
QB	19.93	28.17	62.81
RB	13.58	33.21	26.97
WR	15.15	50.74	26.00
TE	11.55	22.45	11.75
K	5.63	12.35	7.54
D/ST	5.56	11.30	8.91

What I found was that AVT was significantly more accurate than the experts across the board! Most notably is the marked accuracy over Expert2 in the QB position (approx. 3x's more accurate) and Expert1 in the WR position (more than 3x's more accurate). These results strongly support my original belief and observation that the AVT is worthwhile and successful; the thousands of dollars of prize money verify it.

With results so compelling, one must wonder what exactly makes AVT much better than the experts. I offer my thoughts:

For starters, conventional methods require a lot of human guesswork. Take Randy Moss' projection, for example, in the 2004 NFL season. I observed one expert source projecting Moss to have 111 receptions, 1,534 yards receiving, 15 TDs, and 34 yards rushing in the 2004 NFL season. I wouldn't say this is a bad projection. However, we need to consider that each of these statistical categories requires precise judgment and analysis, and one bad mistake could skew the most important result of all – Moss' total fantasy points scored. My point here is that no matter how well someone knows a player or how much he watches him in training camp, it is very difficult to project with accuracy what he's going to do in every statistical category. Heck, even the players who know themselves better than anyone else would have a tough time making accurate projections.

AVT, on the other hand, applies a methodology that doesn't involve any human guesswork. It takes away the margin of human error by relying entirely on the strong foundation of statistics and probability. One specific area it relies on is long-term effects. Take a look at the NFL season. After all, this is what the AVT tries to predict. Each season is filled with over 25,000 plays. There is a good chance the AVT can predict, with accuracy, the NFL's season-ending results with this many plays. How so? I'm going to use a coin flipping example to help you understand why the last statement has merit.

Suppose we had to predict, within a five percent margin of error, the percentage heads will flip up after "x number" of flips. We would correctly guess 50 percent because we know a coin will come up heads half the time. So, I went ahead and flipped a quarter 100 times to put our prediction to the test (which you can easily do on your own as well). The results are charted in Figure 5. You can see the flip-by-flip recordings in Appendix C.

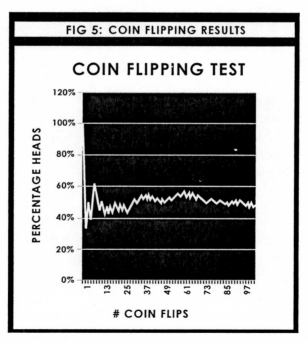

FIG 5: COIN FLIPPING RESULTS

You'll see in these results that our prediction of 50 percent heads was off by more than a five percent margin of error after six of the first ten flips. This shows how difficult it is to predict things in the short-term because anything is liable to happen. The long-term gives us much better results. The results are so much better that you'll find our prediction of 50 percent to always be within a five percent margin of error after the 26th flip, right on up until the 100th flip. This result should be self evident in Figure 5 because you can see the line moving closer and closer to the coin's expected outcome of 50 percent as the number of flips increase. The more flips, the better the chance of predicting the coin's results with a low margin of error.

This example should now help you understand why there's a good possibility the AVT can predict the NFL with a low margin of error. Again, the NFL season is filled with 25,000+ plays, and so there is a good chance its season-ending results will settle somewhere close to the actual expected outcome.

This begs the question: What is the expected outcome of the NFL?

That is the "million dollar" question. It is every expert's and projector's goal to determine the NFL's expected outcome because that is exactly what should be projected. Unfortunately, this task is not as easy as it is with a coin. The NFL isn't like a coin where we easily know the expected outcome based on its physical characteristics. Rather, the NFL is a complex entity that doesn't keep the same characteristics from year to year. It also involves the unpredictability of humans playing and coaching the game.

Therefore, to determine the NFL's expected outcome, the AVT once again puts its stock in statistics and probability, this time using *statistical inferences*. Statistical inferences are conclusions drawn from one set of data in order to predict the results of something else. In practical terms, the AVT uses past NFL results in order to predict what's going to happen this season.

To explain the concept of statistical inferences, let's go back to the coin flipping example. We didn't have to use statistical inferences because we already knew the physical properties of a coin to give it an expected outcome of 50 percent heads. But suppose we didn't know what a coin looked like or know any of its physical properties. Let's say all we knew was that there were two possible results: heads or tails. How could we possibly guess, with some accuracy, the percentage heads will flip up in the future? The answer lies in statistical inferences, of course. We use the coin's historical results to make an educated guess on what's going to happen in the future. Thus, we would infer from Appendix C's results that heads will flip 48 percent of the time in the future. Of course, the optimal guess is 50 percent but our projection of 48 percent sure isn't that bad considering "we didn't know what a coin looked like or any of its physical properties." Indeed, the AVT may not know what the NFL looks like, but it sure can help us project its results with great accuracy through statistical inferences, as already seen in Figure 4.

WHY THREE YEARS?

Do you expect your ten-year old Chevy Nova to work as well this year as it did in its first or third year? Well, if you don't, then you will probably understand my reasoning for why you should judge a player based on his performance in the last three years. As you know, AVT can observe any number of years of historical data in determining its average values. You also know that I recommend observing three years' worth of data just like in Figure 1. The following section is going to explain why.

Years back when I was first introduced to the AVT, after reading an article by Christopher Annunziata and Wade Iuele, my inclination was to observe as many years as possible in determining the projections. After all, I knew that the more I observed something the closer its results should fall towards the expected outcome, just like in the coin flipping example. However, I quickly realized there's a flaw in this kind of thinking. You see, unlike a coin which always has the same characteristics, shape, and expected outcome over time, the NFL is rather a complex entity with many changing parts including new owners, coaches, players, rules, play books, stadiums and even fans. This meant that the NFL is likely to see new trends and "expected outcomes" develop over time. So I had to be careful not to observe NFL data that is too old when implementing the AVT system; observing old data may not help in predicting today's NFL because today's NFL probably operates differently.

In contrast, observing too few NFL seasons may not be appropriate either. Just take a look at the coin flipping results in Figure 5. They were often found to fall far from the expected outcome when few flips were observed. So if we were to observe, say, just one year's worth of NFL data then the results are liable to fall far from the NFL's expected outcome; even though an NFL season is filled with thousands of plays, it's still conceivable that the NFL could "malfunction" on any given year resulting in unusual statistics.

Indeed, there had to be a happy medium; I just didn't know where that medium was.

I concluded the best way to go about this situation was to graph, observe, and analyze the fantasy output of the 1st, 12th, and 24th ranked players in major fantasy positions over the course of ten years (see Figures 6-10). Then, I would use this data in testing various AVTs to ultimately determine what the optimal number of years to observe is.

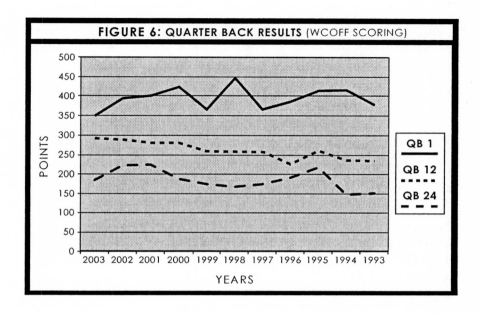

FIGURE 6: QUARTER BACK RESULTS (WCOFF SCORING)

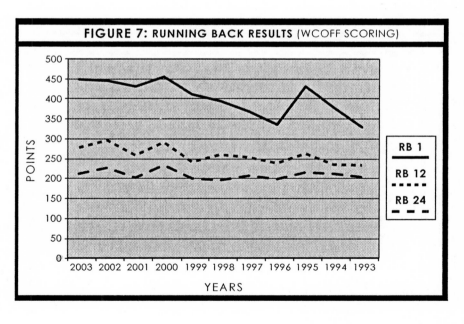

FIGURE 7: RUNNING BACK RESULTS (WCOFF SCORING)

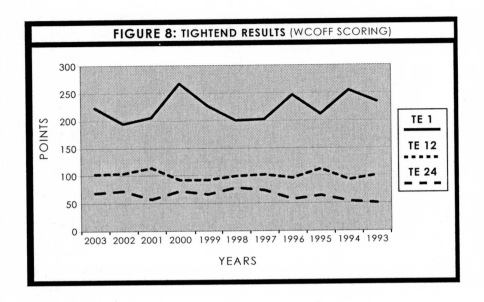

FIGURE 8: TIGHTEND RESULTS (WCOFF SCORING)

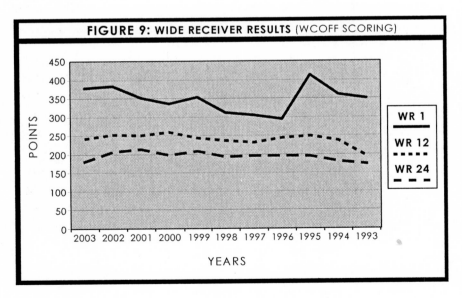

FIGURE 9: WIDE RECEIVER RESULTS (WCOFF SCORING)

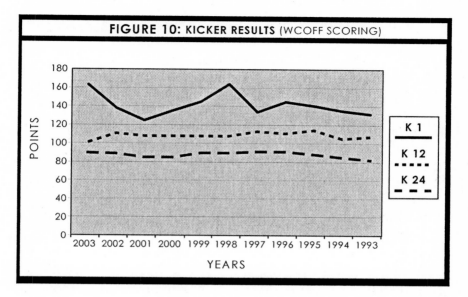

FIGURE 10: KICKER RESULTS (WCOFF SCORING)

As suspected, we can see short-term fluctuations and long-term trends in Figures 6-10. For example, long-term upward trends are clearly visible in Figure 7. Short-term fluctuations are significantly apparent in all figures, especially when observing the top-ranked players in each position.

This last observation is worth a little more analysis. While the top-ranked players show very erratic behavior with its peaks and valleys, the 12th and 24th ranked players show smoother and more consistent lines. I came to the conclusion that this is a consequence of constraints, or scoring boundaries, put on the lower ranked players. Let me explain. The highest fantasy point scorer has no scoring boundaries. He is free to break any NFL and fantasy football records he can. This freedom allows the top player to score extremely high one year and relatively low the next year, thus creating the peaks and valleys you see in the charts.

All other players are bounded by higher-scoring players.

The second-best fantasy scorer is restricted by the top player's score. To put it differently, the No. 2 fantasy scorer cannot exceed the No. 1 scorer, otherwise he'd no longer be the No. 2

scorer, he'd become the No. 1 fantasy scorer. The No. 3 ranked scorer is restricted by both the No. 1 and No. 2 players' scores, and so on. Since the lower ranks have to deal with more constraints, their range of scoring is more limited. Hence, the smoother lines for the lower ranked players.

What does this observation have to do with determining the optimal number of years for AVT purposes?

It tells us there's too much of a potential margin for error when using only one year's worth of data to predict the next season, and this is especially true when projecting the top ranked players. For example, suppose we used a one-year AVT to predict WR1 in 1995. You can easily see how troublesome this would be by simply looking at Figure 9. You will see that WR1 scored well over 400 points in 1995, which would become our one-year AVT projection, but unfortunately in the following season WR1 scored less than 300 points. This 100+ point margin of error could be detrimental on draft day.

Of course, this type of risk is lessened for the lower-ranked players because they fluctuate less from year to year. However, as fantasy football drafters, we should be more concerned with the higher-ranked players; these are the guys expected to carry our fantasy squads to victory. Like paying top dollar for a Corvette instead of a Chevette, we must get our money's worth from our expensive purchases. Therefore, we must remain focused on determining the optimal number of years to observe, especially for projecting the top-ranked players.

In ultimately determining the optimal number of years, I performed various tests on one-year, two-year, three-year, four-year, and five-year AVTs. (Now, due to all of these statistical studies, I guess you can officially compare me to that mad scientist from *Back to the Future*, Doc Brown!) The compiled results should give us a good idea as to which AVT works the best.

Let me give you an example. One of the tests involved projecting TE1 in the 2001 season. In performing this test, I obtained the necessary numerical data from Figure 8, as shown in Figure 11.

POSITION & RANK	1996	1997	1998	1999	2000	2001
FIGURE 11: FANTASY POINTS SCORED BY TE 1						
TE 1	249	201	200	225	267	?

The goal was to see how well the various AVTs did in projecting the fantasy points scored by the top tight end, TE1, in 2001. Of course, we know the correct projection is 206 fantasy points as seen in Figure 8. It was now time to see how close the various AVTs came in projecting the correct result.

According to a one-year AVT the top ranked TE is projected to score 267 fantasy points. This is simply due to the fact that TE1 scored 267 fantasy points in 2000. This projection has a margin of error of 267 - 206 = 61 fantasy points. Let's see how the other AVTs fared.

A two-year AVT takes the average of the 1999 and 2000 seasons. Thus, we get the following projection: (225+267) / 2 = 246 fantasy points. This result has a margin of error of 246 - 206 = 40 fantasy points. This is a much better projection than the one-year AVT, but I'd say it still has a wide margin of error. Let's try a three-year AVT. The projection for the top TE would be (225+267+200) / 3 = 231 fantasy points. Its margin of error is 231-206 = 25 points. The results seem to be getting better as the number of years observed increases. A four-year AVT results in the following projection: (267+225+200+201) / 4 = 223 fantasy points. The margin of error is now only 223- 206 = 17. A five-year AVT offers the following projection on TE1: (267+225+200+201+249) / 5 = 228 fantasy points. This has a margin of error of 228 - 206 = 22 points. Finally, the projection got worse.

After doing similar tests on several other generic positions and ranks, the compiled results are shown in Figure 12.

FIGURE 12: ABSOLUTE MARGIN OF ERROR (WCOFF FANTASY POINTS)					
PROJECTION	1-year AVT	2-year AVT	3-year AVT	4-year AVT	5-year AVT
2001 TE1	61	40	25	17	22
2003 RB1	4	13	5	16	26
2003 RB12	21	2	2	11	15
2003 WR1	6	10	21	22	31
2002 QB1	6	18	4	16	7
2003 WR24	27	30	26	28	25
TOTAL ERROR:	125	113	83	110	126

As you can see, the optimal methodology is a three-year AVT. It had a total margin of error of just 83 fantasy points; clearly the lowest among all the AVTs. The one-year and two-year AVTs were obviously affected by short-term scoring fluctuations. The four-year and five-year AVTs were most likely off kilter because of the long-term trends. This is exactly why I recommend and use a three-year AVT. I like to know, on the one hand, that I'm using enough data to avoid short-term fluctuations, but on the other hand, I'm not being affected by data that is too old.

[As a side note for those hardcore mathematicians: There is a statistical approach known as *regression analysis* that would project fantasy points taking into account the upward and downward long-term trends. This mathematical process can get quite complicated especially compared to the AVT methodology I suggested which uses a simple *straight-line analysis*. For what it's worth, since I am not the great mathematician Stephen Hawking, I choose not to implement regression analysis because I consider it overkill. (Of course, this opinion could always change.) Therefore, I will not provide any details on the subject in this edition. Maybe one day it will be the subject in my next book, but who knows? If you are interested in learning more about regression analysis I suggest buying a good statistics book such as: *STATISTICS – Principals and Methods* by Richard A. Johnson and Gouri K. Bhattacharyya.]

CLOSING THOUGHTS ON AVT

I want to elaborate on why I believe many experts don't use or promote the AVT, especially after showing you how well it works. I can think of six reasons:

First, maybe they didn't know about it? Simple enough.

Second, it might be egotistical since some fantasy footballers think they are the greatest and like to blow smoke up their own behinds. As a result, many times people, especially "experts," naturally feel they know more than the rest of the world. I will admit I sometimes fall in this category. As a consequence, these experts may not want to believe something as simple as AVT can do better than their own system. So they stubbornly ignore it. Also ego-related is that people like to be in control. Since AVT does all the work, there is little control left for the expert.

Third, some experts might feel as if they have uncovered the recipe for New Coke and want to keep the AVT to themselves. Therefore, it's quite conceivable the experts are using AVT but are keeping it secret just as I have for the past several years. Why give away such a good thing when you can keep it all to yourself, right?

Fourth, fantasy footballers fork out a lot of dough for expert projections. Experts may not want to disclose the AVT method for the simple reason that people may no longer have to pay them for projections. Use me as a prime example. I used to pay for projections back in the day. Now, I don't have to because of the AVT system.

Fifth, I've heard experts argue that the AVT doesn't "balance" the stats. Let me give you an example of what they mean. An expert, when doing projections, should take into account that a quarterback's passing stats need to equal the sum of all his receivers' receiving stats. In other words, for every yard passed there should be a yard received. This "balancing act" ensures that all stats and projections are in good working order. The conventionalist will argue this strategic use of balancing stats is not possible when using the AVT. This is absolutely not true. While the AVT methodology itself cannot take into account the balancing of NFL statistics, you'll soon learn that such balancing still has its effect when ranking players. This will be covered in the next chapter.

The sixth and final reason is that experts may claim AVT doesn't properly recognize the talent pool of the NFL. Here's an example. Suppose the NFL has five stud RBs who are "all but guaranteed" to score more than 200 fantasy points this season, assuming they stay healthy. Let's also say that the NFL has only experienced an average of three RBs with more than 200 fantasy points in the last three years. Part of the reason is because the talent pool wasn't as strong. Another part of the reason is that all the best RBs haven't been able to stay healthy through an entire season together. Observing this scenario, the conventionalist will most likely project five RBs to score over 200 points. In contrast, a three-year AVT may only project three RBs to score over 200 points. Who's going to have the better projections: the AVT or the conventionalist? Many people will say the conventionalist has the upper hand, but I beg to differ. Although the talent pool may be stronger this year, let's not forget that history has a good chance of repeating itself. In other words, there's a reasonable chance that one or more of this year's stud RBs will get injured or even under-perform. The point is that a lot of things are likely to happen that will keep a surplus of talented players down to "normal" season-end results, giving the advantage to AVT.

CHAPTER 4 – RANKING PLAYERS

Ever see David Letterman's rankings for the Top Ten Reasons *Why Fantasy Footballers Score the Hottest Dates on Saturday Nights?* Me neither. But pay attention. Even Letterman can learn a thing or two about ranking players here, and he knows a bit about football.

Ranking players is the process of analyzing NFL players and listing them in order of fantasy importance. Players are separated and ranked according to position. The higher a player is ranked the more important, or more valuable, he is deemed in that position on draft day. In other words, the higher a player is ranked, the more likely you are to draft him first.

While there are various ways to rank players, the process itself seems to be a top priority for fantasy footballers. In a 2004 Footballdiehards.com message board poll 114 fantasy football managers were asked, "What do you spend most of your time working on before the draft?" Their choices were Projections, Rankings, Draft Strategy, or Other. A majority of the field said they spend most of their time on player rankings (61%) with draft strategy coming in second (23%). You can see the complete results in Figure 13.

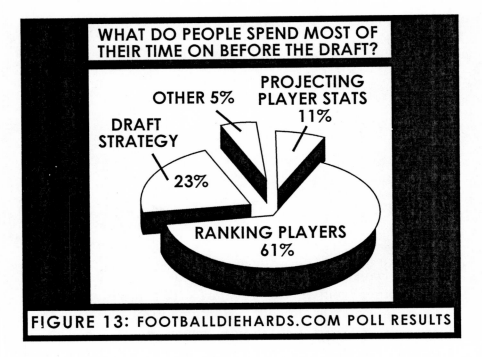

WHAT DO PEOPLE SPEND MOST OF THEIR TIME ON BEFORE THE DRAFT?

OTHER 5%

PROJECTING PLAYER STATS 11%

DRAFT STRATEGY 23%

RANKING PLAYERS 61%

FIGURE 13: FOOTBALLDIEHARDS.COM POLL RESULTS

These results are interesting because, oddly enough, ranking players shouldn't require that much work and analysis. In fact, ranking players should take less than half the amount of time spent on draft strategy. Another poll asked several managers in the group of 61 percent what they did to rank players. While no two managers were exactly alike, most seemed to follow the same basic methodology: first they'd find a set of expert rankings to their liking, then they'd read up on NFL player profiles and stay abreast with NFL news, and finally they'd tweak the expert rankings to fit their own opinion leading up to draft day.

The key facet to this general approach is that the methodology limits itself to the simple and fun processes. Finding expert rankings, watching the news, and tweaking lists are all relatively easy and fun to do. What does this have to do with the amount of time they spend on ranking players? Everything!

Fantasy footballers spent most of their time on ranking players because the process was fun to them. This is a clear indication that managers tend to play fantasy football more for the fun of it as opposed to the optimal approach to win. Sure, it's easy to analyze *ESPN Gameday*. It's enlightening to read player profiles. It's cool to learn about personal things like how Tiki Barber was his high school valedictorian. It's fun to watch and listen to the Swami's Predictions. These are all things that make playing fantasy football fun especially when ranking players. What about the more difficult and time-consuming tasks? There was little or no mention about projecting player statistics in order to determine a set of rankings – which is the conventional way to rank players. Nor was there any mention about creating a set of player rankings from scratch. Everyone seems to go straight to "watching tv and tweaking the expert rankings."

Ironically, it turns out that this short cut may be the best way to rank players. The reason is because extra efforts and analyses usually do not overcome the margins for error in ranking players. The truth is, few people including the experts can consistently out-perform everyone else when doing player rankings. For example, you'll find a plethora of significantly different player rankings from experts and fantasy managers during the pre-season. There is so much disparity in opinion that even the most competent experts are likely to end up ranking certain players 20+ spots apart. The bottom line is that there's no telling whose rankings are going to be better. Indeed, most of the experts have an equal or near-equal chance to be the best.

So, why should you or anyone else put forth the extra effort in ranking players? The truth is: you shouldn't. The many margins for error and the difficulty in predicting players dilute most of the skill needed to over-achieve in ranking players. So it should go without saying, there are few rights and wrongs for ranking players – rather mostly opinion. If you have one, use it. If you don't have an opinion, feel free to copy any expert list of your choosing.

Like thinking Ashlee Simpson actually sang live on "Saturday Night Live," the general public is sometimes wrong on many things. Where the general public is wrong is the amount of time spent on player rankings. Again, 61% said they spend most of their time on player rankings. There are two reasons why this isn't a good thing. First, player rankings shouldn't require extra efforts because those efforts often go for naught. You already know this. Managers who spend too much time on player rankings often do it for the wrong reason. They do it not because they necessary feel it's the most important step in preparing for the draft but because it is the most fun step in preparing for the draft. This is a trap you should avoid because there are things more important than ranking players. This brings us to the second reason why you don't want to put a lot of time and energy into player rankings, and that is because *the way you rank players is not nearly as important as the way you draft players (draft strategy)*. You'll learn more about draft strategy in the chapters that follow. For now, realize that fantasy drafts can still be conquered with mediocre rankings.

Of course, this is not to say a half-fast approach in ranking players will be beneficial to you. Anyone who takes too much of a lackadaisical approach in ranking players will consistently have bad player rankings – which can ruin your chances for a championship season. So, please, don't be confused with the point being made here. You still need to exercise some level of due diligence in player rankings. The better you can rank players the more icing you'll have on your cake. However, you shouldn't worry about spending that extra effort in trying to determine the best set because it usually doesn't pay off.

I recommend any of the following four approaches for ranking players:

1. Stay the course.

This suggests you continue to follow whatever ranking system you currently use assuming a) you have one, b) it works reasonably well, and c) you don't spend too much time on it. However, if you feel your system needs improvement (as most do), then consider trying one of the other methods that follow, or at least consider integrating some of the attributes of these methods into your own system.

2. Copycat the expert.

The second method is to simply use the rankings from your favorite expert. Although this may be the easiest route, it doesn't mean it's the worst. In fact, it could turn out to be the best route. While experts – and anyone else for that matter – were bashed in Chapter Three for their failure to project great statistics, they do a great job at ranking players. So why not take advantage of their expertise and analysis? Sure, there's a lot of variation in expert opinion but, again, that's an unavoidable aspect due to margins for error. Almost any set of expert rankings can arguably be considered the best. Just make sure that if you follow an expert's set of player rankings, it is based on fantasy scoring similar to your league. Otherwise this approach will turn counter-productive. Also, be sure to use an updated set of rankings. In other words, don't use magazine rankings that were printed two months before the draft or even web-site rankings that were listed two weeks before the draft. You need something that has been updated within hours, or days at the worst, of the draft to ensure yourself an accurate cheat sheet. Footballdiehards.com is a great site for updated sets of player rankings including those from Emil Kadlec, Bob Harris, and myself.

3. Follow convention.

Third, you can pretend you are Chris Berman, the Swami himself, and gaze into your crystal ball for projected stats. Here, you can follow conventional wisdom by projecting stats on each player, converting those stats into fantasy points, and ranking the players accordingly. Of course, this process entails all the legwork we try to avoid by using AVT from Chapter Three. But if convention remains your cup of tea then feel free to drink it. However, if you use personal player projections for ranking the players be sure to eventually replace those projections with AVT projections on the cheat sheet. If you have to ask yourself why, then flip back and re-read Chapter Three.

4. Utilize Zarzycki's ranking system.

The fourth approach is to follow my methodology for ranking players. In general, I like to observe five main criteria when determining a player's ranking: physical talent, mental approach, football stats, health, and job situation. All these "ingredients" blend into unique mixtures that create each NFL player's recipe for fantasy success – or failure. For instance, do you remember Rod Tidwell from the movie Jerry Maguire? He had many personal issues that influenced his performance on the field. If he was a fantasy football receiver, then anybody choosing him could be aware of his motivation that enabled him to have a great individual season in that movie. Consider the aforementioned factors that influence success, and maybe your chosen player will "show you the money."

Furthermore, I try to integrate a high level of objectivity with the right mix of "gut feeling." One of the things I like most about my methodology is that it includes many of the best processes used in the previous methods listed – an eclectic approach. For instance, you'll see that I like to factor in other expert rankings and opinions before ultimately ranking all players.

Another key to properly ranking players is to not be distracted by real-life events and player personalities when valuing a player. Managers are not rewarded if their players give a lot of autographs, have great chemistry in the locker room, do community work or start a charity (even though that's nice of them to do). Conversely, managers are not penalized if their fantasy star doesn't smile at the fans, get along with the media, or wear the right clothes. So, ignore those United Way commercials and post-game interviews and focus on the real deal – what fantasy points can a player achieve.

The remainder of this chapter will describe my ranking system in full detail. It will give you complete insight as to how an expert ranks players from the ground up. Even if you don't agree with many of the processes, you should still be able to carry over a few concepts, guidelines, and ideas to help improve your current ranking system.

STEPS AND GUIDELINES FOR RANKING PLAYERS

Follow these steps for each position separately.
Step 1 – Determine how many players to rank

It doesn't make sense to rank 300 WRs when only 90 of them will be drafted. It's like inspecting every doughnut at Krispy Kreme's before you choose your beloved jelly or glazed doughnut. You simply don't have to do it. Therefore, by knowing this limitation you will save time in avoiding ranking more players than you have to. Furthermore, this consolidates the cheat sheet.

Follow this general rule when determining how many players to rank:

Rank enough players to supply each manager with twice the maximum number of starters allowed.

For example, if each manager could start two RBs in a twelve-team league then twice the maximum number of starting RBs in the league is 2 x 2 x 12 running backs. Therefore, 48 RBs should be ranked on the cheat sheet. Suppose this league had a flex starter (RB/WR/TE). Now each team can start up to three RBs (2 RBs plus a flex RB). Here it would be wise to rank 2 x 3 x 12 RBs, or 72 RBs, on the cheat sheet.

Here's one last example to make sure you get the idea. The WCOFF has 12 teams per league and the starting line-up is 1 QB, 2 RBs, 3 WRs, 1 TE, 1 FLEX (RB/WR/TE), 1 K, & 1 D/ST. After integrating the flex player, you'll find the maximum players that can be started for each of the positions is 1 QB, 3 RBs, 4 WRs, 2 TEs, 1 K, & 1 D/ST. Multiplying these number by the number of teams in the league, and then doubling that number, a WCOFF cheat sheet should have 24 QBs, 72 RBs, 96 WRs, 48 TEs, 24 Ks, and 24 D/STs ranked. The one exception might be that you probably don't have to rank 48 TEs and just 24 would suffice owing to the fact that TEs aren't likely to be drafted as a flex player. (See step two of the RV Method in Chapter Seven for an explanation as to why this is).

Step 2 – Create initial rankings

Once you know how many players to rank in a position, you can begin determining who those players are going to be. This is like narrowing down your doughnut choices to jelly, glazed,

Boston or Bavarian Crème. I like to initially rank players according to their fantasy points scored per game over the past three years. This offers an excellent foundation because it appropriately ranks players even if they missed games due to injury/suspension. This process also ensures more credit will be given to those players who excel in your fantasy scoring system. For example, if your league offers one fantasy point per reception you'll find the pass-catching running backs are ranked higher than those who don't catch the ball often.

Emil Kadlec's *Stat Ledger* program is a great internet tool for determining the stats you need for this step (footballdiehards. com). Or, check out my site, DraftingToWin.com, for additional information.

Step 3 – Replace generic names with actual players

After you've determined an initial set of rankings, you can begin to insert those names in place of the generic names as created from doing AVT projections. Names such as RB1 and RB2 will be replaced with players like Clinton Portis and Shaun Alexander. Figure 14 lists a before-and-after.

BEFORE			AFTER		
Position &Rank	AVT Projection		Rank	RB	Projection
RB1	456		1	LaDainian Tomlinson	456
RB2	401		2	Marshall Faulk	401
RB3	342		3	Priest Holmes	342
RB4	324		4	Clinton Portis	324
RB5	312		5	Ricky Williams	312
RB6	307		6	Edgerrin James	307
RB7	303		7	Travis Henry	303
RB8	297		8	Deuce McAllister	297
RB9	284		9	Shaun Alexander	284
RB10	283		10	Ahman Green	283

FIGURE 14: CHEAT SHEET CHANGING FROM GENERIC TO ACTUAL

```
QB1 D. CULPEPPER

QB2 G. FREROTTE


RB1 M. BENNETT

RB2 M. WILLIAMS

RB3 O. SMITH


WR1 R.MOSS

WR2 D.BATES

WR3 K.CAMPBELL

WR4 N. BURLESON

WR5 K. HOWRY


TE1 J.KLEINSASSER

TE2 H.GOODWIN


FB C.STACKHOUSE


K1 A.ELLING
```

FIGURE 15:
2003
MINNESOTA VIKINGS
DEPTH CHART

Steps 4-6: Depth chart analysis

One of the most useful tools for ranking players is the NFL depth chart. The depth chart is as important to a fantasy footballer as it is to an actual head coach. It ranks players per position per NFL team. To give you an example, Figure 15 was the depth chart for the Minnesota Vikings at one point during 2003 season.

Depth charts tell us who's on the NFL roster, who's starting, who's backing up, et cetera. There is so much information to gain from depth charts that the next three steps make use of them. You can obtain updated charts from a variety of sources including NFL.com, ESPN.com, and Footballdiehards.com.

Step 4 – Weed Out Players

Do you remember that scrawny 5'7", third team point guard on your high school junior varsity basketball team? Well, he probably should have been cut. Similarly, the cheat sheet may contain several players who no longer deserve to be ranked. I call the process of removing these players "weeding." A player can be weeded for a variety of reasons including season-ending injury, suspension, demotion and/or retirement. In all these cases, NFL depth charts can be used to determine which players should and should not be weeded.

Keep in mind, when you weed a player, then all players below him will shift up the rankings list by one slot.

I recommend these general guidelines for weeding out players based on their position on the depth charts:

QUARTERBACK, TIGHT END AND KICKER

Weed any QB, TE and K that is not in the No. 1 slot. Why? NFL teams only start one of them. Therefore, the backups, or No. 2 slots rarely get a chance to play, let alone score any fantasy football points.

However, you may want to keep an eye on No. 2 slots if the guy is in a heated battle for the starting position. It's not rare for players to slide up and down the depth charts during pre-season football. When it happens, make sure you adjust accordingly. Do you remember Drew Brees' situation in 2004? He basically wasn't expected to start after the Chargers acquired first rounder Philip Rivers, but when Rivers held out for contract negotiations Brees took over the No. 1 slot and never looked back. Brees took the Chargers to the playoffs and had himself a career year.

RUNNING BACK

NFL coaches tend to play just one RB and sometimes two to three RBs. Therefore, weed any RB who is not in the top three slots. You can weed RBs who are in the No. 2 and No. 3 slots if they are not on a team that uses a committee approach that features all of them sharing the workload. These situations are known as a RBBC or runningback-by-committee. Think Jerome Bettis and Charlie Garner here. All guys involved in a RBBC are going to be on the playing field earning fantasy points; thus, they deserve to remain somewhere on the cheat sheet.

Wide Receiver

WR is the deepest position in the NFL. By "deep," I mean there are a lot of players that get playing time and score fantasy points. NFL teams often finish a game with at least four WRs in the stat box. Therefore, be very conservative in weeding WRs. Weed only those WRs in the fifth slot or lower. So, get rid of your Joey Dunklebergers or your Carlos Valdezes. Who? My point exactly.

Step 5 – Plant Players

As much as the stoner fantasy footballer wishes that "planting" is where fantasy footballers store their wacky weed, it is not. Planting is the process of finding and inserting new players into the cheat sheet. These players are most likely to be rookies out of college, professionals drafted from another football league (NFL Europe, Arena League, CFL), or already-existing NFL players who moved up the depth chart after a year or more of hard work. The reason they are not in the initial rankings list from step two is because they haven't acquired enough fantasy points in recent years. I'll refer to players that should be planted as "newcomers."

Keep in mind, when you plant a newcomer, then all players below him will shift down the rankings list by one. There will inevitably be one player who gets pushed off the cheat sheet assuming you strictly adhere to the rule in step one regarding how many players to rank. That's perfectly acceptable and encouraged, actually, because it keeps the cheat sheet consolidated.

Planting is a two-part process. The first part is determining who is worthy of being planted. This is pretty easy. To do this, use the same guidelines from step four; only use them to plant instead of weed. For instance, in step four you would weed out any QB not listed in the #1 slot. Here you would consider planting any QB in the # slot. In step four, you would weed out any RB not in the top slot or a RBBC. Here you plant any RB in the top slot or in a RBBC. Make sense?

The second part is much more ticklish. You need to determine where to plant the newcomers. Where a newcomer is ranked usually depends on his chance of making an impact and how big an impact he can make. By "impact" I mean competing well against other starting fantasy players throughout the course of a full season. To make an impact in fantasy football is to score close to what many of the other top fantasy players are scoring. For instance, let's say the twelve starting QBs in your 12-team fantasy league finished the season with an average fantasy output of 200 fantasy points. This would mean that a newcomer would have to score near 200 fantasy points to have made an impact for your fantasy squad. To make a bigger impact is to score more than 200 points.

Here are my general guidelines for planting NFL players:

QUARTERBACK

With all respect to Kurt Warner and Ben Roethlisberger, fantasy football has seen few QB newcomers make an impact. This means you'll have to be very careful and conservative if and where you decide to plant one. Fantasy managers tend to overrate them, believing that they are likely to make an impact, and rank them too high on the cheat sheet. This is usually the result of media hype. The media will tend to give new NFL starting QBs a lot of attention especially because they will make an immediate impact in the NFL, and rightfully so. Unfortunately, making an impact in the NFL doesn't always translate into making an impact in fantasy football. A perfect example is Roethlisberger's tremendous rookie season in 2004 when he nearly led the Pittsburgh Steelers to the Super Bowl.

While he held the NFL's best winning percentage among all starting QBs that year, he barely finished the fantasy season in the top 20 WCOFF rankings. The truth is, QB newcomers rarely make an impact in fantasy football.

Let's take a closer look.

From 1999-2004 only seven quarterbacks finished in the top 20 (WCOFF scoring) as a newcomer. See figure 16 for the yearly breakdown.

Rank	1999	2000	2001	2002	2003	2004
1-10	K. Warner	D. Culpepper	0	0	0	0
1-20	J. Garcia T. Couch	0	C. Weinke	0	B. Leftwich	B. Roethlisberger

FIGURE 16: NEWCOMER QBS WHO MADE AN IMPACT

These results are pretty staggering when you consider there are only 10-12 starting QBs in a typical fantasy league. This means that a newcomer must finish in the top ten to make any kind of a seasonal impact. Only Kurt Warner and Daunte Culpepper have been able to accomplish that feat in the six-year span shown in Figure 16.

Of course, there are many newcomer QBs who can, and do, make an impact in fantasy football in any given week. However, when we rank players on the cheat sheet it is for the ENTIRE season – not just for any given week. Thus, the results from Figure 16 ultimately tell us it's not very wise to plant newcomer QBs high up in the rankings.

Let's get into why QBs have difficulty succeeding early in their NFL careers. First, the NFL playbook is full of complex plays and timing routes so it takes time to learn. Second, NFL defenses are equally complex and can defend against the QB using tricky schemes. Third, the NFL moves light years faster than college leaving the newcomer slow to react. Fourth, newcomers often take a conservative approach in order to minimize their own mistakes. Coaches add to this effect by often calling a conservative game in order to "protect" a young quarterback from mistakes and injury.

So, where should you rank a newcomer QB?

First realize that any NFL starting QB deserves to be ranked in at least the top 32 because there are only 32 starting QBs in the NFL. You just have to be cautious in ranking him in the top 20 and especially the top 10. Just like a fresh on-the-scene swimsuit model is hot doesn't mean she is the next Heidi Klum, right? Well, top rankings are reserved only for those players who are likely to make an impact and not for the hot rookies. Truthfully, I have never ranked a newcomer in the top ten. Furthermore, I am only inclined to rank a newcomer in the 11-20 range if he has exceptional talent (Michael Vick); has recently played in another professional league like the CFL or Arena League (Kurt Warner/Tommy Maddox); or if he has been in the NFL for at least a year learning from the sidelines (Chad Pennington/Daunte Culpepper). These guys possess that something extra that sets them above the rest of the newcomers. In most cases, however, I will stick to ranking newcomers in the lowest echelon, the 20-32 range.

RUNNING BACK

Unlike the QB position, newcomers are likely to make an immediate impact when given the opportunity in the RB position. It is not rare to find a rookie RB finish the season in the top ten fantasy scoring. That's because the running back position doesn't involve intricate thinking, planning, and practicing like the QB position. This is not to take away from the position. It's just that it is easier for young talented athletes to excel right away in the RB position. Figure 17 shows newcomer running backs who made an impact in fantasy football from 1999-2004.

Rank/Year	1999	2000	2001	2002	2003	2004
1-10	Edgerrin James	0	LaDainian Tomlinson	Clinton Portis	0	0
11-20	Olandis Gary	Mike Anderson Jamal Lewis	Dominic Rhodes Anthony Thomas	0	Domanick Davis	W. McGahee
21-30	Ricky Williams	Travis Prentice	Michael Bennett Travis Henry	Marcel Shipp	0	0

FIGURE 17: NEWCOMER RBS WHO MADE AN IMPACT

Notice there are eight more impact RBs than QBs. One reason for this result is that the RB position is easier to master than the QB position in the NFL, as already mentioned. Another reason is the inclusion of ranks 21-30 in observing impact players as seen in Figure 17 as compared to just observing the top 20 ranked players like in Figure 16. Actually, only the top 10 ranked QBs should really be considered as impact players in Figure 16. Bottom line, RBs do not have to finish the season ranked as high as QBs to be considered an impact player.

Why are more rankings observed in the RB position than the QB position? Fantasy football starts more RBs than QBs. A typical fantasy roster will have two to three starting RBs per team compared to just one QB. This means a twelve-team fantasy league will have 24-36 starting RBs and just 12 QBs. Therefore, a RB who ranks in the 21-30 range still makes an impact because he is still in scoring proximity of some of the other starting RBs.

As far as where to plant a newcomer RB, it very much depends on the depth chart and the job situation. For those RBs listed in the No. 1 slot, you must find out if his NFL coach plans on using him as a workhorse (one who gets most of the team's carries) or as part of a RBBC (where carries are shared among players). In almost any situation, you can find the answer by keeping abreast with NFL news and team reports. You'll typically find about one-third of the NFL teams use a RBBC while the other teams give most of the carries to one guy. The workhorses are the players you should salivate over. They are potential fantasy RB studs who have the opportunity to accumulate a lot of fantasy points due to all the carries they are expected to get. Think Clinton Portis, Edgerrin James or LaDainian Tomlinson in their heyday. Any RB labeled as a team's workhorse should automatically be ranked in the top 20. You should strongly consider ranking a workhorse in the top 10 if you hear, read, and see positive news on this player.

If a newcomer RB is a part of a RBBC, then it's not as important where he's listed on the depth chart. Whether he's the No. 1, 2, or 3 guy in a RBBC, he's going to share the workload regardless. I would have to analyze each of the players in the RBBC and see what might come out of it. If the news indicates the newcomer has a lot of potential to eventually carry the team – a good indication would be the coach praising him in the pre-season – then this is an obvious chance that the RBBC could eventually turn solo, and the newcomer may turn out to be a weekly workhorse by the end of the season. Here, I would consider ranking him in the 20-35 range based mostly on this potential. However, this type of situation is a rarity, and in most cases a RBBC will remain a RBBC throughout the year. RBBCs aren't very attractive to fantasy football managers due to shared workload. Unless one of the players in the committee gets injured (odds are against it) don't expect any of them to become big impact fantasy players. I will rank a RB in a RBBC somewhere in the 20-30 range if he's in the No. 1 slot of a two-man RBBC and the 30-40 range if he's in the No. 2 slot. For three-man RBBC it's caveat emptor. Here, playing time is extremely diluted due to shared workloads among three players so be very careful on who you take. To make matters worse in a three-man RBBC, you still can't expect a big jump in value if one of the players in the RBBC gets injured because time will still be shared among two players. Thus, I'm apt to rank newcomers that fall into this situation very low on the cheat sheet. I'll rank him in the 25-35 range only if he's in the No. 1 slot, otherwise he's going to be planted somewhere in the thirties, forties, or even fifties.

Has Ron Dayne ever won anything for your fantasy football team? Well, if he hasn't, then it is because he is always sitting behind Tiki Barber and doesn't get the chance to play. Hence, if a RB is in the No. 2 or No. 3 slot on a team that doesn't follow a committee approach, then you have to see if there's any chance for him to move up into the No. 1 slot. Again, the No. 1 slot is the coveted position here because it receives the bulk of the workload. A newcomer represents very little value if there's very little chance he will move into the No. 1 slot. For instance, if the only way he could move up is by an injury to the starting player then I would put very little emphasis on his value and ranking. On the other hand, if the newcomer is on a team that is still looking for a No. 1 starter then he may be deserving of a higher ranking based on potential. Some teams will put that No. 1 slot up for grabs to the RB that best competes in the pre-season. Any newcomer that finds himself in such competition and actually has a chance of becoming a stud RB deserves respect on the cheat sheet. Look to rank such a player in the 20-40 range depending on the situation.

If the newcomer is a No. 2 RB who is not in contention to take over the starting role, then he still may be of value to your fantasy squad. Specifically, he can be valuable as a handcuff to your starting fantasy RB. A handcuff is a fantasy player who backs up your fantasy starter. Suppose you drafted the workhorse RB on the Seattle Seahawks as your starting fantasy RB. The No. 2 RB of the Seahawks can be of value to your squad because of his insurance value. If your starter gets injured, then the No. 2 RB can take over where the No 1. RB left off. Remember, one's loss is usually another's gain in fantasy football. A good handcuffer is one who's able to obtain nearly all of another player's value in the event of an injury leaving you, the fantasy manager, without a loss.

However, there is a problem in ranking handcuffs because his value is dynamic. That is, his value and ranking changes considerably depending on the players you draft in the early rounds. Looking back at the prior example, what if you didn't draft the No. 1 RB on the Seahawks? In this case you should not have much of an interest in drafting the No. 2 RB because he really offers no value to you unless, of course, you think he would make great trade bait to the manager who drafted the Seahawk's No. 1. Bottom line, without the No. 1 RB, the No. 2 RB doesn't present much value because he doesn't offer any immediate fantasy results nor any kind of insurance value. However, if you draft the No. 1 RB for the Seahawks, the No. 2 instantly becomes a valuable pickup for your fantasy squad. Based on this dynamic aspect, you really shouldn't worry too much about where to rank handcuffers. Rather, it's best to take a reactive approach. Rank them relatively low on the cheat sheet but keep an eye on them. Pump up their value and ranking if you draft a handcuff's respective No. 1 RB. If you don't draft the No 1 RB, you should only consider drafting a No. 2 if it's late in the draft, if you have an open roster spot to fill, if you feel this No. 2 RB could make a huge impact if he ever had the chance to start, or if you can use him as trade bait. To reiterate, where you initially rank handcuffers isn't all that important because your value and ranking of them will change depending on who else you draft. I will explain the process of drafting handcuffs in more detail in Chapter Ten.

NFL FULLBACKS

With all apologies to Daryl "Moose" Johnston and J.P. Comella, we have to remember that while the NFL still utilizes the fullback position, fantasy football does not. Therefore, those players listed as fullbacks on NFL depth charts must ultimately be treated and ranked like a running back. Of course, knowing someone is a fullback in the NFL certainly does affect where you should rank him as a fantasy running back. In general, fullbacks do not make as much an impact as traditional running backs. This is mostly because the fullback position demands more blocking for the ball carrier as opposed to being the ball carrier. As we all know, fantasy sports don't exactly award points for blocking.

Adding to this effect is that when fullbacks do carry the ball, it's usually for short yardage plays.

This is not to say that all fullbacks don't offer any kind of value. In fact, a fullback can offer quite a bit of value if he catches a lot of passes (good for scoring systems that award 1 fantasy point per reception) or scores a lot of short yardage TDs. If you find a fullback who fits either of these profiles, he may be worthy of a rank in the 30-50 range depending on how many fantasy points you think he is likely to score. For the most part, even the top NFL fullbacks are backup fantasy running backs at best. To give you an idea, Dallas Cowboys FB Richie Anderson was the highest scoring fullback in the 2004 WCOFF season, yet he only finished as the 47th best fantasy running back.

WIDE RECEIVER

The WR position is the deepest of all positions. The position is so deep that many NFL teams consistently show three to four receivers with decent numbers in the stat box at the end of each game. Because of this, fantasy league commissioners tend to establish starting lineup rules that allow managers to start more WRs than any other position with as many as four in some leagues. With so many starting WRs, this means there is a very wide range of rankings that make an impact. Usually WRs who finish the season in the top 40 made an impact. Figure 18 is a list of all newcomer WRs that finished the season in the top 40 from 1999-2004.

Rank	1999	2000	2001	2002	2003	2004
1-10	0	0	0	0	Anquan Boldin	0
11-20	0	0	0	0	Andre Johnson	Michael Clayton
21-30	Kevin Johnson	0	0	0	0	Lee Evans
31-40	Torry Holt	Darrell Jackson Peter Warrick	Chris Chambers Rod Gardner	0	0	Larry Fitzgerald Roy Williams Keary Colbert

FIGURE 18: NEWCOMER WRS WHO MADE AN IMPACT

There are a total of 13 newcomer WRs who made an impact in the six-year span shown in Figure 18 with more than half of them falling in the lowest echelon, the 31-40 range. Considering this is supposed to be the deepest position, these results show how extremely hard it is for newcomers to make an impact in this position. Why is this?

Wide receivers are closely related to quarterbacks in that they both have a steep learning curve. In fact, the two positions are linked together. One passes the ball to the other. It requires chemistry, quick thinking, precise passing, precise running, and concentrated execution in order for each pass to be completed. Strong chemistry usually takes years to develop. Let's also remember that the NFL playbook instills complex plays, timing patterns, and proper positioning when it comes to pass plays. This is the only way to consistently beat opposing defenses which are filled with the world's smartest, fastest, and most gifted football defenders. Thus, it usually takes a WR two to three years before he adapts to this level of competition and starts scoring a decent level of fantasy points.

All of the above is very significant when deciding where to plant newcomer WRs on your cheat sheet. Here's a quick and fast rule: *never rank a newcomer in the top 30*. As you can see in figure 18, it's a rarity when a newcomer cracks the top 30. There's no need to push the envelope.

I must warn you, however, that it will be difficult to strictly adhere to this rule. Each season there's a crop of players out of college with phenomenal skills and raw talent. They'll certainly be hyped up by NFL scouts and media. Don't let this affect your fantasy know-how. Keep reminding yourself that it doesn't matter if he's seven feet tall and runs a 4.3 forty, he's still a long-shot to excel in his first year as a fantasy player.

Personally, I like to analyze where a WR was taken in the NFL draft when deciding where he should be ranked on a fantasy cheat sheet. If a receiver was drafted in the top 15 picks of the NFL draft, then he may be worthy enough of a ranking somewhere in the thirties. These guys are "freaks" who are very dangerous on any given play. Their biggest advantage might be that NFL franchises that spend a high pick on a WR are typically in need of a starting wide receiver *right now*. This means he'll get plenty of opportunities on the field in order to rack up fantasy points. This extra playing time compensates for the position's steep learning curve.

Other top prospects are WRs who have great skill but don't have quite enough potential to be the very best. These are guys who are drafted in the mid-to-late first round and possibly the early second round of the NFL draft. Look at the player as well as the team that drafted him. The key ingredient is how much playing time this guy is likely to see. If the team doesn't have a solid core of starting WRs already, you may consider ranking the newcomer in the thirties due to expected playing time. In most cases, a ranking in the forties or fifties will best suit his situation.

With all other newcomers it's truly a crap shoot. I couldn't tell you where to rank them other than not in the top 40. The best thing to do is read player reports during training camp being very careful not to fall for any hype. Rank a newcomer higher if you feel he has a chance to get some decent playing time. It's all about PT, baby. Look for NFL teams that are in disarray. Some teams may not have a solid No. 1 or even No. 2 WR. In this situation there can be sometimes four or five guys fighting for the coveted top two WR slots. Keep an eye out for any newcomers slipping into this situation. If he proves himself in the pre-season and develops good chemistry with his QB, then things just may turn out to be all right. This is exactly what happened with the Arizona Cardinals in 2003. They had about five WRs competing for the top two spots. In fact, I was fully aware of this situation in the 2003 WCOFF draft. I took two Cardinal newcomers (Jason McAddley and Larry Foster) hoping that one of them would rise to the top and turn into a nice sleeper pick. You know what? I was right! One of the newcomers turned into a stud! Unfortunately for me, it was the Cardinals late second-round pick Anquan Boldin who, quite frankly, I thought was the longest shot of all to succeed. He eventually earned the No. 1 slot and turned into one of the best WRs in the NFL. He scored eight TDs and received over 1,300 yards. Plus, he set a rookie record in receptions (101). Most importantly, he finished the year in the top 10 fantasy WRs. So even though I wasn't lucky enough to get Boldin, my strategy was right in that one of the Cardinal WRs was going to turn out nicely.

TIGHT END

Tight ends are similar to wide receivers in that they get a majority of their points from running pass routes and receiving the ball. In other words, TEs also face a steep learning curve due to the intricacies involved in learning the position. However, the similarities between the two positions may end there. Most other aspects of the two positions differ greatly. Here are three you need to be most aware of. First, TEs are not a deep position. NFL teams will utilize just one and sometimes two tight ends. Second, TEs are often used more for blocking rather than receiving. Third, if and when a TE does catch the ball it's often a short yardage "check-down." Owing to these three characteristics, TEs are not apt to make big plays and score a lot of fantasy points. Also, due to the limitations of the position only those who finish the season in the top 10 are really considered impact TEs. So there aren't many impact TEs available especially from a crop of newcomers. Now, I know Jeremy Shockey made a huge impact for the Giants his rookie year, but you should think of him as the exception rather than the rule. Therefore, you should not rely on tight ends to earn you serious points.

Figure 19 is a list of every newcomer TE that has made an impact from 1999-2004.

	1999	2000	2001	2002	2003	2004
1-5	0	0	0	Jeremy Shockey	0	0
6-10	0	0	0	Randy McMichael	0	0

FIGURE 19: NEWCOMER TES WHO MADE AN IMPACT

As you see, there are only two impact players, and they both hit the NFL scene in 2002.

Obviously, these results show us that we should be very wary about planting TEs in the top ten. Consequently, you should only concern yourself with newcomers that are listed as the No. 1 TE on a NFL team's depth chart. Even then you may not want to rank him high especially if he's known as more of a blocker than a pass catcher. Remember, blocking is great for the NFL but it's worthless in fantasy football. On the other hand, if he's a big, tall guy who has shown great pass-catching abilities in college, then consider planting him anywhere in the 6-20 range. This situation depends on how good he is as a receiver and how his NFL team plans on using him. For instance, when the New York Giants drafted Jeremy Shockey, Head coach Jim Fassel was outspoken about changing the offensive game plan to accommodate their new weapon. Subsequently, the Giants went from last to first in TE pass plays, and Shockey went on to finish the season as a top five fantasy TE. If you find a TE that fits the same bill, then don't hesitate to take a chance on him by ranking him in the 6-10 range.

KICKER

Kickers are almost as useless to fantasy teams as a snow shovel is in Hawaii. However, we still have to value and rank them accordingly. Uniquely enough though, a fantasy kicker's value is more dependent on the NFL team he plays for rather than his own skills. The strongest most sure-footed kicker is worth very little if his team doesn't get him into field goal range. Almost as bad is a kicker that plays on an explosive offense that scores too many touchdowns. That's because a kicker's value comes from kicking lots of field goals and not extra points.

Ideally, the best fantasy kickers will be involved in an offense that is strong enough to get into the red zone (inside the 20 yard line) but not strong enough to punch it into the end zone. Unfortunately, it's very difficult to predict such an offense. I look for teams that have a strong running back and weak quarterback, or vice versa. These are teams that may have enough talent to move the ball down the field, but there's that "missing piece" that may keep them from scoring TDs. As a consequence, their field goal kicker will rack it up with lots of opportunities.

Some people might even look to see if a guy kicks for a team that plays in a dome because weather conditions are minimized. A kicker in a dome is less likely to be affected by wind, snow, and rain throughout the course of the season.

The most consistent rule of thumb has been that the stronger a team's offense the more fantasy value its kicker has. In fact, many experts rank kickers according to the strengths of their respective team offenses. Usually, teams that have enough firepower to score a lot of touchdowns will still get their fair share of field goals. Even if the team scores too many TDs and the kicker puts up a lot of extra points, that's still a lot better than a team that can't even make it into field goal range, and the kicker doesn't do anything.

This is not to say we should ignore the skill level of the kicker entirely. We still must look at his talents. Can he kick the ball far? Can he kick it with accuracy? What are his field goal and extra point statistics from his prior team? There are a lot of attributes you could look for in a kicker such as years of experience, career field goal percentage, longest field goal made, and career field goal percentage of attempts 40+ and/or 50+ yards long.

The cool thing about a kicker's history is that it's very tell-tale. If he can kick forty yarders in high school or college then he most likely can kick forty yarders in the NFL. Again, try not to put too much stock in his skill because his team has much more of an affect on his fantasy value. Owing to this, it isn't necessary to analyze how many newcomers have made an impact in a six-year span such as Figures 16-19. Rather, you can simply analyze all kickers, whether they are newcomers or veterans, based on their talent and the NFL team they play for.

DEFENSE/SPECIAL TEAMS (NOT APPLICABLE)

The only occasion you would find yourself dealing with a newcomer D/ST is when an expansion team enters the NFL. This occasion is so rare that there is no need to provide any information on it.

Steps 6 – 11: Repositioning

By now your cheat sheet should have just about every player accounted for, including newcomers and veterans. Whether or not these guys are in their right places is yet to be analyzed. Since you spent a lot of time positioning newcomers, it's now time to position, or reposition, the veterans and all those NFL players that were in the initial rankings from step two.

Step 6 – Historical rankings

Newcomers are tricky to predict because there's no telling how they'll perform in the NFL. This is obviously not the case with NFL veterans. These players have a history to look at – something that is valuable in determining where he should be ranked. However, it's also important not to get caught up in analyzing NFL stats and numbers. There are so many categories and columns of numbers to analyze you can end up with brain freeze. Instead, I recommend simplifying things by observing historical fantasy rankings. This offers an overall picture that's easy to review. The point is to base this year's ranking simply on where he has ranked in the past several years.

Since the initial ranking list was created by analyzing each player's fantasy-points-per-game data over the last three years, chances are most of the veterans will be in close proximity to where they should be ranked. Nevertheless, there are always holes to patch up. For example, suppose player A was ranked 10th on the initial list. After planting and weeding you notice he still lies in 10th place on the cheat sheet. Now let's say you saw that he finished as the 1st, 2nd, and 12th ranked fantasy player in each of the previous three years, respectively. In this case I would consider ranking him better than 10th because he proved to be a top-two receiver twice in the last three years. Then again, my opinion might tell me Player A is on the decline because he took a big dip the last year. Maybe Player A is getting too old. Maybe he had a serious injury. Maybe his team was at fault by not throwing to him enough, or maybe he was worrying about his hip-hop career too much. It will boil down to your personal opinion. You'll simply have to analyze the player's situation, keep abreast the NFL news, and make a ranking decision.

Just because Mike Vrabel has three touchdowns in three career receptions doesn't mean he should be a Hall of Fame Tight End. So, watch out for players who play in gimmick situations or players with fewer than 10 games worth of experience during the last three years. It's very possible his average-fantasy-points-per-game is skewed high or low due to his short stint; thus, he may have been placed too high or too low on the initial ranking list. Research each player as much as possible in order to see if he needs repositioning. You can follow a lot of the guidelines presented in the newcomer section since many of them apply to veterans as well. For instance, all the guidelines for kickers can be applied to both newcomers and veterans.

This is also the time to strongly think about your league's scoring and its rules. For example, if you are in a keeper league you should slide the younger players up the rankings and significantly drop those players who are nearing their retirement. The reason for this is simple. Rookies and young stars can be kept for the long-term while older veterans only offer immediate value. Bottom line, any rule you can exploit in your league is to your advantage.

Step 7 – Veteran depth charting

Depth charts are such a powerful tool in helping rank newcomers, how can we not use the same tool for veterans? I recommend following the general guidelines in Figure 20, which tell you where the veteran should be listed on the depth chart according to where he is currently ranked on the cheat sheet. If you find a player's current ranking and depth chart position do not match up according to Figure 20, then you might want to reposition him accordingly. As always, you'll simply have to evaluate the situation and make your own decision as to where to rank him.

	If you ranked him here:	He should be here on the depth chart. ...
QB	1-32	1st
QB	33+	2nd
RB	1-20	1st
RB	21-40	1st or 2nd
WR	1-10	1st
WR	11-20	1st , possibly 2nd
WR	21-30	1st or 2nd
WR	31-40	1st, 2nd, or 3rd
TE	1-32	1st
K	1-32	1st
D/ST	N/A	N/A

FIGURE 20: GUIDELINE FOR RANKING VETERANS

I remind you that these are general guidelines and unique situations may present exceptions to the rule. For instance, there might be a stud fantasy QB who is currently a free agent in the NFL. This means he should still probably be ranked in the top ten even though he's not on any NFL depth charts. The moment he gets picked up by a NFL team he'll instantly move into the No. 1 slot.

Step 8 – Target potential

While historical analysis and depth charting provide a good strategy for ranking players, the true experts know the best edge comes from factoring in hidden potential. For example, some experts seem to know just what running back plays his best on grass instead of turf, and some managers know that a 6'5" receiver is playing in a conference where the average height of the opposing corner back is 5'9". This goes to show that although many players who have potential aren't necessarily good enough to be ranked in the crème de la crème, they can certainly finish there. The key is to rank these potential sleepers high enough so that you snag them right before your opponents were planning to. However, you should also be careful not to rank them too high because, let's not forget, they only offer potential at this point. You don't want to waste high draft picks on players who may not turn into anything. I recommend ranking players with potential just a few notches higher than you might normally rank him. I'll provide more detail on how to target and draft sleepers in Chapter Nine. In the meantime, here are some guidelines that will help you find hidden potential in each position:

QUARTERBACK

Quarterbacks are like women. Guys can never seem to figure them out. For instance, quarterbacks can have a complete failure of a year one season and a stellar season the next. Many times this is due to a QB moving into a new environment. That's exactly what happened to Rich Gannon. Gannon had quarterbacked for various teams in the NFL for 10 years and never made a big impact. Then he signed on with the Oakland Raiders in 1999, and his career blossomed. He racked off four straight seasons as a top five fantasy QB. Of course, no one could have imagined he'd turn out to be this great. Nevertheless, moving to a new environment – the Raiders – should have raised a red flag that it's conceivable for him to turn over a new leaf.

Moving to a new environment doesn't necessarily mean moving to a new team. Some QBs enter a new environment because their teams significantly changed the roster during the off-season. This can result in a whole new team chemistry and atmosphere for the QB. Look for positive team changes that can lift a QB to new heights. If a team has significantly improved its O-line, wide receivers, or even upgraded its running back, that could lead to better QB numbers. An improved O-line will offer more protection and more time to pass the ball. An improved WR core will offer more receiving potential down the field. Ironically, the best weapon of all may be a stud RB. RBs are good for sustaining long drives down the field, hence more plays and opportunities for the QB to rack up fantasy points. The very best RBs will also give the QB lots of short dump offs that can turn into big passing plays. Remember, all yards ran after the catch, still get credited as passing yards to the QB.

Another thing to look for in a QB is how many years of experience he has starting in a professional football league. This experience can come from just about any professional league including the NFL, Arena Football, CFL, and NFL Europe. Just take a look at how Tommy Maddox excelled in the NFL after getting some experience in the now defunct XFL. Guys with professional experience are beyond the steep learning curve leaving them in a position to run on all cylinders. This ultimately gives them a realistic shot at the top ten, maybe even top five in fantasy scoring.

RUNNING BACK

To be a RB sleeper usually means to be on the right team at the right time. Two scenarios that come to mind are a RB being taken by a team that is looking for a starter or a RB being on a team where the starter gets injured, demoted, or traded away. Since RBs face a very short learning curve in succeeding in the NFL (meaning, newcomers and veterans can be treated similarly), the section on RB newcomers in step five provides all the guidelines you need to know in searching for those who have the best potential to excel in the position.

WIDE RECEIVER AND TIGHT END

Veteran WRs and TEs tend to reach a scoring plateau after four to five years of playing in the NFL. For example, a TE who's been a great blocker in the NFL for four years isn't going to turn into a great pass-catcher in his fifth year. Basically, what you see is what you get when it comes to WRs and TEs after they've played several years. This makes it very easy to value and rank those players who've been in the league for four or more years. Simply keep his current ranking in close proximity to where he's finished in the past. Bottom line: there's very little hidden potential in the vets.

Your main focus in targeting potential should be on the super-talented WRs and TEs who are in their 2nd and 3rd years in the NFL. These are likely to be guys that were top prospects out of college a couple of years ago. Sure, they might have struggled in their rookie or sophomore seasons in the NFL, but they are still riding that proverbial learning curve. As you'll see in Chapter Nine, this curve tends to be overcome after a two to three year process. In fact, I tend to draft a handful of young WRs who are in their second and third seasons for this reason alone. Try to focus on those players that are on NFL teams that have openings for a starting position. Playing time is extremely crucial for a WR to reach his full potential. If his team doesn't show any confidence in him or plays him on a limited basis then he may never get the opportunity to blossom into that sleeper you were hoping for on draft day.

PLACE-KICKER

Again, kickers are mostly dependent on their team's offensive ability to fly down the field and land in field goal range. I like to target all kickers who are on teams with a good QB but a not so good RB, or vice versa. Again, these type of offenses tend to have enough talent to move down the field into field goal range but lack that extra weapon to punch it in the endzone. This equates to plenty of field goals and lots of hidden potential for a kicker.

DEFENSE/SPECIAL TEAMS

Deciding which D/STs to rank in the top ten is like deciding which members of 'N SYNC you wish to see fall off the planet first. They all deserve consideration if you think about it long enough. I rank Joey Fatone first by the way. Needless to say, D/STs is the most difficult of all positions to rank. To give you an example, in 2003, Fantasy Football Pro Forecast Magazine took pre-season D/ST rankings from thirteen of the most well-respected and successful fantasy football experts in the world including yours truly. All the rankings were combined into one "average" that established the experts' choice. These results were compared to actual results as shown in Figure 21.

Rank	Expert Rankings	Actual Finish
1	Tampa Bay	6
2	Philadelphia	17
3	Miami	5
4	Pittsburgh	16
5	Carolina	19
6	Atlanta	10
7	Baltimore	3
8	Green Bay	15
9	Oakland	24
10	New England	1

FIGURE 21: 2003 EXPERT D/ST VERY TOUGH TO PREDICT

As you can see, half the teams did not finish even close to the top ten. Furthermore, of the teams that did finish in the top ten, they still did not finish relatively close to their pre-season ranking.

Why are D/STs difficult to rank?

I can give you two reasons. First, it's much more difficult to predict an entire team of players than it is to predict just one guy. There are many more factors, issues, and unknowns involved with a team of players. Thus, there's a greater margin for error in predicting results. Second, top ten D/STs score a big chunk of points via TDs. Whether it's a kickoff return or an interception returned for a TD, the point is, these kinds of TDs are extremely lucky as well as unpredictable. Almost any given team in any given year can hit a lucky streak of defensive and special teams' TDs that catapult them into the top ten, thus making them even more unpredictable.

There are two morals to this story. First, don't break your back worrying about ranking D/STs. The position is incredibly unpredictable so don't waste your time. Second, it's not all that bad if you end up picking a D/ST that's ranked very low. Again, almost any team has a decent shot to finish as a top ten fantasy squad as shown in the right column of Figure 21. So don't be afraid to sit back and let your opponents take all the top-ranked teams while you draft from other positions first.

Step 9 – Observing the media, NFL news and press conferences

Some fantasy footballers have lives, and some don't. Yet, those who sit in front of the tube all day have a distinct advantage over the fantasy footballer who is taking his grandmother's poodle out for a walk or sipping Bahama-Mamas on some island filled with white sand. Not coincidentally, keeping abreast with the NFL news and media plays a critical part in almost every step, so I listed it here as its own category, not only to emphasize its true importance but also to point out some of its potential pitfalls.

The NFL is under constant scrutiny by the press. It receives more publicity and attention than any other major sport in the USA. This has its advantages – and disadvantages – for fantasy football managers. Any knowledge you can garner from the TV, internet, newspaper, radio, or watching live play is power...assuming you use it wisely. You will constantly be adjusting and tweaking your rankings as you learn more about the players and teams from the news. For example, if you hear Bill Belichick announce he's going to make it a team goal to throw more passes to a certain receiver, then move the receiver up in the rankings. If you hear Tom Coughlin say Tiki Barber is having difficulty recovering from a hamstring injury, then slide him down. If you hear Chris Mortensen announce that a player might be in trouble with the law because he was caught with a hooker and wearing ladies underwear, then you might want to drop him in the rankings due to "distractions." Gathering news, interpreting it, and using it to adjust rankings is an ongoing process until the day you draft players. Actually, it continues after the draft, but right now we are only concerned with how the news affects the draft day cheat sheet.

The real trick is sifting through the news, figuring out what's relevant, and trying to determine how much it should affect your rankings. You have to be responsible with what you see and hear. Some news is hearsay; other news is redundant (that is, your cheat sheet already factored it in); and sometimes things are blown out of proportion. The media is full of drama queens. It all boils down to your own judgment, intuition and opinion. An excellent source for up-to-date NFL news and notes is Footballdiehards.com's very own Bob Harris. Harris is regarded as one of the best, if not the best, NFL news gatherers for fantasy football web sites. He also offers a mighty credible opinion on much of the news he reports. Basically, any significant news regarding the NFL and its players will be hunted down by Harris and posted in his *FlashUpdate* (TFLreport.com) and at Footballdiehards.com.

I still have to remind you that even much of the news reported by Harris, which originates from NFL beat writers and reporters from around the country, is liable to fall under media hype. For example, this happens a lot when a rookie quarterback comes to town. He'll get a lot of hype and attention. Do I need to mention Ryan Leaf or Eli Manning here? Well, as a fantasy manager, you must keep reminding yourself that rookie QBs are likely to need several years to develop so ignore this type of hype – and that's if they develop at all! (Ahhhem—Leaf—mmm, excuse me.) Another example where the media may hype the situation in the wrong direction is when there's a new head coach. For instance, if a "defensive-minded" head coach takes over a team that already has a good offense, the media tends to stir the pot of controversy by trying to hint that the new head coach will ruin the chemistry of the offense. I remember this happened to Peyton Manning and the Colts when defensive guru Tony Dungy took over the team as head coach in 2002. The media slammed this franchise because many felt that by bringing in Dungy it would ruin an offense that was already great. Yet, Peyton Manning and the Colts offense never missed a beat. In fact, the Colts eventually broke several individual and team passing and receiving records in 2004 including Manning breaking Dan Marino's TD record, all under the leadership of Dungy.

On the flipside, the media tends to favor an offense more than it should if an "offensive-minded" coach takes control of a struggling NFL franchise. In 2001 the Washington Redskins snagged one of football's most brilliant offensive minds by signing the Florida Gators' Steve Spurrier. Consequently, the media continuously hyped up Spurrier's genius mind for developing the "fun-n-gun" offense. Many fantasy footballers fell into the trap by taking guys such as Patrick Ramsey, Stephen Davis, and Rod Gardner very early in the draft. All these guys underperformed, at least to what the media hyped them up to be, and the Washington offense ultimately flunked. Two years later, Spurrier resigned.

I personally follow this simple rule when it comes to NFL head coaches: Ignore them and the hype that follows!

Step 10 – Dealing with the injury/suspension report

It's extremely important to stay abreast of all NFL injuries/ suspensions, especially while ranking players. Injury reports tell us how many weeks a player will be out or is expected to be out in the form of something like "expected to miss four to six weeks." Be very careful about injury return dates and how it affects your fantasy season. If the NFL regular season begins in two weeks then a "four to six weeks" prognosis is really only "two to four weeks" because you only care about how many weeks he'll miss during the regular season.

Sometimes you'll find reports disclosing that a player is ahead of schedule in his rehabilitation process. It's up to you to determine if that's wishful thinking or the truth. If it's from the "horse's mouth," it could be wishful thinking. If it's from the team doctor, then I might put a little more faith in the statement.

You also have to be cautious about injuries that may take additional time to heal. For instance, fantasy managers entered the 2003 season with the general perception that Atlanta's stud QB Mike Vick would be out only six to eight weeks with a broken leg. You know what, I didn't see the initials "M.D." following these managers' last names. Subsequently, six weeks into the season, Vick admitted, with a tear in his eye, he would need more time to heal. He didn't return until three weeks left in the season, well after most managers dropped him off the roster.

As a fantasy owner, you'll come across a wide range of injuries such as high ankle sprains, torn ACLs, and several degrees of concussions. Some injuries are hard to figure out; others are very easy to deal with. For instance, I wouldn't put too much worry on a bruised forearm to the non-throwing arm of a quarterback or third degree burns due to a botched back waxing on a pretty boy receiver. However, a pulled hamstring on a wide receiver could nag him throughout the entire season. It's up to you to decide which injuries to be more careful about when drafting players. Since few of us are doctors, we can only trust the reports and prognosis provided by the NFL team and its medical staff. If you have additional resources, feel free to take advantage of them. I know this one accountant who consults his family doctor on the various injuries of his fantasy players. In return for injury advisories the doc gets some free tax advice. It's funny how networking sometimes connects various professions.

Now let's get into how to actually rank those players who are injured. It's not as straight- forward as you may think. Start by ranking the injured player as if he weren't injured at all. In other words, rank him where you would normally, had the injury not occurred. This will let you see what his projected fantasy points would be if he played a full and healthy season. Obviously, since he's injured we'll have to take a chunk of these points away. This "chunk" should be in proportion to the number of weeks he's expected to miss in relation to the entire fantasy season. For example, if a player is expected to miss eight weeks (half a fantasy season) you should remove fifty percent (8 divided by 16) of his projected fantasy points. If a player is expected to miss two to four weeks of the season, then assume he's going to miss three weeks. Thus, you should remove three sixteenths (3 divided by 16) of his projected points. Once you've removed the appropriate percentage of points you have what is called his "post-injury projection." This is how many points he's projected to score when he comes back healthy enough to play.

Now it's a simple matter of ranking him according to his new projection, right?

Wrong!

A common mistake – I see it all the time – is that fantasy owners rank an injured player based on his post-injury projection. ... But that could be a big mistake. Many times an injured player is actually worth more than his post-injury projection. Let me show you why. Let's say your cheat sheet shows Mike Vick projected to score 200 fantasy points and Brett Favre to score 160 fantasy points. Obviously Vick is more valuable. Now suppose Vick gets injured in a pre-season game and is expected to miss the first eight games of the season. His post-injury projection is 50 percent (8 missed games divided by 16 total games) of a healthy season which turns out to be 100 fantasy points. Here's the catch: Vick is still worth more than a healthy player who's projected to score 100 fantasy points. Moreover, it's quite possible Vick is still more valuable than a healthy Favre who's projected to score 160 fantasy points.

The last statement might sound crazy to you, but, rest assured, there are two legitimate reasons why Vick may still be more valuable than Favre. First, Vick is expected to significantly outperform Favre on a week-by-week basis once he returns from injury. Vick is projected to score 100 fantasy points over the final eight games of the season which equates to 12.5 points per game. During this same span, Favre is projected to score only 80 points which is only 10 points per game. This makes Vick more valuable at least for the second half of the season. Even if Vick returned at less than 100 percent health, say he's only 90 percent because the injury nags, he'll still be more valuable in the second half of the season because he'll still average more points per game than Favre. However, as a piece of advice, it's good to assume – for peace of mind when ranking and projecting – that when a player comes back from an injury, he'll play at 100 percent. So let's assume Vick will score 100 fantasy points over the final eight games.

Second, you are allowed to start another QB, let's call him QB15, while Vick is "healing" on the bench during the first eight weeks of the season. This is a huge advantage that most people don't take into consideration when ranking injured players such as Vick. So even if you draft Vick and he only gives you 100 points you'll still be able to rack up additional points from the QB position during the first eight weeks. In practicality, your "starting QB" is the combined effort of Vick and QB15. It is this combined score that should be used to rank Vick on the cheat sheet because you know by drafting him that's the total output you expect to get from your "starting QB" through the entire season.

Before you can adjust Vick's ranking you first need to determine who "QB15" is likely to be and how many points he will score in the first eight weeks. You need to ask yourself, "Who am I most likely to draft as the first back-up player in this position?" It will be this player's projection that should be used as part of the "combined effort." I think the best way to answer this question is also one of the easiest, and that is to simply assume your back-up is going to come from the middle of the group of potential back-ups. For instance, if you are in a ten-team league you should figure the top ten ranked QBs on your cheat sheet will be drafted as starters among the league. The next ten ranked QBs are likely to be the group of back-ups which would be those QBs ranked 11-20 on the cheat sheet. Thus, you can assume you are likely to get someone in the middle of this group, specifically someone like the 15th ranked QB who falls as close to the middle of the group as possible. It's no coincidence then that the generic name and rank is "QB15" in the example given in the prior paragraph.

The next step would be to observe how many points QB15, let's call him Eli Manning, is projected to score. Suppose Manning is projected to score 130 fantasy points. This means he's projected to score 65 fantasy points in the first eight weeks of the season. So by drafting Vick you should also expect to draft Manning, and their combined effort will give you a total of

65 + 100 = 165 fantasy points. Therefore, you should re-rank Vick on the cheat sheet that is closest to a 165 fantasy point projection which, by the way, would be higher than Favre's ranking since he was projected to score only 160 points. I say "closest to" because the AVT projections may not offer one that is exactly equal to 165 fantasy points. But that's okay because "close" only counts in horseshoes, hand grenades, and, of course, fantasy football.

One last point to make about the above ranking process, where an injured player's projection is increased due to a "combined effort," is that it only works if the injured player (i.e., Vick) is projected to score more points per game than the back-up player (i.e., Manning). Otherwise a player like Manning would start every game regardless of when Vick returned and there would be no such thing as a combined effort. Whenever you come across the situation where an injured player's points per game projection isn't high enough for him to become a starter, then you probably shouldn't rank him at all. What good is he to you? First of all he's currently injured. Second, he's not good enough to start when he returns from injury. Nevertheless, if you decide you still want to rank such an injured player make sure you use only his post-injury projection as the basis for his ranking. For instance, you would simply rank Vick according to his post-injury projection of 100 points as opposed to increasing his projection and ranking based on a combined effort.

Step 11 – Checks and Balances

By this point your cheat sheet is the culmination of hard work, research, analysis and opinion. ... But how good do you think it really is? Unless you think you are Michelangelo and your cheat sheet is the fantasy football equivalent of the Sistine Chapel, then your cheat sheet probably needs a lot of adjustments. That's something you need to assess. One way to get this assessment is to find a second unbiased opinion or compare notes with someone else's rankings. However, getting a second opinion isn't as easy as giving your cheat sheet to someone and saying "grade this for me." For instance, you may not be able to find anyone experienced enough to properly critique your "work of art" or, perhaps, they play in your league and you don't want to reveal anything to an opponent. In any case, here are some creative methods for getting that much needed critique. It's a fantasy football system of "checks and balances."

CHECKS

This process involves checking your cheat sheet with other sources of ranked players. There are specifically two excellent sources you should compare notes against.

First, check the rankings of fantasy football experts. You can find expert lists in magazines such as Fantasy Pro Forecast or on web-sites such as Footballdiehards.com or my own site, DraftingToWin.com. Experts are an excellent source to compare your own cheat sheet against because, as stated earlier in this chapter, experts do a tremendous job in ranking players. Just make sure the rankings you compare notes with are based on similar fantasy scoring rules to that of your own (e.g., performance-based). Otherwise the rankings may not be appropriate.

Second, check a mock draft site such as Antsports.com and MockDraftCentral.com. The beauty of a site like either of these is that you can selectively observe the average results of hundreds of mock drafts that are based on the same size and similar scoring rules as your league. Average mock draft results are a "public consensus" of sorts on player rankings which makes it great to compare against your own cheat sheet. For instance, if you notice that Shaun Alexander is the highest drafted RB in 100 mock drafts then that should be considered a strong case to rank Alexander No. 1 on your cheat sheet, or at least close to it. Bottom line, comparing your rankings against the order in which players are being drafted by the hundreds of people is a great tool in cross-referencing a cheat sheet.

After checking the results of expert rankings and mock drafts you'll no doubt find a plethora of differences between those results and that of your cheat sheet. In fact, some of those differences are likely to be pretty significant. So now what? This is when you may have to smack yourself a few times to shake the ego out of your head. Quit pretending you are Sean Salisbury, and try to open yourself to the possibility that you either missed something, or your opinion is off kilter.

The first thing you have to decide is whether or not the difference is significant enough to warrant a possible change on the cheat sheet. Raise a red flag when you discover any of the following discrepancies on your cheat sheet, for any position:

1) A top fifteen player is ranked more than five places off by another source.

2) A top thirty player is ranked more than ten places off by another source.

3) Any ranked player is ranked more than fifteen places off by another source.

When you discover any of these situations, say you notice Alexander is the No. 1 RB in mock drafts and you personally have him ranked seventh, it may mean that you need to adjust your cheat sheet. However, don't all of a sudden cave in and move Alexander to that of what an expert says or the general public thinks. Again, variations in rankings are to be expected and accepted. Remember what I wrote in the beginning of the chapter: even competent experts will have players ranked 20+ slots apart. So, maybe it is your ranking that is in fact right and everyone else's ranking is wrong? *Smack!* Shake out that ego. Go back to your original notes, analyze the player's history, read up on the player's profile a little more than usual, and see if your opinion changes. If it doesn't, kudos to holding your ground. If it does, kudos for not letting your ego stand in the way. In either case, at least you did your due diligence.

Nevertheless, if you find your rankings to be significantly different from *multiple sources,* then there's probably a decent chance you overlooked something and you most likely need to fix your cheat sheet. For instance, if you notice Alexander is No. 1 in mock drafts and in the top three from various experts, then you should give very strong consideration to pushing Alexander at least in the top five on the cheat sheet. At the very least, this adjustment acts as a great hedge against your own potential error in judgment. But even if you strongly feel there is no error, you still might want to adjust your ranking. Not because your opinion could be wrong but because you want to prevent yourself from drafting someone too early. Suppose you like Torry Holt as the No. 1 ranked WR this year while everyone else has him as the No. 8 receiver. In this type of situation, you are liable to take Holt in the first round even though he's likely to fall to you in the later rounds. Therefore, you may want to slide Holt down on the cheat sheet to something like the No. 4 ranking. By lowering Holt, you will prevent yourself from taking him in the first round which is advantageous because you can most likely snag him in the second round or even the third if you feel like risking it.

Another alternative might be to keep Holt ranked as the No. 1 WR on your cheat sheet, but put a note next to his name reminding you not to draft him too early. You should observe where Holt is being drafted in most mock drafts and decide what round might be best for you to draft him in order to minimize the risk of losing him to someone else. For example, if most people are drafting Holt in middle of the third round then you should consider taking him in the second. This way you still get your top-ranked wideout without overpaying for him with a first round draft pick.

....AND BALANCES

Just like you want to cash in your chips for an exact and balanced amount after a successful run at the craps table, so must offensive stats be exact and balanced. Players on the same

NFL team must have balanced statistics. Specifically, passing stats must balance with receiving stats. For example, if Daunte Culpepper throws for 355 yards against the New York Jets you can bet silver dollars to plain donuts those who caught the ball will have a combined 355 receiving yards. The same goes for TDs. For every TD Culpepper throws there's got to be someone on the other end receiving it. So for every passing TD there must be a receiving TD balancing the equation. This balancing effect is like a law of physics or, rather, a law of football. So let's call it the first law of fantasy football – passing stats must balance with receiving stats.

We should be able to use the first law of fantasy football to see if our rankings and projections balance out. For instance, we should be able to look at Culpepper's projected stats and see if it balances out with his receivers' projected stats. Unfortunately, the process is a bit ticklish because our projected stats – the AVT projections – are in fantasy points rather than the basic components needed to apply the first law such as passing yards, passing TDs, receiving yards, and receiving TDs. To understand why this is a bit of problem, let's say you have Culpepper ranked first which gives him an AVT projection of 374 fantasy points. Well, you don't know exactly what "374 fantasy points" means. Maybe it means he'll throw for 3,000 yards, run for 2 TDs, and pass for 22 TDs. Then again, maybe it means he'll throw for 2,500 yards, run for 3 TDs, and pass for 25 TDs. The point is that we don't have the detailed projections needed to apply the first law of fantasy football.

That doesn't mean we can't improvise a little. There are several generalizations, or rules, based off of the first law of fantasy football that can still be used to successfully balance players according to just their ranking without worrying about detailed stats or even AVT projections. Here they are:

Rule No. 1) If a QB is ranked in the top five, then at least one of his receivers should be ranked in the top 20 – OR – his TE should at least be in the top 5.

Rule No. 2) If a QB is not ranked in the top 20, then no more than one of his WRs should be ranked in the top 20.

Rule No. 3) No team should have three WRs ranked in the top 30.

Rule No. 4) If a team has two WRs ranked in the top 25, then its QB should be ranked in the top 10.

Although these rules don't offer an exact science, they do a reasonably good job in balancing QBs with their WRs. For instance, Rule No. 1 ensures that a stud QB is counter-balanced with at least one stud receiver. This makes sense because a stud QB has so many fantasy points to "throw around" that one of his receivers is bound to "catch" a lot of them. The same thing goes for Rule No. 4. If a team's WRs are doing great then that has to be counter balanced with a strong performance by the QB.

On the dark side of things, if a QB isn't projected to do very well then chances are his receivers will also struggle, hence Rule No. 2.

Rule No. 3 goes by the basic limitations that only one individual can catch the ball at a time, all receivers have to share the passing game, and no one can catch all the passes. Since most teams don't throw the ball enough, it's mighty hard for a NFL team to finish the season with three highly-involved receivers. Ironically, we witnessed such an event with the 2004 Indianapolis Colts where wide-outs Marvin Harrison, Reggie Wayne, and Brandon Stokley *amazingly* finished the season in the top fifteen. Keep in mind this Colts team is an exception to the rule – or shall I say future Hall of Famer QB Peyton Manning is an exception to the rule. Bottom line, Manning and his receivers had to practically break every NFL passing and receiving record to achieve this outstanding result.

Let's move on to rushing statistics and analyze whether or not they can be balanced like passing and receiving statistics.

The truth is, rushing stats don't have a statistical counter-balance like passing and receiving stats have with one another. Therefore, we won't find ourselves with a "second law of fantasy football." However, rushing stats do have three practical limitations that allow fantasy footballers to delegate a proper balance in the RB rankings. The first limitation is that only one RB can run the ball at a time. The second is that NFL coaches generally limit their teams to a certain percentage of running plays per game, which roughly falls around 50%. The third is that there are very few running plays of 20+ yards in the NFL. In fact, teams are likely to go an entire game without having a single run of over 20 yards.

Collectively, these limitations tend to keep NFL teams from significantly out-performing each other in total rushing stats. This also allows us as fantasy managers to guess – with a high level of confidence – that no NFL team will have a corps of RBs that significantly out-perform another team's corps of RBs. Sure, some teams will have one RB stud getting most of the work and scoring a lot of fantasy points, while other teams will have several fantasy RBs sharing the load in a RBBC and scoring much fewer fantasy points each. The key point is that the total fantasy output of one NFL team's RBs – whether that's one, two, three or even four guys – will not significantly out-perform another team's RB(s).

With that in mind the following two rules can be used to balance RB rankings:

Rule No. 1) No team should have two or more RBs ranked in the top 25.

Rule No. 2) All teams should have at least one RB ranked in the top 40.

The basis of Rule No. 1 is to prevent anyone from highly ranking two RBs who are on the same NFL franchise. It's practically impossible for an NFL team to sport two stud fantasy RBs due to the three aforementioned limitations in rushing. Furthermore, since it's so difficult for a NFL franchise to operate with two stud RBs, that leaves the door open for just about every franchise to have at least one RB in the top 40, hence Rule No. 2.

By following such balancing *laws, rules, and limitations* you should feel fairly safe that your set of player rankings is balanced and in good working order.

Step 12 – Go Back to Step 4 & Repeat

Ranking players is an ongoing process right up until draft day. The main thing is to keep abreast of the latest NFL news, and adjust the rankings accordingly. You should continuously repeat steps 4-11 in order to ensure yourself of having the most up-to-date and complete set of rankings heading into the draft.

Chapter 5 – Value-Based Drafting 101

It's time to take a more strategic approach, so let's put on our thinking caps. Shortly, you will understand why implementing the right draft strategy rather than relying on pre-draft player rankings will make all the difference come playoff time.

But first, a true story...

It was early in the summer of 2003 when Emil Kadlec asked me to compete in his *Fantasy Football Pro Forecast* magazine's experts' poll. After finishing 2nd out of 552 teams in the '02 WCOFF, it was apparent that my reputation among my fantasy peers had been bumped up a few notches, so I enthusiastically accepted his invitation.

The Fantasy Football Pro Forecast poll was simple in premise: its purpose was to find out which of the hand-picked "experts" could generate the player ratings that produced the most fortuitous final results. I was about to stand toe-to-toe with the likes of Chris Schussman (1st place winner in '02 WCOFF) and Bob Harris (TFL Report), as well as industry standouts MVP Sportsbook, Red Eye Sports, KFFL, FF Champs,

CBSSportsline, Sandlot Shrink, Fantasy Guru, Grandslam, Draft Sharks and Fantasy Insights.

So I made my picks, and admittedly I didn't give much more thought to this poll until bumping into Emil shortly after the end of the season. What he told me that December afternoon played a big part in why I decided to write this book.

"How did I do?"

"Ummm," Emil started. "Well, not good."

Not good? Impossible! Down but not out, I let my curiosity cloak my bruised ego.

"What happened?" I mustered.

The numbers told a somber tale: out of the 13 experts, my poll ranked near the bottom in QBs (12th place), WRs (12th), TEs (10th) and DEF (13th), while salvaging a 5th-place showing at QB. Decimated by injuries, I realized that accurately ranking players so early in the summer was a crap shoot.

"However," Emil continued. "You finished second in the Overall Top 25 Rankings."

My brain struggled to reason what I had just heard: was it possible that, at least pertaining to my poll, my overall "whole" ranking system proved greater than the sum of its individually-ranked parts?

Emil went on to explain that if I were have to competed against the same panel of experts in an actual fantasy draft, my rankings would have likely garnered a second-place finish.

"OK, let me get this straight," I probed, not fully embracing the previous explanation. "I entered the draft with one of the worst sets of player rankings, yet I would likely be in contention for a title in an actual league?"

Do you believe in miracles? Well I don't. Just truth, and the truth is that succeeding in fantasy football is not contingent on high player rankings. Granted, a well-planned (and sometimes luck-driven) ranking system can put you heads and shoulders above your competition, but you can catapult poor, pre-draft player rankings into overall success by following the principles of Value-Based Drafting (VBD).

VBD is a proven mathematical system that determines the most valuable player among all positions. To begin to understand how VBD works you must first fully grasp your goal during the draft. With top-ranked players available in every position, each time you're up to make a selection, who do you take? Tick tock. Do you snag the best QB? Tick tock. What about the top ranked RB or WR? Tick tock. Then again, what if you desperately need a TE? Tick tock.

Your play is to look underneath the surface to determine the true top-ranked player. Those managers who are unprepared for this investigation will not be able to accurately determine the correct choice especially in the short time given to make a pick.

A VBD application (or "app" from this point forward) mathematically allocates values to the players so you can determine the best player overall. In other words, it calculates the top ranked option among all positions – the overall best pick, the crème de la crème.

Here's a simplified example showing you how value-based drafting works:

Suppose you are in a league competing against just one other fantasy owner, the starting lineup consisting of only 1 QB and

1 RB and the draft lasting only two rounds. Let's also suppose your cheat sheet is simply as follows:

FIGURE 22: SIMPLIFIED CHEAT SHEET

Rank	QB	QB Projection	RB	RB Projection
1	QB1	200 points	RB1	100 points
2	QB2	180 points	RB2	60 points

The draft is serpentine-style: You pick first in the first round and last in the second round.

Who do you take with the first pick?

On the surface, QB1 looks like the logical pick because he is projected to score the most points. I've asked this question to a few friends who've been playing fantasy football longer than me and all of them wanted to take QB1. Are they correct?

Let's assume you select QB1, and your opponent follows suit by snagging RB1 and QB2 with the next two picks (When using VBD, ALWAYS ASSUME that your opponent values and ranks the players the same as you do). Inevitably, you take RB2 with the last pick. Let's see who fared better.

Your team, QB1 & RB2, is projected to score 200 + 60 = 260 points.

Your opponent's team, RB1 & QB2, is projected to score 100 + 180 = 280 points.

How can this be? You had the first pick and you felt justified picking the highest-scoring player. You considered QB1 to be the "best" player, yet your opponent ends up having the better team. ... Hmmm. What went wrong?

It turns out that the best player is RB1 not QB1. That's because, according to VBD, a player's *value* is not determined by the number of points he's projected to score; rather, his value is determined by the number of points he's projected to *outscore*. Specifically, you are interested in how many points he will outscore players in his position. QB1's value is 20 points because he's projected to outscore QB2 by 20 points. Thus, when you draft QB1, then you can expect a 20-point advantage over your opponent.

Now let's take a look at RB1. His value is 40 points because he's projected to outscore RB2 by that amount. So by drafting RB1 you get a 40-point advantage over your opponent. This is the premise of value-based drafting. **Draft players in a fashion to outscore your opponent.**

Of course, real fantasy football (can anyone say oxymoron?) isn't as simple as the example just given. There are more owners to compete against, more players to pick from, and more rounds to draft in. Furthermore, there are many ways one can apply the VBD principles. Some applications are good, and others aren't. Unfortunately (or fortunately depending on how you want to look at it), few people completely understand the inner-workings of the VBD in order to maximize efforts on draft day. Today, VBD is quickly growing into one of the most recognized and widely used drafting applications among fantasy football experts.

But, before we delve into any kind of advanced methodology, you first need to understand the basics of VBD, its terminology, and its simplest application – the *Worst Starter Method*. The remainder of this chapter will focus on such introductory material. Chapter Six will detail two intermediate VBD apps that are popular among many people – the Average Starter Method and the "100 Pick" Method. Chapters Seven and Eight will reveal the advanced applications of VBD that I personally customized and regularly use (even experts don't know about these). If you master these advanced concepts, consider yourself a force to be reckoned with on draft day.

But first, let's go over the basics starting with VBD terminology.

There are several terms used in VBD that you need to understand. One is called the "baseline." Each position has its own baseline. The baseline is the reference point at which players in a position are compared in order to determine their values. The difference between a player's projection and his position's baseline becomes his value. In other words, to determine a player's value subtract the baseline from his projection. Think back to the example given earlier. QB1's value was determined to be 200-180 = 20 fantasy points. The baseline used was 180 fantasy points because that's what was subtracted from the player's projection in order to determine his value. Can you determine what baseline was used in determining RB1's value in the prior example? (The answer is in next paragraph.)

Since RB1's value was determined by subtracting 60 fantasy points from 100 fantasy points, the RB baseline is 60 fantasy points.

You'll notice that the QB baseline of 180 fantasy points is equivalent to QB2's projection, and the RB baseline of 60 fantasy points is equivalent to the projected points of RB2. That's because I chose to use "baseline players." Baseline players are specific players chosen to determine a position's baseline. Specifically, the baseline players' projections are used to determine baselines. Please note: *You'll see that some VBD apps make use of baseline players, while others determine the baseline number using an independent formula.*

Players' values as determined from Value-Based Drafting are referred to as "X numbers" or "X values." Getting back to the prior example, QB1's X value = 200-180 = 20 fantasy points. RB1's X value = 100-60 = 40 fantasy points. X values represent how many fantasy points your fantasy team will outscore your fantasy competition. Your mission on draft day is to accrue as much X-Value as possible when selecting players.

X values are used to rank all players from all positions in one collective ranking list, known as the "overall rankings." As a fantasy football manager, your job is mostly to draft the best available player from the overall rankings list each time you pick, at least for the early rounds.

VBD can be applied in a variety of ways, with each variation implementing a different method for determining baselines. The most basic version is called the *worst starter method*. It is an excellent method, especially for beginners, because of its simplicity to grasp, coupled with favorable results. This method determines the baseline player to be the guy who is the "worst starter." Worst starter is defined as the player who's projected to score the fewest fantasy points among all the starting players in the league.

The systematic way of finding the worst starter in each position is to multiply the starting lineup by the number of teams in the league. For instance, suppose you are in a twelve-team league with a starting lineup of 1 QB, 2 RBs, 3 WRs, 1 TE, 1 K, 1 D/ST. After multiplying the starting lineup by twelve teams you'll find that the league will collectively start 12 QBs, 24 RBs, 36 WRs, 12 TEs, 12 Ks, and 12 D/STs. Therefore, the worst starters – or the baseline players – are the 12th ranked QB, 24th RB, 36th WR, 12th TE, 12th K, and 12th D/ST on the cheat sheet.

Once you know who the baseline players are you can begin to calculate X values. Let's say your cheat sheet had RB rankings and projections as listed in the first two columns on the left side of Figure 23. (Note: these projections were calculated using a three-year AVT in the 2003 WCOFF.)

Player	(Pts)	–	(Baseline)	=	X #
RB1	442	–	190	=	252
RB2	375	–	190	=	185
RB3	347	–	190	=	157
RB4	326	–	190	=	136
RB5	316	–	190	=	126
RB6	306	–	190	=	116
RB7	301	–	190	=	111
RB8	293	–	190	=	103
RB9	276	–	190	=	86
RB10	268	–	190	=	78
RB11	262	–	190	=	72
RB12	254	–	190	=	64
RB13	250	–	190	=	60
RB14	246	–	190	=	56
RB15	238	–	190	=	48
RB16	231	–	190	=	41
RB17	227	–	190	=	37
RB18	222	–	190	=	32
RB19	217	–	190	=	27
RB20	213	–	190	=	23
RB21	205	–	190	=	15
RB22	202	–	190	=	12
RB23	199	–	190	=	9
RB24	**190**	–	190	=	**0**
RB25	178	–	190	=	-12
RB26	173	–	190	=	-17
RB27	169	–	190	=	-21
RB28	159	–	190	=	-32
RB29	151	–	190	=	-39
RB30	149	–	190	=	-41
RB31	145	–	190	=	-45
RB32	139	–	190	=	-51
RB33	137	–	190	=	-53
RB34	134	–	190	=	-56
RB35	125	–	190	=	-65
RB36	121	–	190	=	-69
RB37	120	–	190	=	-71
RB38	115	–	190	=	-75
RB39	111	–	190	=	-79
RB40	109	–	190	=	-81

FIGURE 23: DETERMINING RB X VALUES

With the 24th ranked RB being the baseline player, you know that his projection of 190 fantasy points becomes the baseline (shown in **bold** in Figure 23). **This is now the reference point used to determine X values for all RBs.** That is, 190 fantasy points can be subtracted from each RB's projection in order to calculate his X value. All calculated X values are listed in the far right column of Figure 23. You'll notice that players ranked above the baseline have positive X values while players below the baseline have negative X values. Baseline players, if any, will always have a value of zero.

FIGURE 24: CHEAT SHEET WITH X VALUES QB / RB / WR

QB	Pts	X #	RB	Pts	X #	WR	Pts	X #
QB1	400	124	RB1	442	252	WR1	357	191
QB2	381	105	RB2	375	185	WR2	331	165
QB3	358	82	RB3	347	157	WR3	320	154
QB4	346	70	RB4	326	136	WR4	304	138
QB5	341	65	RB5	316	126	WR5	292	126
QB6	335	59	RB6	306	116	WR6	276	110
QB7	316	40	RB7	301	111	WR7	271	105
QB8	308	32	RB8	293	103	WR8	270	104
QB9	300	24	RB9	276	86	WR9	266	100
QB10	294	18	RB10	268	78	WR10	265	99
QB11	285	9	RB11	262	72	WR11	258	92
QB12	**276**	**0**	RB12	254	64	WR12	254	88
QB13	267	-9	RB13	250	60	WR13	251	85
QB14	264	-12	RB14	246	56	WR14	245	79
QB15	257	-19	RB15	238	48	WR15	241	75
QB16	247	-29	RB16	231	41	WR16	238	72
QB17	245	-31	RB17	227	37	WR17	231	65
QB18	242	-34	RB18	222	32	WR18	222	56
QB19	233	-43	RB19	217	27	WR19	219	53
QB20	226	-50	RB20	213	23	WR20	217	51
QB21	222	-54	RB21	205	15	WR21	213	47
QB22	215	-61	RB22	202	12	WR22	211	45
QB23	209	-67	RB23	199	9	WR23	206	40
QB24	205	-71	**RB24**	**190**	**0**	WR24	198	32
			RB25	178	-12	WR25	194	28
			RB26	173	-17	WR26	191	25
			RB27	169	-21	WR27	189	23
			RB28	159	-32	WR28	185	19
			RB29	151	-39	WR29	182	16
			RB30	149	-41	WR30	180	14
			RB31	145	-45	WR31	177	11
			RB32	139	-51	WR32	174	8
			RB33	137	-53	WR33	171	5
			RB34	134	-56	WR34	169	3
			RB35	125	-65	WR35	168	2
			RB36	121	-69	**WR36**	**166**	**0**
			RB37	120	-71	WR37	162	-4
			RB38	115	-75	WR38	159	-7
			RB39	111	-79	WR39	158	-8
			RB40	109	-81	WR40	157	-9

FIGURE 24: CHEAT SHEET WITH X VALUES TE / K / D/ST

TE	Pts	X #	K	Pts	X #	D/ST	Pts	X #
TE1	222	119	K1	148	30	D/ST1	162	47
TE2	176	73	K2	144	26	D/ST2	156	41
TE3	173	70	K3	140	22	D/ST3	151	36
TE4	155	52	K4	138	20	D/ST4	141	26
TE5	150	47	K5	132	14	D/ST5	137	22
TE6	142	39	K6	130	12	D/ST6	135	20
TE7	126	23	K7	127	9	D/ST7	134	19
TE8	117	14	K8	126	8	D/ST8	124	9
TE9	114	11	K9	124	6	D/ST9	123	8
TE10	110	7	K10	121	3	D/ST10	121	6
TE11	107	4	K11	120	2	D/ST11	117	2
TE12	**103**	**0**	**K12**	**118**	**0**	**D/ST12**	**115**	**0**
TE13	96	-7	K13	117	-1	D/ST13	111	-4
TE14	93	-10	K14	114	-4	D/ST14	109	-6
TE15	92	-11	K15	113	-5	D/ST15	109	-6
TE16	86	-17	K16	111	-7	D/ST16	108	-7
TE17	84	-19	K17	110	-8	D/ST17	106	-9
TE18	83	-20	K18	108	-10	D/ST18	105	-10
TE19	80	-23	K19	107	-11	D/ST19	104	-11
TE20	80	-23	K20	103	-15	D/ST20	103	-12
TE21	77	-26	K21	99	-19	D/ST21	101	-14
TE22	70	-33	K22	96	-22	D/ST22	99	-16
TE23	67	-36	K23	95	-23	D/ST23	97	-18
TE24	63	-40	K24	92	-26	D/ST24	96	-19

If you follow the same process for every position, you should end up with a complete set of player rankings, projections, and X values such as that found in Figure 24. You'll notice the baseline players are the same ones as determine in the prior example. They are the 12th ranked QB, 24th RB, 36th WR, 12th TE, 12th K, and 12th D/ST (shown in **bold**).

At this point, you should begin to understand the true advantage of applying VBD principles. All the positions and players can now be grouped together in one list known as the overall rankings. **This is the most important list on the cheat sheet**. Figure 25 ranks the top 25 players from Figure 24 in an overall rankings list.

FIGURE 25:
OVERALL RANKINGS
(WORST STARTER METHOD)

Overall	Player	X #
1	RB1	252
2	WR1	191
3	RB2	185
4	WR2	165
5	RB3	157
6	WR3	154
7	WR4	138
8	RB4	136
9	RB5	126
10	WR5	126
11	QB1	124
12	TE1	119
13	RB6	116
14	RB7	111
15	WR6	110
16	WR7	105
17	QB2	105
18	WR8	104
19	RB8	103
20	WR9	100
21	WR10	99
22	WR11	92
23	WR12	88
24	RB9	86
25	WR13	85

Figure 25 tells you which players are the most valuable regardless of position. So, when it's your turn to draft a player, you'll know which player and position to draft from rather than debating and mulling over the top players available in each position. For instance, if you had the first overall pick in the draft you should jump all over RB1 because he offers the most X value.

An important part of becoming an educated fantasy manager is taking the time to analyze and understand the processes and results of draft strategies and systems. This particular juncture makes a great opportunity to reflect on the strategies and results you've just been introduced to. Of course, you're probably hoping I would do the "analyzing and thinking" for you so here are seven of my own observations and comments regarding Figures 24-25, the Worst Starter Method, and VBD in general:

1) The purpose of any VBD system is to draft players who are going to outscore your opponents so you can win fantasy games. According to the Worst Starter Method, the manager who gets stuck drafting the worst starter, such as QB12 in Figure 24, will gain nothing because all the other managers are expected to draft better players. This is what makes the Worst Starter

Method an acceptable approach for drafting players. It bases the values of players relative to the worst starter. In other words, the Worst Starter Method awards positive X values to those managers who are savvy enough to draft better starters than the worst ones. For instance, anyone who drafts a QB ranked higher than QB12 will be rewarded with positive X values, and deservingly so.

2) While there are only 25 players listed in Figure 25 you should actually include more players in the overall rankings. I recommend listing about 50-70 players in the overall list and drafting from that list until they are all depleted. Typically, you'll want enough players to last at least five rounds of the draft.

3) NEVER draft players with negative X values while implementing a VBD system. This mistake can be avoided simply by not including players with negative X values in the overall rankings. You should treat players with negative X values as you would poison ivy: stay away from them at all costs, for two primary reasons.

First, dealing with negative numbers gets a bit confusing. When push comes to shove, and you're on the clock, determining the better choice between QB24 with an X value of −71 and TE24 with an X value of −40 can be more of a challenge than you would think.

But secondly, and more importantly, a player's value should be determined by how many points he's projected to *outscore* other players in his position. When a player dips below the baseline he is no longer outscoring, but rather he is being outscored. This will result in misleading data.

Let me give you an example supporting this second reason. Looking at Figure 24, suppose the only players remaining in the draft were RB25 (X value of -12), RB26 (X value of -17), WR37 (X value of -4), & WR38 (X value of -7). According to these negative X values you would draft WR37 because −4 is the closest number to being a positive X value. However, when you analyze the situation more carefully, you'll see that RB25 outscores RB26 by five fantasy points while WR37 outscores WR38 by only three points. This indicates the most valuable player should be RB25 because he's the one who's outscoring other players in his position the most — which is the whole premise of value-based drafting. Moral of the story: Stay away from using negative X values.

By the way, just because you aren't allowed to draft players with negative X values via VBD doesn't mean you won't ever have the chance to draft those players. There will be additional draft strategies that you'll utilize on draft day after you've finished with VBD. So don't worry if you see a sleeper or a handcuff sitting there with a negative value, you'll still get a chance to draft him. These secondary and tertiary strategies will be covered in Chapter Ten.

4) You'll find overall rankings dominated with RBs and WRs, especially in the top 25. These positions are laden with value for two primary reasons: baseline players for these positions are relatively far down the list (24th ranked RB, 36th ranked WR), resulting in a larger number of players sitting above the baseline with positive X values, and RBs and WRs are high-scoring positions. While high-scoring players don't offer value per se (as shown in Figure 22) it does allow the opportunity for other players to score a lot less. It's this scoring difference that creates the value to look for when drafting players.

5) Notice there aren't any Ks and D/STs in Figure 25. These positions should rarely find their way in the overall rankings, especially the top 50. The reason for their low values is that Ks and D/STs don't outscore each other by that much. For instance, Figure 24 shows the best kicker scoring just 30 more points than the 12th best kicker. Compare this to the RB position where the best player almost outscores the 12th best by almost 200 fantasy points.

The lesson learned here is that you should wait until the late rounds before drafting a K or D/ST. In fact, I always wait until the latter half of the draft before considering such positions. In any case, if you find one of these positions ranked high on the overall list then double-check your calculations, something isn't right.

6) Notice only two QBs and one TE cracked the top 25 in Figure 25. While QBs and TEs are more valuable than Ks and D/STs, they still don't offer nearly as much value as RBs or WRs. This is because the QB and TE baseline players are ranked relatively high on the list (12th ranked player compared to, say, the 24th or 36th ranked player). As a result, fewer players sit above the baseline with positive X values, taking away most of the potential for a big mark-up in X value.

This should tell you to be careful about overrating QBs and TEs. The most common mistake among fantasy managers is drafting these positions too early, specifically in the first four to five rounds. Expect at least half of your league to take a QB and/or TE in these early rounds. Make sure you're not one of them. Actually, QB1, QB2 and TE1 are probably ranked too high in Figure 25. Overrating the best players in these positions is one of various faults found in the Worst Starter Method. Don't worry. We'll delve into improved VBD apps in the chapters that follow.

7) The overall list is the most important list on the cheat sheet. Therefore, it's important to be aware of what aspects of your fantasy league affect this list. **Specifically, there are three variables that significantly affect the outcome of the overall rankings: the number of teams, scoring rules, and starting roster.** As these variables change, so will the overall rankings. If you play in multiple fantasy leagues with different variables, then you better make sure you create separate overall rankings for each of those leagues. Many fantasy footballers make the mistake of thinking one cheat

sheet is good for every league. This couldn't be further from the truth.

To give you a better idea, let's explore the effect the aforementioned variables have on overall rankings by taking a look at five different leagues. The leagues are as follows with League #1 being used as the control group:

League #1
No. Teams: 12
Starting Roster: 1 QB, 2 RBs, 3 WRs, 1 TE, 1 K, 1 D/ST
Scoring Rules: WCOFF

League #2
No. Teams: 8
Starting Roster: 1 QB, 2 RBs, 3 WRs, 1 TE, 1 K, 1 D/ST
Scoring Rules: WCOFF
Variable: No. teams (lowered to eight).

League #3
No. Teams: 12
Starting Roster: 1 QB, 2 RBs, 2 WRs, 1 TE, 1 K, 1 D/ST
Scoring Rules: WCOFF
Variable: Starting roster (one less receiver).

League #4
No. Teams: 12
Starting Roster: 1 QB, 2 RBs, 3 WRs, 1 TE, 1 K, 1 D/ST
Scoring Rules: WCOFF without point per reception
Variable: Scoring (no point per reception).

League #5
No. Teams: 8
Starting Roster: 1 QB, 2 RBs, 2 WRs, 1 TE, 1 K, 1 D/ST
Scoring Rules: WCOFF without point per reception
Variables: No. teams, starting roster, and scoring (all three variables changed as they were in each of previous three leagues).

Each league's top 25 overall rankings were determined by applying the worst starter method. The first three leagues' applied this method to the rankings and projections listed in Figure 24 since those projections were already determined via three-year AVT based on WCOFF scoring. The fourth and fifth leagues required a different set of AVT projections based on the removal of awarding one point per reception in the scoring. While those adjusted projections aren't listed in the book, the top 25 results for all leagues are listed in Figure 26.

Overall Rank	League #1	League #2	League #3	League #4	League #5
			FIGURE 26: OVERALL LIST COMPARISONS		
1	RB1	RB1	RB1	RB1	RB1
2	WR1	WR1	RB2	RB2	RB2
3	RB2	RB2	WR1	RB3	RB3
4	WR2	WR2	RB3	WR1	QB1
5	RB3	WR3	RB4	QB1	WR1
6	WR3	RB3	WR2	WR2	QB2
7	WR4	WR4	RB5	RB4	WR2
8	RB4	TE1	QB1	WR3	TE1
9	RB5	RB4	WR3	QB2	RB4
10	WR5	WR5	TE1	RB5	RB5
11	QB1	QB1	RB6	WR4	WR3
12	TE1	RB5	RB7	RB6	RB6
13	RB6	WR6	WR4	RB7	RB7
14	RB7	RB6	QB2	RB8	RB8
15	WR6	WR7	RB8	WR5	WR4
16	WR7	QB2	WR5	QB3	QB3
17	QB2	WR8	RB9	WR6	TE2
18	WR8	RB7	QB3	RB9	QB4
19	RB8	WR9	RB10	TE1	QB4
20	WR9	WR10	WR6	WR7	D/ST1
21	WR10	RB8	TE2	WR8	RB9
22	WR11	WR11	WR7	RB10	WR5
23	WR12	TE2	RB11	QB4	RB10
24	RB9	TE3	WR8	RB11	QB5
25	WR13	WR12	QB4	WR9	D/ST2

Again, it's very important to study and understand the results of VBD systems. Figure 26 is no exception, so here are four additional observations on such results. It's this kind of analysis that helped me over-achieve in VBD drafting, and I'm sure it will significantly improve your understanding of VBD as well.

OBSERVATION #1

Notice the WRs in League #3 slide down the rankings (always compare things to League #1 which is the control group). In fact, five WRs fall out of the top 25 completely. This is a result of the starting lineup being reduced from three to two WRs. This lineup change reduces the need to draft WRs essentially making it proper to lower their value and position in the overall rankings.

OBSERVATION #2

Once again, you'll notice WRs sliding down the rankings in League #4. This time it's the result of a scoring change. The removal of the scoring rule that awards one fantasy point per reception significantly reduces the value of WRs. This should seem obvious, as receptions are a main component of WR scoring. TEs, who are receivers in their own right, also lose value in this instance. This is apparent with TE1 sliding down from 12th to 19th place.

RBs and QBs are the beneficiaries of this variable change. These positions subsequently fill in the holes left by WRs and TEs in the top 25.

OBSERVATION #3

Taking a look at League #5, this league combines the efforts of reducing the starting lineup of WRs and removing the scoring rule of one fantasy point per reception. This "double dose" results in a drastic reduction in the value of WRs. The overall rankings of WRs plummeted from 14 down to just four in the top 25. Now do you see the importance of creating separate cheat sheets for different leagues?

OBSERVATION #4

My last observation focuses on League #2 where the number of fantasy teams is reduced from 12 down to 8. While all the positions shift in value, only the TE position is significantly affected, moving up in value. TE1 jumped up to the eighth ranked spot while two additional TEs sneaked into the top 25. Why is this?

Let's break it down. When the number of teams is reduced from twelve to eight, the baseline players for all positions shift up. The baseline players for the QB and TE positions shift from the 12th ranked spot up to the eighth ranked spot. The RB baseline player goes from the 24th ranked spot up to the 16th ranked spot. The WR baseline player goes from the 36th ranked spot up to the 24th ranked spot.

Breaking it down more, we have to analyze the resulting changes in the baselines. Using the data in Figure 24, the RB baseline went from 190 fantasy points up to 231: an increase in 41 fantasy points. Thus, the X values of RBs are reduced by 41 fantasy points.

The WR baseline jumped from 166 fantasy points up to 198, an increase in 32 fantasy points. This results in the X values of WRs being reduced by 32 fantasy points. Following the same analysis on QBs, you'll see that their X values are reduced by 32 fantasy points as well.

Now let's take a look at TEs. The baseline adjusted from 103 fantasy points to 117. This relatively small bump reduced all TE values by just 14 fantasy points. This is a much smaller reduction than what the other positions faced, and as a consequence, TEs gained value and moved up in overall rankings.

CONCLUSION

VBD principles, specifically those regarding the Worst Starter Method, will significantly improve your overall draft results against opponents who do not utilize VBD. That's because you strategically draft in a way to outscore your opponents. You can expect above average results with just mediocre player rankings. Indeed, VBD principles are that powerful. However, winning a league title usually requires some modifications to the VBD system. Be careful, though, as some modifications may or may not improve your results above and beyond that of the Worst Starter Method. The next chapter will introduce you to two existing, modified VBD apps. One is better than the Worst Starter Method. The other is worse. Turn the pages and you'll find out why.

CHAPTER 6 –
TWO MORE VBD APPS

Remember the first time you tried ice cream as a kid? Sure it tasted great, but you also knew you could make it better by adding some delicious toppings. After years of childhood experimentation, you eventually learned which toppings made the sundae better, such as cherries and whipped cream, and which ones made it worse, such as the peat moss lying near Mom's garden. Well, consider this a chapter to introduce you to two of the first experimental "VBD sundaes" created by fantasy football experts: the Average Starter Method and the 100 Pick Method. These variations were created after the *vanilla-like* Worst Starter Method (pun intended, sorry). Naturally, one of them turned out to be pretty good. The other, well, let's just say it involved too many pinches of peat moss.

As you read through this chapter, keep this in mind: the main purpose is not necessarily to teach you how to implement these apps in your own draft; rather, it's to give you a better grasp as to what else lurks out there as well as what makes a VBD app better or worse. It's sort of like seeing which ingredients are good or bad before having to make your own sundae.

Both apps will be applied towards a 12-team league with a starting line-up consisting of 1 QB, 2 RB, 3 WR, 1 TE, 1 K, 1 D/ST. The rankings and projections to be used are listed in Figure 27. Not coincidentally, these are the same league variables and data as applied with the Worst Starter Method in Chapter Five. This allows us to compare results in a controlled environment, so to speak.

QB	Pts	RB	Pts	WR	Pts	TE	Pts	K	Pts	D/ST	Pts
QB1	400	RB1	442	WR1	357	TE1	222	K1	148	D/ST1	162
QB2	381	RB2	375	WR2	331	TE2	176	K2	144	D/ST2	156
QB3	358	RB3	347	WR3	320	TE3	173	K3	140	D/ST3	151
QB4	346	RB4	326	WR4	304	TE4	155	K4	138	D/ST4	141
QB5	341	RB5	316	WR5	292	TE5	150	K5	132	D/ST5	137
QB6	335	RB6	306	WR6	276	TE6	142	K6	130	D/ST6	135
QB7	316	RB7	301	WR7	271	TE7	126	K7	127	D/ST7	134
QB8	308	RB8	293	WR8	270	TE8	117	K8	126	D/ST8	124
QB9	300	RB9	276	WR9	266	TE9	114	K9	124	D/ST9	123
QB10	294	RB10	268	WR10	265	TE10	110	K10	121	D/ST10	121
QB11	285	RB11	262	WR11	258	TE11	107	K11	120	D/ST11	117
QB12	276	RB12	254	WR12	254	TE12	103	K12	118	D/ST12	115
QB13	267	RB13	250	WR13	251	TE13	96	K13	117	D/ST13	111
QB14	264	RB14	246	WR14	245	TE14	93	K14	114	D/ST14	109
QB15	257	RB15	238	WR15	241	TE15	92	K15	113	D/ST15	109
QB16	247	RB16	231	WR16	238	TE16	86	K16	111	D/ST16	108
QB17	245	RB17	227	WR17	231	TE17	84	K17	110	D/ST17	106
QB18	242	RB18	222	WR18	222	TE18	83	K18	108	D/ST18	105
QB19	233	RB19	217	WR19	219	TE19	80	K19	107	D/ST19	104
QB20	226	RB20	213	WR20	217	TE20	80	K20	103	D/ST20	103
QB21	222	RB21	205	WR21	213	TE21	77	K21	99	D/ST21	101
QB22	215	RB22	202	WR22	211	TE22	70	K22	96	D/ST22	99
QB23	209	RB23	199	WR23	206	TE23	67	K23	95	D/ST23	97
QB24	205	RB24	190	WR24	198	TE24	63	K24	92	D/ST24	96
		RB25	178	WR25	194						
		RB26	173	WR26	191						
		RB27	169	WR27	189						
		RB28	159	WR28	185						
		RB29	151	WR29	182						
		RB30	149	WR30	180						
		RB31	145	WR31	177						
		RB32	139	WR32	174						
		RB33	137	WR33	171						
		RB34	134	WR34	169						
		RB35	125	WR35	168						
		RB36	121	WR36	166						
		RB37	120	WR37	162						
		RB38	115	WR38	159						
		RB39	111	WR39	158						
		RB40	109	WR40	157						

FIGURE 27: RANKINGS AND PROJECTIONS

AVERAGE STARTER METHOD

The Average Starter Method determines its baselines by taking the average projection of all the starters in the fantasy league. "Starters" are defined as those players ranked equal to and above the "worst starter" as defined from the worst starter method. So, if the 12th ranked QB is the worst starter, then all QBs ranked in the top twelve are considered starters.

After applying this methodology to the league variables given earlier you'll find that the starters include the top 12 QBs, 24 RBs, 36 WRs, 12 TEs, 12 Ks, and 12 D/STs.

The next step is to determine the average projection for each position. Let's start off with the QB position. Calculating the average projected points of the twelve starting QBs is achieved by taking the sum of their projected points. Using the data in Figure 27 we get the following result:

(400+381+358+346+341+335+316+308+300+294+285+276) = 3,940 fantasy points.

The average can be found by dividing this amount by the number of players observed:

3,940 / 12 = 328 fantasy points (rounded to nearest whole number).

Thus, the baseline for the QB position is 328 fantasy points according to the Average Starter Method. Simple as that!

Implementing the same process for the other positions results in the following baselines: RB = 267, WR = 231, TE = 141, K = 131, D/ST = 135. After applying these baselines to the data in Figure 27, the X values calculated for all the players and positions are listed in Figure 28. The overall list is shown in Figure 29.

QB	X #	RB	X #	WR	X #	TE	X #	K	X #	D/ST	X #
QB1	72	RB1	174	WR1	126	TE1	81	K1	17	D/ST1	27
QB2	53	RB2	108	WR2	100	TE2	35	K2	13	D/ST2	21
QB3	30	RB3	80	WR3	89	TE3	32	K3	9	D/ST3	16
QB4	18	RB4	59	WR4	73	TE4	14	K4	7	D/ST4	6
QB5	13	RB5	49	WR5	61	TE5	9	K5	1	D/ST5	2
QB6	7	RB6	39	WR6	45	TE6	1	K6	-1	D/ST6	0
QB7	-12	RB7	34	WR7	40	TE7	-15	K7	-4	D/ST7	-1
QB8	-20	RB8	26	WR8	39	TE8	-24	K8	-5	D/ST8	-11
QB9	-28	RB9	9	WR9	35	TE9	-27	K9	-7	D/ST9	-12
QB10	-34	RB10	1	WR10	34	TE10	-31	K10	-10	D/ST10	-14
QB11	-43	RB11	-5	WR11	27	TE11	-34	K11	-11	D/ST11	-18
QB12	-52	RB12	-13	WR12	23	TE12	-38	K12	-13	D/ST12	-20
QB13	-61	RB13	-17	WR13	20	TE13	-45	K13	-14	D/ST13	-24
QB14	-64	RB14	-21	WR14	14	TE14	-48	K14	-17	D/ST14	-26
QB15	-71	RB15	-29	WR15	10	TE15	-49	K15	-18	D/ST15	-26
QB16	-81	RB16	-36	WR16	7	TE16	-55	K16	-20	D/ST16	-27
QB17	-83	RB17	-40	WR17	0	TE17	-57	K17	-21	D/ST17	-29
QB18	-86	RB18	-45	WR18	-9	TE18	-58	K18	-23	D/ST18	-30
QB19	-95	RB19	-50	WR19	-12	TE19	-61	K19	-24	D/ST19	-31
QB20	-102	RB20	-54	WR20	-14	TE20	-61	K20	-28	D/ST20	-32
QB21	-106	RB21	-62	WR21	-18	TE21	-64	K21	-32	D/ST21	-34
QB22	-113	RB22	-65	WR22	-20	TE22	-71	K22	-35	D/ST22	-36
QB23	-119	RB23	-68	WR23	-25	TE23	-74	K23	-36	D/ST23	-38
QB24	-123	RB24	-77	WR24	-33	TE24	-78	K24	-39	D/ST24	-39
		RB25	-89	WR25	-37						
		RB26	-94	WR26	-40						
		RB27	-98	WR27	-42						
		RB28	-108	WR28	-46						
		RB29	-116	WR29	-49						
		RB30	-118	WR30	-51						
		RB31	-122	WR31	-54						
		RB32	-128	WR32	-57						
		RB33	-130	WR33	-60						
		RB34	-133	WR34	-62						
		RB35	-142	WR35	-63						
		RB36	-146	WR36	-65						
		RB37	-147	WR37	-69						
		RB38	-152	WR38	-72						
		RB39	-156	WR39	-73						
		RB40	-158	WR40	-74						

FIGURE 28:
X VALUES
(AVERAGE STARTER METHOD)

I offer three observations about the Average Starter Method and its results:

First, notice this method doesn't use baseline players to determine baselines like the Worst Starter Method does. Instead, the baselines are determined by a mathematical formula (in this case, it's taking an average). This means

FIGURE 29: OVERALL RANKINGS (AVERAGE STARTER METHOD)

OVERALL RANK	PLAYER	X VALUE
1	RB1	174
2	WR1	126
3	RB2	108
4	WR2	100
5	WR3	89
6	TE1	81
7	RB3	80
8	WR4	73
9	QB1	72
10	WR5	61
11	RB4	59
12	QB2	53
13	RB5	49
14	WR6	45
15	WR7	40
16	RB6	39
17	WR8	39
18	TE2	35
19	WR9	35
20	RB7	34
21	WR10	34
22	TE3	32
23	QB3	30
24	WR11	27
25	D/ST1	27

that its baselines are probably, *but not always*, going to fall between ranked players. In other words, the baseline is probably not going to be equal to a player's projection. This is perfectly acceptable and does not affect VBD principles and usage. There simply won't be a player with an X value of zero in every position like you would see in the Worst Starter Method.

Secondly, the Average Starter Method has a strong tendency to overrate the QB, TE, and D/ST positions. It's scary to even think about drafting a QB or TE in the first few rounds, let alone rank them in the top ten overall. Well, that's what you'd get if you used Figure 29. To add salt to the wound, a D/ST squeaked its way in the top 25. These overall rankings would result in a very bad draft because you'd likely be the fool drafting a QB, TE, and D/ST in the first three rounds. As I alluded to in Chapter Five, you should avoid drafting QBs and TEs in the first couple of rounds and a D/ST in the first half of the draft. These positions should not be valued so highly because they are easy to fulfill (usually just one starting player is needed) and plenty of serviceable players are usually still available in the later rounds. There are additional reasons that will be touched upon in the following chapters. But the bottom line is: don't be misled into thinking even the best players in these positions are valuable enough to draft in the early rounds. They are not.

Thirdly, notice that the Average Starter Method doesn't offer many players with positive X values. For instance, there are only ten RBs with positive X values in Figure 28. Compare this to the 23 RBs available with positive X values via the Worst Starter Method in Chapter Five (Figure 24). Additionally, there are only 16 WRs with positive X values in Figure 28 compared to 35 WRs via the worst starter method. The same effect can be seen in all the positions. This makes the Average Starter Method very limited in its application because, as discussed in the last chapter, only players with positive X values should be drafted while using VBD. Basically, the Average Starter Method depletes itself very early in the draft with so few players to draft from.

As you can see in the latter two observations, the Average Starter Method has some huge pitfalls. No offense to whoever created the Average Starter Method but maybe it should be renamed the "Below Average" Starter Method. If you are looking for an improved VBD application, then the 100 Pick Method would be a wiser choice.

100 Pick Method

This method was developed by Joe Bryant and David Dodds as revealed in their article "Value Based Drafting Revisited," published in 2003's *Fantasy Football Pro Forecast Magazine:*

> "There are many ways to establish a baseline and the following are the most popular methods: Average

Starter and Worst Starter. But like most popular things, neither of these choices is the ideal baseline. After years of experimenting, we have found that the best baseline is based on the number of players that will be taken at a given point in the draft. We personally use 100 players as this basis, but you can play around with other points if you like. After 7 years, we've settled on using 100 players for most leagues."

Later in the article, Bryant and Dodds introduced a systematic approach for calculating the number of players that will be drafted in the first 100 picks. You can simply look at last year's draft and count the positions. If you don't have such results, they recommend observing mock draft results of a similar league structure.

I would like to take the liberty of adding a third option: observe an expert's top 100 overall list, assuming you can find an expert who bases the list on a league similar to yours. You can expect that players will be drafted in an order that closely relates to the expert's overall rankings because people tend to draft according to what the experts say.

Actually, there's one last alternative and that would be to combine the results of two or more of the aforementioned options and take an average, eliminating any chance of an aberration tainting your data. It is more likely that average results will fall closer to the optimal guess.

In any case, let's assume it was determined that 12 QBs, 29 RBs, 40 WRs, 12 TEs, 4 Ks, and 3 D/STs are likely to be drafted in the first 100 picks of the draft. By the way, these are actual results found from observing various mock drafts of a similar league structure to that of this study. Such results indicate that the baseline players should be the 12th ranked QB, 29th RB, 40th WR, 12th TE, 4th K, and 3rd D/ST. Applying this to Figure 27 we get the list of X values and overall rankings as shown in Figures 30 and 31.

QB	X #	RB	X#	WR	X #	TE	X #	K	X #	D/ST	X #
QB1	124	RB1	291	WR1	200	TE1	119	K1	10	D/ST1	11
QB2	105	RB2	224	WR2	174	TE2	73	K2	6	D/ST2	5
QB3	82	RB3	196	WR3	163	TE3	70	K3	2	D/ST3	0
QB4	70	RB4	175	WR4	147	TE4	52	K4	0	D/ST4	-10
QB5	65	RB5	165	WR5	135	TE5	47	K5	-6	D/ST5	-14
QB6	59	RB6	155	WR6	119	TE6	39	K6	-8	D/ST6	-16
QB7	40	RB7	150	WR7	114	TE7	23	K7	-11	D/ST7	-17
QB8	32	RB8	142	WR8	113	TE8	14	K8	-12	D/ST8	-27
QB9	24	RB9	125	WR9	109	TE9	11	K9	-14	D/ST9	-28
QB10	18	RB10	117	WR10	108	TE10	7	K10	-17	D/ST10	-30
QB11	9	RB11	111	WR11	101	TE11	4	K11	-18	D/ST11	-34
QB12	0	RB12	103	WR12	97	TE12	0	K12	-20	D/ST12	-36
QB13	-9	RB13	99	WR13	94	TE13	-7	K13	-21	D/ST13	-40
QB14	-12	RB14	95	WR14	88	TE14	-10	K14	-24	D/ST14	-42
QB15	-19	RB15	87	WR15	84	TE15	-11	K15	-25	D/ST15	-42
QB16	-29	RB16	80	WR16	81	TE16	-17	K16	-27	D/ST16	-43
QB17	-31	RB17	76	WR17	74	TE17	-19	K17	-28	D/ST17	-45
QB18	-34	RB18	71	WR18	65	TE18	-20	K18	-30	D/ST18	-46
QB19	-43	RB19	66	WR19	62	TE19	-23	K19	-31	D/ST19	-47
QB20	-50	RB20	62	WR20	60	TE20	-23	K20	-35	D/ST20	-48
QB21	-54	RB21	54	WR21	56	TE21	-26	K21	-39	D/ST21	-50
QB22	-61	RB22	51	WR22	54	TE22	-33	K22	-42	D/ST22	-52
QB23	-67	RB23	48	WR23	49	TE23	-36	K23	-43	D/ST23	-54
QB24	-71	RB24	39	WR24	41	TE24	-40	K24	-46	D/ST24	-55
		RB25	27	WR25	37						
		RB26	22	WR26	34						
		RB27	18	WR27	32						
		RB28	8	WR28	28						
		RB29	0	WR29	25						
		RB30	-2	WR30	23						
		RB31	-6	WR31	20						
		RB32	-12	WR32	17						
		RB33	-14	WR33	14						
		RB34	-17	WR34	12						
		RB35	-26	WR35	11						
		RB36	-30	WR36	9						
		RB37	-31	WR37	5						
		RB38	-36	WR38	2						
		RB39	-40	WR39	1						
		RB40	-42	WR40	0						

**FIGURE 30:
X VALUES
(100 PICK METHOD)**

FIGURE 31: OVERALL RANKINGS (100 PICK METHOD)		
OVERALL RANK	PLAYER	X VALUE
1	RB1	291
2	RB2	224
3	WR1	200
4	RB3	196
5	RB4	175
6	WR2	174
7	RB5	165
8	WR3	163
9	RB6	155
10	RB7	150
11	WR4	147
12	RB8	142
13	WR5	135
14	RB9	125
15	QB1	124
16	TE1	119
17	WR6	119
18	RB10	117
19	WR7	114
20	WR8	113
21	RB11	111
22	WR9	109
23	WR10	108
24	QB2	105
25	RB12	103

ADVANTAGES OF 100 PICK METHOD

The overall rankings in Figure 31 look pretty good. There are no QBs and TEs listed in the top ten nor are there any Ks and D/STs in the top 25. This means you don't have to worry about making the mistake of drafting one or more of these positions too early as you might with the Average Starter Method or Worst Starter Method.

Another advantage to the 100 Pick Method is that it offers plenty of players with positive X values to draft from. In fact, it offers exactly 100 players with positive or zero X values, as the name implies. Compare this to the lowly 50 players spewed out by the Average Starter Method. You'll also find that of these 100 players more are found in positions that are deemed more important.

This leads us to the next advantage of the 100 Pick Method: more X value is awarded to positions that are deemed more important. This is the whole basis of the 100 Pick Method. The methodology lowers the baselines of a position when more players are expected to be drafted from that position, deeming it important. In turn, this increases the X values. For instance, notice the baseline player for the WR position was lowered from the 36th ranked player (Worst Starter) to the 40th ranked player as shown in Figure 30. This adjustment essentially increased the X values of all the WRs by nine points, which is the difference in projected points between WR36 and WR40. This increase in X value is easily justified because the position is deemed very important. In other words, more WRs are expected to be drafted than any other position in the first 100 picks, 40 to be exact.

The 100 Pick Method justifiably decreases X values as well, specifically in those positions that aren't deemed that important. The K and D/ST positions are perfect examples. Since only four and three of each position, respectively, are expected to be drafted in the first 100 picks you'll notice that the baseline players are listed near the top of the rankings in Figure 30. This leaves very few players with positive X values along with very little potential for a high mark-up in X value. That's fine because these positions aren't deemed that important, which is why no one seems to be drafting from them in the first place.

Yet another advantage of using the 100 Pick Method is that it gets phased out at just about the right time during the draft. As you'll eventually learn, VBD principles become less important as we go deeper into the draft. We eventually get to a point where players such as handcuffs and sleepers become more important than X values. For example, you might be better off ignoring VBD and handcuffing your stud RB in the ninth round. While this handcuffer could very well have a negative X value, he's still more important to your fantasy squad than, say, the third WR of the Arizona Cardinals who's available with an X value of 11 fantasy points. This is especially true if you already drafted numerous WRs. This methodology also explains why it wouldn't be wise to create something like the "200 Pick Method." VBD simply isn't worth applying in the later rounds of the draft, especially once the 100th pick approaches.

The last advantage regarding the 100 Pick Method is that it applies to flex leagues. This is the only VBD app discussed thus far that actually takes flex players into account, at least in an indirect way. Let's assume your league requires a flex player (RB/WR/TE). This essentially increases the demand to draft more RBs, WRs, and TEs and, as a result, you can expect more players to be drafted in these positions in the first 100 picks. Consequently, in a justifying manner, the 100 Pick Method awards more X value to such positions.

DISADVANTAGES OF 100 PICK METHOD

Having said all that, the 100 Pick Method is still not perfect. In fact, it may come to your surprise that it's far from perfect, for two significant reasons. The first is that it forces managers to follow the lead of other people. Whether it's observing mock drafts, expert rankings, or last year's draft results, all deciding data comes as a consequence of other people's actions and opinions. In other words, the 100 Pick Method puts values on positions according to the values other people put on them first.

Now, I'm not sure about you but doesn't this seem a bit twisted? A VBD app is supposed to give us an advantage over other people because they don't know how to appropriately draft positions and players. I mean, if people did know exactly who to draft then we'd have little chance to out-draft them in the first place, right? But they don't, and we need to be able to take advantage of it. Unfortunately, by following the 100 Pick Method, we make ourselves susceptible to the same mistakes other people make. For instance, how do we even know it's correct for a league to collectively draft 40 WRs in the first 100 picks as observed in mock drafts? We simply have nothing to tell us that this is proper judgment. The only thing we know is that our research tells us 40 WRs are likely to be drafted in the first 100 picks. Hence, the 100 Pick Method establishes the baseline player at the 40th ranked WR.

This brings us to the second disadvantage of the 100 Pick Method: there is nothing that explains or justifies what makes a good baseline. In fact, none of the VBD apps I've found explain anything about why baselines should be where they are or why someone should draft a certain position in a certain stage of the draft. Furthermore, there are tons of other questions left unanswered. Why isn't it good to draft a QB in the first round? Why shouldn't we rank Ks and D/STs very high? Why do I feel like I have to draft strictly RBs and WRs with my first four picks? And is this feeling correct?

Thus, it became very important for me to develop theories and systems that answered these questions. I wanted a VBD system that not only created optimal baselines for each position but justified, reasoned, and explained why these baselines were the way that they were. Moreover, I needed to utilize a system where my opinion pays higher dividends than the opinions of my opponents. This is why I developed The RV Method.

Chapter 7 - Baseline Theory:
Introducing the RV Method

The last chapter presented various experimental "VBD sundaes," as the analogy went, along with which kinds of "ingredients" that a VBD app should have in order for it to leave us with a good taste in our mouths at the end of draft day. Other not so great ingredients were also introduced, which should obviously be avoided if at all possible. Now that we have this working knowledge under our belts, consider this chapter to show us how to create that super fudge sundae!

The specific VBD apps introduced thus far include the Worst Starter, Average Starter, and 100 Pick Methods. Some of these apps were described to have better baselines than others with specific reasons outlining why this was the case. In order to fully understand these reasons, I took it upon myself to better analyze value-based drafting and its various applications. From these efforts I uncovered a stockpile of additional factors and characteristics that make one set of baselines better than another set, inspiring me to customize an optimal set of baselines for almost any kind of league. I call this system the "R Value Method" or "RV Method."

Head and shoulders above those apps previously described, I used the RV Method in the 2003 Expert's Poll previously described in the beginning of Chapter Five. To refresh your memory on the outcome of this poll, I was able to turn one of the worst sets of player rankings into the second best overall rankings. You are about to learn the inner workings of this revolutionary baseline system.

Word to the weary: the concepts within the system are somewhat advanced; therefore, you may have to read this chapter a few times to fully get the gist of things. (If the concepts were easy then everyone would be using them!) I am also aware this chapter is very long, so I broke the RV Method into seven steps. This way you can read things on a step by step basis without being overwhelmed by everything at once. You'll find that each step takes you that much closer towards understanding baseline theory and why baselines are positioned the way that they are. Fully understanding the material will earn you a "black belt" in fantasy football and graduate you into *the* lethal owner on draft day.

BASELINE RANKING (R)

Before we delve into any kind of methodology, let's briefly overview the baseline ranking. Each step of the RV Method strives towards determining a better set of baseline players, and these baseline players will be listed according to their baseline ranking in terms of *R values*. R refers to the number of players to count down on the cheat sheet in order to find the baseline player, or more simply, the ranking of the baseline player. For example, if R = 21 for the QB position, then that means the baseline player is the 21st QB on the cheat sheet. In this scenario, "R = 21 for the QB position" will be designated as "R(QB) = 21," and future baseline calculations using the RV Method will be documented in a similar, concise fashion. Like the Worst Starter and 100 Pick Methods, each position will have its own baseline player, or in this case, its own R value.

RV METHOD

STEP 1) Determine initial set of R values

The first step is determining an initial set of R values. From this initial set we can then work on tweaking and adjusting the R values to obtain an optimum set — which is what defines the RV Method.

I like to use the Worst Starter Method in determining the initial set of R values because of its simplicity. According to the Worst Starter Method, the rank of the baseline player is determined by multiplying the number of starters per position per team by the number of teams in the league (see Chapter Five). So, for example, if you are in a 10-team league that allows two starting RBs then R(RB) = 2 RBs per team x 10 teams = 20 RBs. If you are in a 12-team league that has one starting QB per team then R(QB) = 1 QB per team x 12 teams = 12 QBs. Follow this methodology in determining R values for all fantasy positions.

While the Worst Starter Method is recommended for this step you could also opt for a more advanced VBD app, such as the 100 Pick Method in Chapter Six, to determine your initial set of R values. However, it would be wise to avoid it. The 100 Pick Method defeats the purpose of customizing your own set of baselines as the RV Method allows you to do. The R values would already be heavily adjusted due to the advanced methodology of the app itself. These adjustments may or may not be appropriate. At this point we simply don't know because we haven't delved into any of the factors and characteristics that make up a good set of R values. It makes more sense to start with a clean, basic set of R values such as those from the *vanilla-like* Worst Starter Method. This way you know all the tweaks and adjustments that will be made to the set are strictly according to your concepts, opinions, and principles. If you are wondering what all these concepts and principles are, hold on to your horses, we'll get to that throughout the system.

INTRODUCTION TO WCOFF CASE ANALYSIS

A case analysis will be provided after each step of the RV Method to exemplify how to proceed in determining and tweaking a set of R values. The analysis focuses around a WCOFF-modeled 12-team league consisting of a starting lineup of 1 QB, 2 RB, 3 WR, 1 TE, 1 K, 1 D/ST, & 1 Flex (RB/WR/TE). Use the case analysis only as a guide for determining R values in your own league. As you read through each step think about how you would adjust your own set of R values.

Here's the case analysis for Step 1:

Using the worst starter method we get the following initial set of R values:

R(QB) = 1 QB per team x 12 teams = 12 QBs.
R(RB) = 2 RBs per team x 12 teams = 24 RBs.
R(WR) = 3 WRs per team x 12 teams = 36 WRs.
R(TE) = 1 TE per team x 12 teams = 12 TEs.
R(K) = 1 K per team x 12 teams = 12 Ks.
R(D/ST) = 1 D/ST per team x 12 teams = 12 D/STs.
R(Flex) = 1 Flex per team x 12 teams = 12 Flex players.

Note: From this point forward R values will include values only. Thus, R(QB) = 12 will replace R(QB) = 12 QBs.

STEP 2) Divvy the R value of the Flex player.

If your league doesn't have a flex player, skip to Step Three. If your league does require a flex player, then the current set of R values will have to be adjusted accordingly.

In understanding why R values need to be adjusted take a look at the case analysis where R(Flex) = 12. This indicates that the baseline player for the flex position is the 12th ranked flex player. Unfortunately, this R value is not practical because cheat sheets do not rank flex players but rather only positions that can be designated as flex players such as the RB, WR, and TE positions. *One cannot apply the flex player's R value to the cheat sheet.* The solution is to apply, or divvy up, the R value of the flex player position to the positions that can be played as the flex player, allowing the R value of the flex player to ultimately be applied to the cheat sheet.

In understanding how to allocate these 12 units you'll need to refer to player rankings and projections. To better demonstrate the process, and in order to stay consistent with the case analysis, let's look at the player rankings and

RANK	RB	PTS	WR	PTS	TE	PTS
1	RB1	438	WR1	371	TE1	207
2	RB2	390	WR2	343	TE2	179
3	RB3	364	WR3	310	TE3	165
4	RB4	330	WR4	296	TE4	142
5	RB5	322	WR5	289	TE5	137
6	RB6	308	WR6	273	TE6	130
7	RB7	304	WR7	268	TE7	125
8	RB8	289	WR8	260	TE8	117
9	RB9	275	WR9	256	TE9	115
10	RB10	264	WR10	254	TE10	114
11	RB11	254	WR11	253	TE11	112
12	RB12	250	WR12	248	**TE12**	**107**
13	RB13	245	WR13	244	TE13	101
14	RB14	239	WR14	238	TE14	98
15	RB15	230	WR15	236	TE15	97
16	RB16	224	WR16	229	TE16	90
17	RB17	221	WR17	223	TE17	89
18	RB18	216	WR18	217	TE18	85
19	RB19	214	WR19	215	TE19	82
20	RB20	206	WR20	212	TE20	80
21	RB21	197	WR21	208	TE21	77
22	RB22	193	WR22	205	TE22	70
23	RB23	190	WR23	200	TE23	66
24	**RB24**	**180**	WR24	192	TE24	65
25	RB25	169	WR25	190	TE25	207
26	RB26	164	WR26	187		
27	RB27	162	WR27	185		
28	RB28	157	WR28	184		
29	RB29	151	WR29	180		
30	RB30	149	WR30	179		
31	RB31	147	WR31	176		
32	RB32	143	WR32	172		
33	RB33	142	WR33	171		
34	RB34	136	WR34	168		
35	RB35	131	WR35	167		
36	RB36	126	**WR36**	**164**		
37	RB37	124	WR37	162		
38	RB38	120	WR38	158		
39	RB39	116	WR39	157		
40	RB40	113	WR40	155		
41			WR41	153		
42			WR42	152		
43			WR43	148		
44			WR44	145		
45			WR45	142		

FIGURE 32: RANKINGS AND PROJECTIONS (RB, WR, TE)

projections I used in the 2004 WCOFF (Figure 32). Since we're only concerned with observing positions that can be played as a flex player, only the RB, WR, and TE positions are listed. Generic names and ranks (RB1, RB2, etc.) were substituted because actual player names are irrelevant to this part of the study.

Your first task is to observe the current set of baseline players as determined via the Worst Starter Method in Step One, designated in bold in Figure 32. This set of baseline players is supposed to be satisfactory in that it allows managers to draft a starting team of players without dipping into negative X values. To demonstrate how this works, let's assume all twelve managers decide to draft their starting RBs, WRs, and TEs as quickly as possible. With the starting lineup consisting of two RBs, three WRs, and one TE, this action leaves a total of 24 RBs, 36 WRs, and 12 TEs off the board in the first six rounds. Notice that with all these players being drafted so quickly, there is still no threat of us being forced into drafting players below the baseline players.

While to this point the system seems to have held true, the problem with the Worst Starter Method is that it doesn't take the flex player into account. Continuing with the previous example, we could very well find ourselves with a cheat sheet that has the top 24 RBs, 36 WRs, and 12 TEs all drafted before we even get a chance to draft our flex player. Thus, we could be forced into a Cardinal sin: drafting a player that has a negative X value.

The solution? Lower the baselines of the RB, WR, and TE positions. To do this we simply divvy the flex player's R value to these positions. This maneuver lowers the baselines just enough so we can draft the flex starter without being forced into negative X values.

Our case analysis will better exemplify how this works. We have twelve units' worth of R value to divvy. In this case, let's allot six units to the RB position, four to the WR position, and two to the TE position, leaving the following new set of R values: R(RB) = 30, R(WR) = 40, R(TE) = 14. If the league drafted the top 24 RBs, 36 WRs, and 12 TEs by the end of the sixth round you are still left with six RBs, four WRs, and two TEs who don't have negative X values, guaranteeing that at least one of these eligible flex players will fall to you in the seventh round.

But how can we assess what is the ideal divvying proportion? Was our suggested allocation of six units to the RB position, four to the WR position and two to the TE position the perfect formula? There is, in fact, an *optimal proportion* of divvying. To determine this proportion, let's analyze the projections of the players available to draft as the flex player. Then we can figure out exactly how many units should be divvied to each position. Let's take a look:

Suppose you have the first pick in the seventh round, and let's assume the top 24 RBs, 36 WRs, and 12 TEs are already drafted off of the list in Figure 32. Who would you want to draft as your flex starter? You would find that the top prospects from each position are RB25 (who's projected to score 169 fantasy points), WR37 (a projected 162 fantasy points), and TE13 (a projected 101 fantasy points). Since you'll get the most points from RB25, he's the smart selection as the flex starter. This strategy only makes sense because by drafting RB25 your starting fantasy squad will likely score more points.

Now suppose you have the second pick in the seventh round instead of the first pick, and RB25 was already drafted. Who would you want to draft as the flex starter? Again, you would want to take the player with the highest projection, in this case, RB26.

With this strategy in mind, the best way to divvy the twelve R-value units is to allocate them one at a time to the R value of the position that has the player with the highest projection.

This methodology allows you to draft the best candidate for the flex position. So in our case analysis the first unit would go to the RB position because RB25 has the highest projection. The next unit would also go to the RB position because the next highest scoring player is RB26. If you follow this procedure for all twelve units, then you'll have divvied out the flex player's R value in an optimal manner.

After observing Figure 32, the twelve players with the highest projections consist of six RBs and six WRs as shown in Figure 33. Therefore, we should divvy out six units to the RB position and six units to the WR position for the R values in our case analysis.

FIGURE 33:
BEST AVAILABLE FLEX PLAYERS

PLYR	PTS
RB25	169
RB26	164
WR37	162
RB27	162
WR38	158
WR39	157
RB28	157
WR40	155
WR41	153
WR42	152
RB29	151
RB30	149

Notice that the TE position receives no credit in R value. The truth is, the TE position rarely competes for the flex position; therefore, it should usually not be granted any additional R value. From our example, you can see that the best available TE is only projected to score 101 fantasy points. This projection is a far cry from the projections of the top candidates for the flex position as observed in Figure 33. Therefore, it would be a waste to award the TE position with any of the flex position's R value.

This perception of the TE position as a weak option was apparent on each draft day in my first two years of the WCOFF, where not one manager played a TE as a flex starter. However, there were a few managers who bucked the trend in 2004, starting TE-flex starters such as Antonio Gates, Tony Gonzalez, Jason Witten, Randy McMichael, and Eric Johnson. Could this be an indication of an upward trend for TEs in the NFL? Only time will tell.

Using the above information we can now adjust the R values for our case analysis. From what we learned, we specifically need to add six units to the RB and six units to the WR position.

CASE ANALYSIS CONT'D

Before: R(QB) = 12, R(RB) = 24, R(WR) = 36, R(TE) = 12, R(K) = 12, R(D/ST) = 12, & R(Flex) = 12.
After: R(QB) = 12, R(RB) = 30, R(WR) = 42, R(TE) = 12, R(K) = 12, & R(D/ST) = 12.

CUSTOMIZING R VALUES

The first two steps have essentially determined the initial set of R values. It's now time to advance on to the real nitty-gritty. The following material introduces all the factors that you need to consider in tweaking, adjusting, and customizing R values to ultimately achieve an optimal set of baseline players.

STEP 3) Increase a position's R value if its starting fantasy players are projected to miss a lot of NFL games.

The reasoning is as follows:

When a fantasy starter misses an NFL game, a back-up player becomes necessary. The more games your starter misses, the more backup support you need. The more backup support you need, the more players you need to draft. The more players you need to draft, the higher the R value needs to be so you don't dip into negative X values.

To prove the point another way, I offer the following three scenarios with each focusing on the QB position.

Scenario One – No risk of missing games

Suppose there are no reasons why a starting fantasy QB would miss a game. In other words, QBs have no bye weeks, injuries, suspensions, illnesses, or anything else that would cause him to miss a game. Albeit unrealistic, this scenario presents a risk-free situation for the fantasy manager; therefore, no backup QB is required. Thus, each manager only has to draft one QB. Looking at the case analysis, R(QB) = 12 remains satisfactory because there is no threat of dipping into negative X values. That's because a 12-team league only needs to draft twelve QBs.

Scenario Two – High risk of missing games

Suppose QBs are at a high risk of missing a lot of games. Let's say we can expect QBs to miss half the season due to any combination of bye weeks, injuries, illnesses, and suspensions. Here owners *must* draft a backup. I emphasize *must* because backups will be needed to fill in for half the season and will play a significant role. Assuming managers need to draft a minimum of two QBs, a 12-team league would see at least 24 QBs being drafted. Thus, R(QB) must at least be equal to 24 in order to avoid dipping into negative X values.

Scenario Three – Medium risk of missing games

Obviously scenarios one and two present unrealistic, opposite extremes. Let's make the risk a little more realistic. Suppose the bye week is the only risk a QB has of missing a game. Assuming the fantasy football season (including playoffs) is 16 weeks long, it can be expected that a backup QB will be needed for 1/16th of the season. Under this scenario managers should still consider drafting a back-up QB but it's not a *must* situation as it was in scenario two. Why? Because a backup is needed for only a small percentage of the season, approximately 1/16th or six percent of the games. If a manager doesn't draft a backup QB, then it only hurts the team for six percent of the season. This is not so bad especially when compared to Scenario Two where not drafting a backup QB meant being hurt for half the season.

So how should the R value be adjusted in Scenario Three?

Since backups aren't needed nearly as much as Scenario Two, the R value doesn't have to be nearly as high. However, because of the bye week, the R value should still be higher than that determined in Scenario One where there was absolutely no risk of a QB missing a game. Therefore, Scenario Three's R value should fall somewhere between 12 and 24.

I created a formula to determine exactly where a position's R value should fall. It is called the *Bench Equation* and it looks like this:

$$NewR = OldR \times [CW / (CW - MG)].$$

In this formula there are three variables: OldR, CW, and MG.

"OldR" is the current R value. For instance, the case analysis says that our current R value for the QB position is 12.

"CW" stands for the Championship Week. It is the week the fantasy championship game is played. This number is also equivalent to the number of weeks played in the entire fantasy season including the playoffs. Most fantasy leagues will have CW = 16.

"MG" stands for Missed Games. It is the number of games a player in general is likely to miss each year. As you'll learn, each fantasy position has its own unique MG value.

Before we determine Scenario Three's MG value let's apply it to the other two scenarios. This will give you more insight into using the Bench Equation. You'll also see how simple the formula really is to use.

All three scenarios assume the fantasy championship is played in Week 16, thus CW = 16. Also, OldR = 12 in all three scenarios because that is the value of R for the QB position in the case analysis. The only variable left to figure out is MG, so let's revisit our three earlier scenarios:

Scenario One

Since there are no bye weeks, injuries, etc., we can assume the QB will not miss any games. Thus, MG = 0. Using the Bench Equation we have R(QB) = 12 x [16/(16-0)] = 12 x [1] = 12. This confirms our original R calculation in that the R value should remain equal to 12.

Scenario Two

Here, the number of missed games is heightened to where the starter is expected to miss half the season. Thus, MG = 8. Using the Bench Equation we have R(QB) = 12 x [16/(16-8)] = 12 x [16/8] = 12 x [2] = 24. Again, we see that the Bench Equation matches our previous R calculation shown in Scenario Two.

Scenario Three

Let's finally apply the bench equation to Scenario Three so we can determine its adjusted R value. The only missed game will be the bye week. Therefore MG = 1. Using the Bench Equation we have R(QB) = 12 x [16/(16-1)] = 12 x (16/15) = 12.80.

At this point, let's take a moment to register what we have, starting with our R value of 12.80. First, don't worry about having an R value with a fraction. The RV Method will continue to tweak and adjust R values to the nearest hundredth. Not to worry: at the end of the system all R values will be rounded back to whole numbers to determine who the exact baseline players should be.

Secondly, I want to explain the significance of increasing an R value by a small amount such as 0.80. To do this, I like to view R values as being a pressure gauge. A higher R value indicates more pressure to draft from a position. A lower R value indicates less pressure to draft from a position. So, R(QB) = 12.80 indicates there is slightly more pressure to draft from the QB position than Scenario One where R(QB) = 12. I use the word "slightly" because 0.80 is a slight increase from 12. The 0.80 worth of additional pressure comes from needing a back-up QB for just one week, which is a small problem to deal with nonetheless. Compare this to Scenario Two where R(QB) = 24. This is a significant increase in pressure because the R value has doubled in value from 12 to 24. I view Scenario Two as having twice more pressure to draft a QB than Scenario One. This should be apparent since a backup QB is needed to replace the starter for half the season. So, as you can see, by viewing the R value as a pressure gauge, you can better understand what the various values and fractions indicate in the overall scheme of things.

DETERMINING ACTUAL MG VALUES

All three prior scenarios made it easy to determine the MG value because the QB's expected number of missed games (MG) was without doubt. Unfortunately, predicting missed game totals in reality isn't so easy for the QB position or any position for that matter. While we know every NFL player will miss at least one game on his bye week, we aren't exactly sure how many additional weeks each may miss due to other variables. It's practically impossible to determine with 100 percent accuracy, like we did in all three scenarios, what each position's actual MG value is going to be in the upcoming season.

So how should we approach predicting MG values? Unlike standardized games such as roulette or blackjack, human beings have tendencies and have, at different levels, some predictability.

I recommend looking at each position's historical results and using that data to predict MG values. This method relates to how AVT projections were determined back in Chapter Three – by using statistical inferences. We can observe the average number of missed games per player in a position, and use that as an educated guess as to how many games a player is likely to miss in the upcoming year. This number becomes the position's MG value. I also recommend observing the last three years' worth of data for similar reasons as described in Chapter Three for AVT.

In analyzing the historical data of each position, it's important to observe only the top-ranked players or specifically those players you would have been willing to start in each of those years. Why is this important? It's the games missed by the starting players that require a fantasy manager to draft back-up support which, to reiterate, is the primary reason for increasing R values. It's irrelevant to observe how many games a bench player misses because he is already on the bench.

To find exactly those players who "you would have been willing to start" in each of the last three years, you'll need access to historical player rankings or cheat sheets. This will allow you to go back and see all the players that were ranked high enough for you to start. Ideally, you'll want to observe cheat sheets that were applied to the same *exact* scoring rules as the league you are playing in right now. A cheat sheet that is based on a different league with a different scoring system could result in skewed player rankings.

If you don't have historical cheat sheets or any kind of player rankings handy, especially going three years back, then you can use the MG values determined in the next few paragraphs. While this may not be the ideal set of MG values for your particular league and situation, they should still be reasonable enough to use, but only if you play in a performance based fantasy league.

Assuming you have cheat sheets in hand, the next step is to observe the current set of R values as determined in Step Two. This set details exactly how many of the top-ranked players you should observe in each position for each of the past three years. For instance, the case analysis shows R(QB) = 12. Therefore, in determining the MG value of the QB position, we should observe the top 12 pre-season ranked QBs in each of the last three years. The reason for this methodology is that Step Two's R values give us a clue as to how many of the top-ranked players we would be willing to start.

For the purpose of adjusting R values in the case analysis, which pertains to the WCOFF, the following material will break down how I went about determining actual MG values for QB, RB, WR, TE, K, and D/ST positions. The sets of historical player rankings to be observed are those I used for the actual 2002, 2003, and 2004 WCOFF seasons as shown in Appendix D.

Referring back to the set of R values listed at the end of Step Two, it's a matter of tallying the number of missed games for each preseason's top 12 QBs, 30 RBs, 42 WRs, 12 TEs, 12 Ks, & 12 D/STs. This information can easily be accessed on websites such as NFL.com and ESPN.com. Simply click on a player's profile and you should be able to access his career stats. Focus on the number of games he played each season: this is all the information you need to determine a player's missed number of games. For example, if you find Player A to have played 12 games in 2004, that means he missed five games since the NFL season is 17 weeks long. (Note: Ideally, NFL Week 17 should be ignored in this observation because fantasy seasons typically do not extend beyond Week 16. Unfortunately, most NFL sites provide only seasonal stats in player profiles. Not to worry: the margin of error of including Week 17's stats in this particular observation is practically negligible in the overall scheme of things.)

As you make these observations, log all the missed games from the last three years into a chart such as Figure 34. The MG values will be the average number of missed games among the group of players observed in each position. Using the data in Figure 34, let's take a look how the MG value for the QB position is determined.

	FIGURE 34: MISSED GAMES FOR TOP PRE-SEASON QBs					
RANK	TOP RANKED QBS IN 2002	# MISSED GAMES	TOP RANKED QBS IN 2003	# MISSED GAMES	TOP RANKED QBS IN 2004	# MISSED GAMES
1	K. Warner	10	D. Culpepper	3	D. Culpepper	1
2	D. Culpepper	1	D. McNabb	1	P. Manning	1
3	J. Garcia	1	P. Manning	1	D. McNabb	1
4	D. McNabb	7	R. Gannon	10	M. Hasselbeck	3
5	P. Manning	1	A. Brooks	1	S. McNair	9
6	A. Brooks	1	K. Warner	15	T. Green	1
7	R. Gannon	1	B. Favre	1	T. Brady	1
8	B. Griese	4	S. McNair	3	A. Brooks	1
9	B. Favre	1	M. Hasselbeck	1	M. Vick	2
10	T. Green	1	T. Green	1	C. Pennington	4
11	S. McNair	1	T. Brady	1	M. Bulger	3
12	K. Stewart	10	J. Garcia	4	J. Garcia	6
	TOTAL:	39	TOTAL:	42	TOTAL:	33

Notice that all QBs missed at least one game regardless of the season in which he played in or what his pre-season ranking was. This is due to the mandatory bye week. Any additional missed games are due to injury, illness, suspension, etc. In any case, the QB's MG value is determined by adding up all the missed games in all three years and dividing by the total number of QBs observed. The total number of missed games is 39 + 42 + 33 = 114 games. The total number of QBs observed is 12 QBs per year multiplied by 3 years equals 36 QBs. Thus, the QB's MG value is 114 / 36 = 3.17 games. This MG value means a starting fantasy QB should be projected to miss 3.17 games in the upcoming season.

Implementing a similar process for all the positions resulted with the data and calculated MG values as shown in Figure 35.

	2002 MISSED GAMES	2003 MISSED GAMES	2004 MISSED GAMES	Total # MISSED GAMES	Total # PLAYERS OBSERVED	MG VALUE
FIGURE 35: CALCULATED MG VALUES FOR 2005 WCOFF						
Top 12 QBs	39	42	33	114	36	3.17
Top 30 RBs	68	99	129	296	90	3.29
Top 42 WRs	61	92	117	270	126	2.14
Top 12 TEs	24	28	38	90	36	2.50
Top 12 Ks	18	12	15	45	36	1.25
Top 12 D/STs	12	12	12	36	36	1.00

As you can see in Figure 35, each position shows a different MG value; some significantly more than others. The major proponent differentiating each position's MG value is the likelihood of certain players getting injured and the potential seriousness of those injuries. Each position entails its own risks. QBs' susceptibility to concussions, RBs' risk of ACL tears, WRs' and TEs' liability to pulled hamstrings and Ks' chances of a freak injury are all examples to consider. You should be aware that D/STs can't get injured because they are comprised of a group of players: if one individual within the bunch gets hurt another player quickly replaces him (although key injuries to the unit may affect other selection criteria).

The prior paragraph includes just a few examples of the many possible injury scenarios that can occur to various players in various positions. When you factor in all the potential scenarios, you'll find that players in certain positions tend to miss more games than players in other positions, as evident in Figure 35. To put it differently, the cumulative risk in some positions is greater than others because the nature of the positional duties, providing higher MG values than others. For instance, we already know D/STs are invincible to injury so their MG value is at the minimum possible of MG = 1 (due to the bye week). You'll find that kickers are a lot less susceptible to injury than any of the remaining positions, thus earning an MG value of 1.25. On the contrary, QBs and RBs tend to get injured the most, each enduring the most hits and tackles throughout the course of a season. These are the only positions where its top-ranked players are expected to miss more than three games on average.

We can now apply the set of MG values in Figure 35 to the case analysis using the Bench Equation. Before doing so, note that you can apply these same MG values towards adjusting your own set of R values assuming you do not have the appropriate resources to determine your own unique set. However, keep in mind these MG values may only be valid for a limited number of years due to possible long-term trends in the NFL, as was discussed in Chapter Three. For example, players may begin to show a trend towards missing fewer games as NFL trainers integrate more improved standards for strength and conditioning. Improved medical attention can also minimize the time players take to recuperate from an injury. On the flipside, if players continue to get stronger and faster there's a bigger risk for injury as the game itself gets more physical. I would advise only using these MG values for a limited number of years, then reassessing a new set based on possible new NFL trends starting around 2008.

CASE ANALYSIS CONT'D

Before: R(QB) = 12, R(RB) = 30, R(WR) = 42, R(TE) = 12, R(K) = 12, & R(D/ST) = 12.
After: Using the Bench Equation and the MG values in Figure 35, we end up with the following calculations for our new set of R values:

$R(QB) = 12 \times (16/(16\text{-}3.17)) = 14.96$
$R(RB) = 30 \times (16/(16\text{-}3.29)) = 37.77$
$R(WR) = 42 \times (16/(16\text{-}2.14)) = 48.48$

$R(TE) = 12 \times (16/(16-2.50)) = 14.22$
$R(K) = 12 \times (16/(16-1.25)) = 13.02$
$R(D/ST) = 12 \times (16/(16-1.00)) = 12.80$

STEP 4) Decrease the R value when a position offers sleepers

Sleepers should trigger a decrease in the R value in a position.

The reasoning is two-fold: First, by reducing a position's R value we are also lowering the X values of the players in the position. By lowering the X values in a position, we make ourselves more likely to draft from other positions since they have higher X values, essentially stalling ourselves from drafting from a position when we lower its R value. This method of "stalling" is a great strategy because there is a lot of good value (sleepers) available to be had later on, and we tend to be rewarded by drafting more players later than earlier when sleepers are likely to be sitting around.

Secondly, as sleepers move up the rankings they force the pre-existing top-ranked players to slide down, consequently lowering the effective value of the top-ranked players. Reducing a position's R value acts as a hedge against this downfall because it appropriately lowers the X values of those top-ranked players. The remaining material within this section will focus on how to optimally achieve this hedge.

To fully understand why and how lowering the R value works to your advantage, we must analyze X values and observe what happens when R values are altered by the sleepers. Suppose a section of our cheat sheet looks like Figure 36:

FIGURE 36: CHEAT SHEET WHEN R(QB) = 13

RANK	QB	PROJECTION	X #
1	QB1	374	101
2	QB2	358	85
3	QB3	341	68
4	QB4	332	59
5	QB5	327	54
6	QB6	324	51
7	QB7	317	44
8	QB8	314	41
9	QB9	306	33
10	QB10	299	26
11	QB11	288	15
12	QB12	280	7
13	QB13	273	0
14	QB14	269	-4

Figure 36 uses R(QB) = 13, meaning that the 13th ranked QB is the baseline player. This also means that all QB X values are calculated relative to QB13's projection of 273 fantasy points. In other words, those players projected to score more than 273 points will have a positive X value and those projected to score less than 273 points will have a negative X value.

But, inevitably, it happens every year: players unpredictably slide up and down the rankings throughout the season. Some players perform better than expected, and others perform worse than expected. For this particular example, suppose QB7 has outperformed QB3, QB4, QB5, & QB6. However, QB15 and QB17 performed extraordinarily well and finished atop everyone (think Kurt Warner in his breakout year). Lastly, QB8 was a bust and finished the season as the 25th ranked QB. All other QBs performed as expected relative to each other.

Had you known the players were going to finish the season like this, your cheat sheet should have looked like Figure 37.

FIGURE 37: EFFECTIVE QB CHEAT SHEET

RANK	QB	PROJECTION	X #
1	QB15	374	101
2	QB17	358	85
3	QB1	341	68
4	QB2	332	59
5	QB7	327	54
6	QB3	324	51
7	QB4	317	44
8	QB5	314	41
9	QB6	306	33
10	QB9	299	26
11	QB10	288	15
12	QB11	280	7
13	QB12	273	0
14	QB13	269	-4

Figure 37 tells us the effective rankings and X values of the players, or the rankings and X values we should have given the players – assuming we had a crystal ball into the future.

Now suppose you drafted QB4 according to the cheat sheet in Figure 36. As you can see from Figure 37, QB4 effectively finished the season as the seventh best QB. So you drafted QB4 expecting an X value of 59 fantasy points (Figure 36) but it turns out his X value should have only been 44 fantasy points (Figure 37). This means that you lost 15 points in X value. The same can be said for most of the other highly-ranked QBs. For example, you could have drafted QB1 expecting an X value of 101 fantasy points but he effectively only offers 68 fantasy points. Thus, you would have lost a whopping 33 fantasy points in X value if you drafted QB1 and started him throughout the season. Figure 38 shows the losses (or gains) in X value that would be incurred if you drafted and started each of the top 12 ranked QBs throughout the season.

FIGURE 38: GAIN/LOSS IN X VALUE WHEN R(QB) = 13

QB	X # [Figure 36]	Effective X # [Figure 37]	Gain/Loss In X #
QB1	101	68	-33
QB2	85	59	-26
QB3	68	51	-17
QB4	59	44	-15
QB5	54	41	-13
QB6	51	33	-18
QB7	44	51	7
QB8	41	N/A	N/A
QB9	33	26	-7
QB10	26	15	-11
QB11	15	7	-8
QB12	7	0	-7
Net:			-148

Since X values represent the number of fantasy points you plan to outscore your opponents, it is a given that any loss incurred very much hurts the performance of your fantasy squad. Since most of the top-ranked QBs in Figure 38 are shown to incur a loss, we can conclude that Figure 36 doesn't make for a good cheat sheet.

The two main causes for the losses in the top players' X values, as well as the causes for Figure 36 not being a good cheat sheet, are sleepers QB15 and QB17. When these two sleepers move atop the rankings, they force all the top-ranked players to move down two notches subsequently causing a reduction in their effective X values. Consequently, you would incur a loss in X value by drafting any top-ranked player with two exceptions.

The first is QB7 who was able to move up in the rankings by outperforming QB3, QB4, QB5 and QB6. This ends up giving him an increase in X value of seven fantasy points. The second exception is if you drafted QB8. Ironically, QB8 is a complete bust who performed horribly. His performance is so bad – he finished as the 25th ranked QB – that you would likely start someone else as the season progressed. So, depending on who else you drafted or picked up in free agency, it's still possible for you to do fairly well in the QB position. For example, you may have been fortunate enough to draft QB15 or QB17 as your backup in which case you would have done very well. In this case QB8's stats are considered "not applicable" because he is likely to be benched for most of the season due to his horrendous output.

The bottom line? *Most of the top-ranked QBs show a significant loss in X value.* Their net loss, excluding QB8, is a whopping 148 fantasy points as shown in bottom row of Figure 38. This is a lot of downfall that you don't want to deal with as a fantasy manager. If you are to give yourself a good chance to win your fantasy league, you must find a way to eliminate, or at least minimize, these potential losses in X value.

What could we have done differently to minimize the potential losses in X values?

One answer is obvious: we could have ranked the players better. In fact, if we were able to rank the players exactly like Figure 37, then there would be no issues. But this isn't the practical solution. It's always easy to blame player rankings in retrospect. The truth is, probably no one could have predicted sleepers QB15 and QB17 to finish the season as the two best QBs. Nor would it be practical or realistic to say that we should have somehow figured out that QB8 was going to bust. Furthermore, you would only be pulling your hair out if you dwelled over little things like ranking QB7 ahead of QB3, QB4, QB5, and QB6. The thing you have to remember is that ranking players is significantly based on opinion, so don't lose any sleep over the mistakes you find at the end of the season: the errors inevitably affect everyone.

The practical answer to minimize the potential losses in X values is to lower the R value of the QB position.

You'll find that the more you reduce the R value, the more you reduce the potential losses caused by sleepers. As stated earlier in this section, reducing R values acts as a great hedge. Let's take a look at how it works.

FIGURE 39: CHEAT SHEET WHEN R(QB) = 12

RANK	QB	PROJECTION	X #
1	QB1	374	94
2	QB2	358	78
3	QB3	341	61
4	QB4	332	52
5	QB5	327	47
6	QB6	324	44
7	QB7	317	37
8	QB8	314	34
9	QB9	306	26
10	QB10	299	19
11	QB11	288	8
12	QB12	280	0
13	QB13	273	-7
14	QB14	269	-11

Suppose you reduce R(QB) from 13 to 12. The new cheat sheet would look like Figure 39.

All QB X values are determined relative to QB12's projection of 280 fantasy points. More importantly, let's take a look at the losses in X value (if any) that are associated with Figure 39. The results are shown in Figure 40.

FIGURE 40: GAIN/LOSS IN X VALUE WHEN R(QB) = 12			
QB	X # [Figure 39]	Effective X # [Figure 37]	Gain/Loss In X #
QB1	94	68	-26
QB2	78	59	-19
QB3	61	51	-10
QB4	52	44	-8
QB5	47	41	-6
QB6	44	33	-11
QB7	37	51	14
QB8	34	N/A	N/A
QB9	26	26	0
QB10	19	15	-4
QB11	8	7	-1
QB12	0	0	0
Net:			-71

As you can see in Figure 40, the net loss in X values among the QBs is now only 71 fantasy points compared to 148 points in Figure 38. This result comes from the fact that projected X values are lowered when the R value is reduced, and when projected X values are lowered, so are the potential losses in X values (as shown in the right column in figure 40). So, by reducing the R value, you lower your expectations on the pre-season top-ranked QBs. The advantage? You are not as disappointed at the end of the year if a QB doesn't finish the season ranked as highly as he was projected.

Our work isn't done yet, as Figure 40 still shows a collective net loss of 71 as well as very few QBs individually showing a gain in X value. So there is still a considerable amount of potential downfall, or disappointment, which needs to be avoided. Let's try reducing the R value by another unit, making R(QB) = 11 (Figure 41).

RANK	QB	PROJECTION	X # WHEN R=11	EFFECTIVE X # [Figure 37]	GAIN/LOSS IN X #
\multicolumn{6}{c}{**FIGURE 41: GAIN/LOSS IN X VALUE WHEN R(QB) = 11**}

RANK	QB	PROJECTION	X # WHEN R=11	EFFECTIVE X # [Figure 37]	GAIN/LOSS IN X #
1	QB1	374	86	68	-18
2	QB2	358	70	59	-11
3	QB3	341	53	51	-2
4	QB4	332	44	44	0
5	QB5	327	39	41	2
6	QB6	324	36	33	-3
7	QB7	317	29	51	22
8	QB8	314	26	N/A	N/A
9	QB9	306	18	26	8
10	QB10	299	11	15	4
11	QB11	288	0	7	7
12	QB12	280	-8	0	8
Net:					17

By making R(QB) = 11, the top-ranked QBs now show a net gain of 17 fantasy points in X value. Another positive aspect about Figure 41 is that seven of the top-ranked QBs will no longer disappoint by season's end (QB4, QB5, QB7, QB9, QB10, QB11, QB12). In other words, if you drafted any of these QBs, you would outscore your opponents more than expected. This is because their effective X value (5th column, Figure 41) is better or equal to your projected X value (4th column, Figure 41). Finally, we've found the kind of results imperative to winning a league title!

At this point one might wonder: why not reduce the R value even more if that will further improve the potential gains in X value?

Hmmm, good question. Reducing the R value again will certainly improve the results in the gain/loss column for X values, but (surprise!) there's a catch. Let's reduce the R value to R(QB) = 9 and analyze the results in Figure 42.

FIGURE 42: GAIN/LOSS IN X VALUE WHEN R(QB) = 9				
QB	PTS	X #	EFFECTIVE X # (Figure 37)	GAIN/LOSS IN X #
QB1	374	68	68	0
QB2	358	52	59	7
QB3	341	35	51	16
QB4	332	26	44	18
QB5	327	21	41	20
QB6	324	18	33	15
QB7	317	11	51	40
QB8	314	8	N/A	N/A
QB9	306	0	26	26
QB10	299	-7	15	22
QB11	288	-18	7	25
QB12	280	-26	0	26
Net:				215

At first glance, Figure 42 appears to show extraordinary results due to the 215 point gain in X value in the right column. However, the "surprise" that occurs when you reduce the R value too much is that the X values also become very low (illustrated by comparing the X values in Figure 42 to the X values we originally had in Figure 36).

Why is having low X values a problem?

Let's think back to the principles of value-based drafting. X values are used to create the overall rankings list which tells managers who to draft. If a position's X values become too low, then that position would be at a risk of having no player represented in the overall rankings list. The other positions are likely to have a lot more players with higher X values and subsequently will occupy most of the overall rankings list. So if we were to lower the X values of the QB position to the extent shown in Figure 42, we are basically taking away our incentive to draft QBs, defeating the purpose of ranking and projecting them in the first place.

Naturally, some form of balance or optimal reduction in R value must exist. Remember, on the one hand we want to decrease R values so we minimize our potential losses in X value (listed in the right columns of Figures 38, 40, 41, 42). On the other hand, we don't want to decrease the R value too much because the X values will be depleted (like that of Figure 42).

So what is the optimal reduction of the R value?

I found the optimal reduction occurs when the R value is lowered just enough so that the net gain/loss in X value of the top-ranked players is closest to zero. I also found that this can best be accomplished by simply **observing the sleepers**. Specifically, by counting the total number of spots all sleepers move up in the top-ranked positions (let's tag this number the "SMU," or "Spots Moved Up") then dividing by the number of top-ranked positions (the "TRP," or "Top-Ranked Positions"), this result gives us the optimal reduction we are looking for.

This process can be exemplified in Figure 37. To keep the process as systematic as possible, let's define "sleeper" as any player that didn't qualify among the top-ranked spots on the cheat sheet but finished there by season's end.

To determine the SMU, or how many places sleepers QB15 and QB17 moved up, we first need to establish the number of top-ranked positions, or TRP. I prefer using the R values as a result of Step Two in determining how many top-ranked places there are in each position because this set of R values gives us a good idea as to how many players will be started among the league. Looking at the case analysis in Step Two gives us TRP = 30 for the running back position, TRP = 42 for wide receivers and TRP = 12 for all other positions. Right now we are focused on the QB position.

Now let's figure out SMU using Figure 37. We know that there are twelve top-ranked spots in the QB position. Therefore, QB15 moved up a total of twelve places within the top-ranked positions to get to the top spot. It's important to be aware that even though QB15 moved up a total of 14 places from his original 15th ranked position, we only count twelve places because that's how many he moved *within the top- ranked spots.*

Following the same methodology, you'll find that QB17 moved up eleven places within the top-ranked spots to make it to the second position. Thus, we find that their total SMU = 12 + 11 = 23. Dividing SMU by TRP gives us 23 / 12 = 1.92. Thus, optimal reduction in R(QB) is 1.92 units, meaning it would have been optimal to reduce R(QB) from 13 to 11.08.

Hold the phone: there is one huge caveat with what we just did. Not one of us is Nostradamus, right? So how could we possibly know the SMU results before the season begins? The answer is simple: we couldn't. The only reason when know the season's outcome in the prior example is because of the hypothetical results revealed in Figure 37, something we realistically wouldn't have in our hands during the preseason.

How does one realistically determine SMU for the upcoming season?

Just like predicting so many other things in fantasy football, predicting SMUs relies on statistical inferences. I recommend always observing the last three years' worth of historical data. Just observe SMUs in the various positions during the last three years and take the average of those observations to predict the future. Keep in mind, SMUs can only be determined if you have the following two data sources in a given year:

1. A cheat sheet, or some sort of preseason ranking.
2. Year-end player rankings.

For the purpose of the case analysis, let's gear our attention towards determining SMUs in the various WCOFF positions during the 2002, 2003, and 2004 seasons. These SMUs will then be averaged to ultimately determine "SMU / TRP." We already have the appropriate preseason player rankings (Appendix D). These rankings show us the top- ranked players who aren't eligible to be sleepers. For instance, all QBs ranked in the top twelve cannot be considered sleepers. All other QBs are eligible.

The next step is to observe the season ending rankings of the WCOFF fantasy players for each season. This step includes observing the sleepers and particularly how many spots each moved up within the top-ranked positions. Such observations are shown in Appendix E, with the final results listed here in Figure 43.

FIGURE 43: SMU & TRP RESULTS (CASE ANALYSIS)						
	QB	RB	WR	TE	K	D/ST
2002 SMU	16	41	156	20	18	35
2003 SMU	15	91	275	13	34	35
2004 SMU	25	96	176	19	22	41
Total SMU	56	228	607	52	74	111
2002 TRP	12	30	42	12	12	12
2003 TRP	12	30	42	12	12	12
2004 TRP	12	30	42	12	12	12
Total TRP	36	90	126	36	36	36
Total SMU/ Total TRP	1.56	2.53	4.82	1.44	2.06	3.08

The bottom row of Figure 43 indicates the optimal number of units by which each position's R value should be reduced within the case analysis. Let's review an earlier point to better demonstrate what this means:

Sleepers should trigger a decrease in the R value in a position. By reducing a position's R value we are also lowering the X values of the players in the position. By lowering the X values in a position, we make ourselves more likely to draft from other positions since they have higher X values, essentially stalling ourselves from drafting from a position when we lower its R value. This method of "stalling" is a great strategy because there is a lot of good value (sleepers) available to be had later on, and we tend to be rewarded by drafting more players later than earlier when sleepers are likely to be sitting around.

Notice that the WR and D/ST positions require the most significant reduction in R value according to Figure 43. The reason for this is that these positions offer more sleeper activity than any other position.

One final note pertaining to Figure 43: these results are optimal when applied towards leagues similar to the WCOFF. If your league involves different lineups, rules, or scoring, then it may be wise to perform your own SMU and TRP calculations for adjusting R values. For example, if you are in a ten-team league starting two WRs without any flex players, it would be wise to observe 20 WRs for each of the last three years (whereas 42 WRs were observed to get the results in Figure 43). This simple change can and will skew the results.

Of course, if you do not have access to historical cheat sheets or preseason player rankings for the last two or three years, then you should still use the results listed on the bottom row of Figure 43 in adjusting your set of R value. While this may not be ideal for your particular league, it is still better to apply than not doing anything. Just make sure you start keeping records of preseason cheat sheets and season ending rankings so not to fall into this dilemma in future draft preparations. Also, in order to avoid errors based on old NFL trends, the results in Figure 43 should not be used beyond the 2008 season.

CASE ANALYSIS CONT'D

Before: R(QB) = 14.96, R(RB) = 37.77, R(WR) = 48.48, R(TE) = 14.22, R(K) = 13.02, R(D/ST) = 12.80.
After: Subtracting each position's R value by the respective number calculated in the bottom row of Figure 43 we get the following set of adjusted R values:

R(QB) = 14.96 - 1.56 = 13.40
R(RB) =37.77 − 2.53 = 35.24
R(WR) = 48.48 - 4.82 = 43.66
R(TE) = 14.22 - 1.44 = 12.78
R(K) = 13.02 − 2.06 = 10.96
R(D/ST) = 12.80 − 3.08 = 9.72

STEP 5) Increase the R value of shallow positions.

This step has us increasing the R value of certain positions that are deemed "shallow." Shallow indicates that the position offers a very limited number of serviceable fantasy players. By "serviceable" I mean any player that consistently garners at least a few fantasy points each week. RB Antowain Smith in 2003 and TE Chad Lewis in 2004 are prime examples of players who were just inside the bubble of serviceability. They don't have to be top point scorers or even average scorers, but they must avoid getting shut out in most weeks to be considered serviceable. Of course, any player that scores a lot of points is definitely serviceable.

Let's take a look at the nature of a shallow position to understand why its R value should be increased.

Shallow positions are liable of being "sold out" on draft day. In other words, managers are at risk of not being able to draft enough serviceable players before it's too late, presenting a unique now-or-never drafting situation. Managers who don't properly account for this situation will end up not having enough serviceable players to fill a starting line up throughout the season – a predicament that could be detrimental to winning fantasy games due to a plethora of dreaded goose eggs. This potential disaster obviously puts a lot of *pressure* on a manager to draft from a position, which is exactly why the R value needs to be increased (Remember the *pressure gauge* analogy described in Step Three?). An increase in the R value will increase the X values of the players in the position, naturally pushing the position and its players upward in the overall rankings list. Thus, the sooner, faster, and more often that position will be drafted. This aggressive drafting approach is the exact remedy for a shallow position; it avoids the risk of not drafting enough serviceable players in time.

However, not all shallow positions have to have its R value increased. I found three conditions that must be met before a fantasy position should truly have its R value increased. Ask yourself the following three questions regarding each position:

1) Is the position shallow?

2) Will it be difficult to pick up a serviceable player in the free agent pool?

3) Is drafting backup players very important?

If the answer is "YES" to all three, then your play is to increase a position's R value. Such a scenario presents extreme pressure to draft from a position.

If the answer to any of these questions is "NO," increasing the R value of that position is not recommended and skipping to Step Six would be the wise choice of action.

Let's take a closer look at each of these questions:

Question No. 1) Is the position shallow?

To determine if a position is shallow you need to figure out how many serviceable players there are likely to be available at the start of the draft. Then you need to estimate how many of them will be drafted. If the results show a deficit, then the position should be deemed shallow.

You can expect there to be exactly 32 serviceable players available in the QB, TE, and D/ST positions. The reason for this is that the NFL has 32 franchises, and each franchise starts and plays only one QB, K and D/ST per week. This means there will only be 32 players scoring fantasy points in each of these positions on any given week. Thus, we can safely conclude that each of these positions offers exactly 32 serviceable fantasy players, with one exception to the rule: the D/ST position. Some fantasy leagues severely penalize D/STs for surrendering too many points or yards, in which case it's possible to have less than 32 serviceable D/STs. A handful of the worst NFL defenses are not going to be serviceable because they won't be able to consistently score positive fantasy points. So be sure to analyze your scoring rules regarding D/STs.

As far as the other positions (RB, WR, TE) there are a variety of ways to determine how many serviceable players might be available on draft day. One option is to closely analyze the NFL, all its teams and players, and estimate how many players are likely to see enough playing time in order to become serviceable. For instance, here are two excerpts from articles I wrote on predicting the number of serviceable TEs and WRs using this type of analysis:

1) Many NFL franchises tend to play more than one TE each week, lifting the potential number of serviceable TEs above 32. However, this is countered by the fact that some of these TEs are used primarily as blockers (a skill, while valuable, left unrewarded in fantasy football). Therefore, we should consider this counter balance and maintain that approximately 32 serviceable TEs will be available during the draft.

2) The WR position is the deepest of all positions, so by definition it is not considered a shallow position. All NFL teams start and regularly target at least two WRs on a consistent basis making those WRs serviceable. Additionally, about two thirds of the NFL, or about 21 teams, will significantly involve a third WR in the game plan, thus earning him serviceability status. Lastly, I estimate an average of five NFL teams to consistently throw to as many as four WRs throughout the NFL season, resulting in all four WRs scoring enough fantasy points to be considered serviceable (think the Rams' quartet of Tory Holt, Isaac Bruce, Kevin Curtis and Shaun McDonald). Adding everyone up gives us (32 x 2) + 21 + 5 = 90 possible serviceable fantasy WRs.

Such analyses are very time consuming and speculative. You need to have a good working knowledge of the NFL in order to move ahead in this fashion. Consequently, I recommend using a simple formula that has proven its accuracy over the years:

All players projected to score at least one fourth the points of the top point scorer in a position can be considered serviceable.

This is not an exact science, but it seems to work very well in most instances. For example, if you glance down at your cheat sheet and see Shaun Alexander projected to be the highest scoring RB with 400 fantasy points, then all RBs projected to score at least 100 points can be considered serviceable.

In some cases, however, projections and scoring systems don't make this formula suitable. In general, you should find approximately 32 QBs, 50 RBs, 90 WRs, 32 TEs, 32 Ks, and 32 D/STs to be serviceable and available on draft day. Use this generalization as a cross reference to your results.

Keep in mind, the aforementioned assumptions, formulas, and analyses are liable to change over time. For instance, RBBCs could lose popularity, decreasing the number of serviceable RBs. Two tight-end formations could become a prevailing scheme among NFL coaches increasing the number of serviceable TEs. Any such playbook movements or other trends can and will affect the size of the serviceable player pool.

Even the QB and K positions, which seem all but locked with 32 serviceable players per position, could potentially increase. How? NFL coaches could one day find that it's better to play two different players in these positions (more common in college football) possibly increasing the number of serviceable players. This actually happened with the Tennessee Titans in 2003, when coach Jeff Fisher used Gary Anderson to kick field goals shorter than 45 yards and Joe Nedney/Craig Hentrich to kick anything longer. However, there were not enough 50-yarders to go around to deem either Nedney or Hentrich serviceable.

But would a coach really use two different QBs each game? Anything is possible. Consider the case where one QB could be used to build a lead and another QB could be used to maintain a lead – a less than far-fetched scenario. Let's use the evolution of Major League Baseball as an analogy: In the early half of the twentieth century, fans were accustomed to seeing one pitcher toss complete games on a regular basis. In fact, pitchers throwing back-to-back games would hardly raise an eyebrow among fans. Relievers, middle men, and closers were terms yet to have been uttered, before that one afternoon when one coach deciphered the advantages of utilizing different pitchers in certain situations. The concept snowballed, and today MLB franchises build teams around closers and relievers. If such a trend were to occur in the NFL QB position, where two of them were consistently playing for the same team on a weekly basis, then we could see a trend of there being more than 32 serviceable QBs. What's my point? Always keep your eyes peeled for the latest NFL trends and adjust accordingly.

After determining the number of serviceable players for each position, the next step is to determine how many in each group are likely to get drafted. Again, if you figure a position has a deficit of players, then it should be deemed shallow.

Projecting how many players are going to be drafted is highly dependent on the league's starting lineups, roster size, and scoring rules. There are two methods you can follow:

The best method is to analyze historical drafts from the actual league you are playing in, assuming the league has been running several years without any significant changes in the rule book. Simply look at a past draft and count the number of players that were drafted in each position. This will give you an excellent idea as to how many serviceable players are likely to be drafted in each position. For example, after observing several drafts in the 2002 and 2003 WCOFF I knew heading into the 2004 draft that roughly 25 QBs, 73 RBs, 90 WRs, 20 TEs, 15 Ks, and 17 D/STs were going to be drafted. In making such an observation, it's acceptable to assume all players drafted are going to be serviceable even though some of them won't be (e.g., handcuffers – they aren't projected to score many points yet are still drafted). Thus, I assumed 25 serviceable QBs were going to be drafted in the 2004 WCOFF draft with similar assumptions on the other positions.

If you don't have access to historical drafts, a great alternative is to observe the results of mock drafts. The process is the same, count the number of players drafted in each position. Just make sure the mock draft you observe (or participate in) is of a similar league and has the same number of drafting rounds.

At this point you should be able to determine if a position is shallow or not. If you find that there are 32 serviceable QBs available but only 25 are going to be drafted, as I did in the WCOFF, then the position has a surplus of seven serviceable QBs and should not be deemed shallow. If you find 50 serviceable RBs to be available while expecting 73 RBs to be drafted, as I also did in the WCOFF, then the position has a deficit of 23 RBs and should be deemed shallow.

A surplus/deficit template on various sized leagues is provided in Figure 44. The results are based on observations on various WCOFF and online mock drafts. In fact, the data regarding 12-team leagues is strictly based on the average results of random WCOFF drafts. All results assume a 20-man roster and a starting lineup of 1 QB, 2 RB, 3 WR, 1 TE, 1 K, 1 D/ST, and 1 Flex.

FIGURE 44: SURPLUS/DEFICIT TEMPLATE (SERVICEABLE PLAYERS)						
League/Pos Availability	QB 32	RB 50	WR 90	TE 32	K 32	D/ST 32
10-Team surplus/deficit	22 +10	64 -14	73 +17	14 +18	13 +19	14 +18
12-Team surplus/deficit	25 +7	73 -23	90 0	20 +12	15 +17	17 +15
14-Team surplus/deficit	30 +2	75 -25	91 -1	28 +4	28 +4	28 +4
16-Team surplus/deficit	38 -6	83 -33	103 -13	32 0	32 0	32 0

The top row labeled "availability" indicates the number of serviceable players expected to be available at the start of the draft. The rows labeled 10-team, 12-team, et cetera, indicate how many serviceable players are projected to be drafted in that size league. The rows below that labeled "surplus/deficit" indicate how many serviceable players are likely to be left when the draft is over. A positive number indicates a surplus of players. A negative number indicates a deficit. Those positions with a deficit are likely to run out of serviceable players on draft day and should be considered shallow, as indicated in bold lettering.

Note, Figure 44 is to be used as a template only, and necessary adjustments should be made accordingly. For example, if your league allows you to draft more than 20 players, you need to increase the number of serviceable players drafted. Some leagues enforce a roster of less than 20 players, in which case you need to decrease the number of serviceable players drafted.

Here are five additional notes and observations regarding Figure 44:

1. Eight-team leagues were excluded from this analysis. Leagues this small tend to offer a surplus of players in just about every position including the usually shallow RB position. There is so much value to be spread around in the draft that there's no need to increase the R values. In fact, drafting and managing a fantasy team isn't all that difficult. With so few teams each manager tends to be loaded with stud fantasy players. As far as I'm concerned, eight-team fantasy leagues don't exist because it involves very little skill to draft a studded team.

2. The running back position has a deficit of serviceable players across the board, further emphasizing the value of the position. The demand of the RB position is always greater than its supply, which helps explain why so many fantasy managers praise and value the position so highly.

3. Notice the big jump in the number of serviceable players being drafted in the K and D/ST positions from a 12-team league to a 14-team league. Approximately 15-17 in each position are anticipated to be drafted in a 12-team league. This number nearly doubles in the 14-team league where 28 of each position are expected to be drafted.

This occurs because managers in a 12-team league understand there is no threat of all serviceable Ks and D/STs being drafted, therefore many managers plan on getting away with drafting only one of each position so they can wisely draft more player in the other positions. They are also aware that when the time arises for a back up K or D/ST, these positions will be generous in the free agency pool.

This view completely changes in a 14-team league. Managers soon realize the slight possibility that all the serviceable Ks and D/STs could be drafted, especially with the presence of any cut-throat managers who aim to hoard as many Ks and D/STs as possible in an attempt to stick it to other squads. This potential risk is a large determinant in all managers drafting two Ks and D/STs each. Ironically, I still recommend drafting only one K and D/ST in a 14-team. It's been my experience that a couple serviceable players of each position tend to still be available in free agency. This maneuver will allow you to draft more players and potential sleepers from other more important fantasy positions such as WR and RB. As long as a few Ks and D/STs remain undrafted, you should be safe. Just keep a look out for those cut-throat personalities.

4. Notice that the QB position in the 14-team league is listed in bold, indicating a shallow position even though it shows a surplus of two serviceable players. The reason for this is that while only 30 QBs are projected to be drafted, all 32 serviceable QBs can easily end up being drafted. Therefore, it's probably wise to play it safe and assume the position is shallow.

You can assume the TE, K, and D/ST positions in a 14-team league could end up being shallow as well, but their situation usually isn't as threatening as the QB position. I found that these positions are rarely depleted of all its serviceable players even though the possibility lurks. I'd say its best to treat these positions as not being shallow; thus, you shouldn't reduce their R values in this step of the RV Method. Again, just keep a look out for cut-throat managers on draft day so you are not left high and dry.

5. Finally, look at what's likely to occur in a 16-team fantasy league. Basically, you can expect every single serviceable player in every position to be taken by the end of the draft. Only the

most buttoned-up will survive this draft because everyone is liable to be left short-handed in multiple positions.

Before moving on to Question No. 2, you should log all your answers to the first question, "Is the position shallow?" in a YES/NO chart. For example, you can see such a chart designated in Figure 45 for all the various-sized leagues as presented in Figure 44 (keeping in mind your chart will be only for one league):

FIGURE 45: IS THE POSITION SHALLOW?				
	10-Team League	12-Team League	14-Team League	16-Team League
QB	NO	NO	YES	YES
RB	YES	YES	YES	YES
WR	NO	YES	YES	YES
TE	NO	NO	NO	YES
K	NO	NO	NO	YES
D/ST	NO	NO	NO	YES

Question No. 2) Will it be difficult to pick up a serviceable player in the free agent pool?

Remember, this question only needs to be answered for those positions you answered "YES" to in Question No. 1. All positions tagged with a "NO" need no further analysis, so skip to Step Six of the RV Method to continue adjusting those R values.

Question No. 2 is a very important one to ask because if serviceable players are easy to pick up after the draft, then that obviously relieves any pressure to get them during the draft. Hence, the R value doesn't have to be increased. But since we already answered "YES" to Question No. 1 that should indicate most or all of the serviceable players are going to be drafted, rendering a free agent pool thin of serviceable players and maintaining the pressure and need to increase the R value. ... or so it would seem.

The depletion of serviceable players on draft day doesn't necessarily mean additional ones won't rise up in free agency. The NFL is filled with well over 500 offensive players who play fantasy-related positions, and while most of them start the season sitting more often than not on the bench, opportunities always seem to arise where a multitude of players become serviceable. A bench player can see the NFL limelight any time a starter gets injured, needs rest, plays poorly, or gets replaced by the coach via a simple lineup change. These scenarios happen often, and when a bench player gets thrown in the game, his fantasy value could shoot up the charts if he excels. While some gel into true gems, many are likely to garner just enough playing action to be considered serviceable on the fantasy level. In any case, these rising stars make it possible to find a serviceable player in the free agent pool even though it seems unlikely immediately after the draft.

It's equally important to consider how difficult it might be to pick up any serviceable players that sprout up in free agency. Remember, any player in the free agent market is up for grabs, according to (most) league rules. Some leagues may allow the worst records first choice to pick up a player while other leagues may apply a blind bidding process. Nonetheless, the more valuable a free agent, the tougher it usually is to pick him up.

A common scenario entails a stud RB getting injured, thrusting his back up into the starting role: this once bottom-feeder will be tugged at by free agent bidders like a wishbone. But for every golden nugget, there are those "lunch pail" players who do nothing spectacular but scrape together enough fantasy points to be considered serviceable. Chances are you'll be able to pick up, for example, the Kansas City Chief's fourth wideout with ease. The bottom line: consider not only how many serviceable players are likely to appear in free agency, but how difficult it will be to snag them - it doesn't do you any good if you can't pick them up.

With the above in mind, let's start answering Question No. 2 for various leagues and positions. You'll find some positions are difficult to pick up serviceable free agents in while others seem very generous, and certain scenarios depend on the size of the league. Again, the following analysis will concentrate only on certain size leagues as indicated with a "YES" in Figure 45. In other words, you won't find an analysis on whether or not it will be difficult to pick up a serviceable kicker in a ten-team league; this would not be applicable.

QUARTERBACK

The QB position is not conducive to offering additional serviceable players as the season progresses. The nature of this position is for the original 32 serviceable QBs to play as long as possible in the NFL without anyone else replacing them. If a serviceable QB does sprout up in the free agent pool, it will be at the expense of a pre-existing serviceable QB, always limiting the position to 32 serviceable players. You can expect managers to be chomping at the bit to pick up any new serviceable QBs especially in a 14 and 16-team league. Thus, it will likely be very difficult to pick up a serviceable QB.

RUNNING BACK

I found that serviceable RBs are very difficult to pick up in leagues that have 14 or more teams. Two reasons: First, all of them will definitely be drafted. Secondly, those that pop up in free agency will be hoarded like there's no tomorrow.

The RB position may or may not be difficult to pick up serviceable free agents in after a 12-team draft, contingent on the league rules. For instance, if scoring rules include one point per reception, then there's usually a handful of the lesser glamorous RBs floating around who are serviceable, specifically those who like catch the ball out of the back field a few times each game (think Dallas Cowboys Richie Anderson). Another factor to consider is how competitive the other managers in your league are. If you are playing against any experienced fantasy footballers then you probably should assume it will be difficult to acquire serviceable RBs in the free agent market. To put it another way, if you were playing against me, then you'd have to worry about me scooping up Anderson first.

Serviceable RBs are usually available in the free agent market for ten-team leagues. This may come as a surprise since Figure 44 shows a somewhat hefty deficit of 14 RBs on draft day. However, it's been my experience that as little as two to three weeks into the season many managers drop their worst RBs, even though they might be serviceable. Furthermore, it's not uncommon for additional serviceable RBs to sprout up as the NFL season progresses whether its due to a newly formed RBBC or a second stringer filling in for an injured starter. The key facet here is that many of these up and coming serviceable RBs are relatively easy to pick up since there are only nine other competing managers.

WIDE RECEIVER

The deepest position of all, WR is naturally also the most bountiful when it comes to supplying managers with serviceable fantasy players after the draft. The situation arises because of two connecting factors: first, the NFL allows two or more WRs to simultaneously play on the field at once, and second, coaches exercise this right to the fullest extent. This is apparent anytime you see three and four wide receiver sets on the field. Each WR on the field is liable to score plenty of fantasy points.

With so many WRs getting their proverbial shot, it shouldn't come as a surprise that serviceable WRs are always popping up in free agency. The one exception is if you play in a 16-team league that allows a 25+ man roster. Under this extreme circumstance it might be difficult to find a serviceable WR in free agency because all third and fourth string WRs are likely to be drafted; not to mention you'll be up against 15 other fierce managers in vying for anyone that pops up. Other than this extreme and unusual circumstance, it shouldn't be that difficult to find a serviceable WR, even if most of them are seemingly expected to be taken on draft day.

TIGHT END

If you play in a 14-team league or smaller, then you should have no difficulty in finding and picking up a serviceable TE in the free agent market. If you play in any of the larger leagues, then expect difficulty.

KICKER

The K position is just like the QB position; it is not conducive to offering additional serviceable players as the season progresses. The nature of this position is for the original 32 serviceable Ks to play as long as possible in the NFL without anyone else replacing them. If a serviceable K does sprout up in the free agent pool, it will be at the expense of a pre-existing serviceable K, always limiting the position to 32 serviceable players. All managers will be chomping at the bit to pick up any new serviceable Ks assuming it's a 16-team league. Thus, we can conclude it will be extremely difficult to pick up a serviceable K.

DEFENSE/SPECIAL TEAMS

The D/ST position is similar to tight ends in that it should be easy to find serviceable players in free agency for leagues 14 teams and smaller and difficult in larger leagues such as 16 teams. One key difference making it more difficult to find serviceable D/STs in larger leagues, relative to TEs, is that D/STs are strictly limited to no more than 32 serviceable D/STs. So once they are all taken on draft day there's no looking back; you are either fortunate to have two D/STs, or you have to endure a full season with only one of them.

Actually, you may not even be guaranteed 32 serviceable D/STs on draft day. Some fantasy leagues severely penalize D/STs for surrendering too many points or yards, in which case it's possible - even likely - to have less than 32 serviceable D/STs. A handful of the worst NFL defenses are not going to be serviceable because they won't be able to consistently score positive fantasy points. In fact, this could be a cause for concern in 14-team leagues if the number of serviceable D/STs is expected to be lower than 28. So be sure to analyze your scoring rules and league size before making a final decision on whether or not this position will offer serviceable D/STs in free agency.

As with Question No. 1, the final step is to log all answers to the second question, "Will it be difficult to obtain serviceable player in the free agent pool?" Figure 46 shows the answers as applied to the previous charts and information. Again, it's only necessary to answer those situations that resulted in "YES" from the first question, as all other scenarios are not applicable.

FIGURE 46: WILL IT BE DIFFICULT TO OBTAIN A SERVICEABLE PLAYER IN FREE AGENCY?

	10-Team League	12-Team League	14-Team League	16-Team League
QB	N/A	N/A	YES	YES
RB	NO	YES	YES	YES
WR	N/A	NO	NO	NO
TE	N/A	N/A	N/A	NO
K	N/A	N/A	N/A	YES
D/ST	N/A	N/A	N/A	YES

Question No. 3) Is drafting back up players very important?

In this third and final question, a "YES" answer ultimately determines whether or not the R value of the position should be increased. As previously stated, this question only needs to be answered for those positions you answered "YES" to in Question No. 2. "NO" answers need no further analysis, so skip to Step Six of the RV Method to continue adjusting those positions.

Why do we have to ask ourselves if backup players are important?

If backups aren't important, then much of the pressure to draft from a position is relieved. In other words, there is no urgency to draft players when all you have to worry about is drafting starting players. This is especially true for any positions that only require one starting player. This type of non-urgency simply makes it a wasted effort in increasing the R value because we should only increase the R value if we feel the pressure to draft (again, think pressure gauge).

Assuming back ups are important, you should without a doubt increase the R value. Increasing the R value applies pressure to draft from a position which ultimately forces you to take an aggressive approach. Aggressive drafting prevents you from getting stuck without the appropriate amount of back up support in case one or more of your fantasy starters cannot play.

The importance of drafting backup players can be measured by the frequency a starter is likely to miss a game. That's because backup support is needed anytime a starter misses a game. So, backup players are very important when starters tend to miss a lot of games. Vice versa, backups aren't all that important if you can be reasonably sure your starter(s) will play most of the season.

Luckily, we already have all the data we need from Step Three with the missed game values (MG values). To reiterate, MG values tell us how many games a fantasy starter is likely to miss throughout the season. Thus, we can conclude it's important to draft backups in those positions that have high MG values and not important in those positions with low MG values. Let's start with positions that have low MG values.

Referring to the data in Figure 35, the two lowest MG values, by far, are 1.25 and 1.00 for the K and D/ST positions, respectively. This means you should expect your starting K or D/ST to miss about one game each throughout the entire season (which so happens to be the bye week). Indeed, not having a back up player in these positions would likely only result in one week's worth of scoring frustration. This situation hardly presents any pressure to draft a second K or D/ST. We can safely conclude that back up players are not important in the K and D/ST positions, and raising the R values of these positions isn't really necessary.

Now let's take a gander at those positions with the highest MG values: the QB and RB positions. Their MG values are 3.17 and 3.29, respectively, indicating they are expected to miss approximately three times as many games as Ks and D/STs. This certainly a situation that warrants an obvious need for back ups, so we should make it a point increase their R values.

Note the WR and TE positions in Figure 35. Their MG values lie in the middle realm, 2.14 and 2.50, respectively. Back ups in these positions may or may not be important. Fortunately, we do not have to decipher what these MG values mean because these positions are declared "not applicable" in all size leagues, as indicated in Figure 46.

At this point we know which positions back ups are important in and which positions they aren't. Summarizing the results regarding Question No. 3 gives us Figure 47.

FIGURE 47: ARE BACK UP PLAYERS VERY IMPORTANT?				
	10-Team League	12-Team League	14-Team League	16-Team League
QB	N/A	N/A	YES	YES
RB	N/A	YES	YES	YES
WR	N/A	N/A	N/A	N/A
TE	N/A	N/A	N/A	N/A
K	N/A	N/A	N/A	NO
D/ST	N/A	N/A	N/A	NO

Figure 47 displays those leagues and positions that garnered a "YES" to all three questions, ultimately telling us that the RB and QB positions need to have their R values adjusted. All other positions can be ignored.

INCREASING R VALUES

The question now becomes: How much do we raise R(QB) and R(RB)?

There's really no set formula or hard and fast rules on raising the R values in either position. After years of mathematical studies, I've settled on the following set of guidelines:

For the RB position, increase the R value five percent in a 12-team league, ten percent in a 14-team league, and 15 percent in a 16-team league. For the QB position, increase the R value five percent for a 14-team league and ten percent for a 16-team league.

(For those who are not mathematicians, multiply an R value by 1.05 to increase it by five percent, 1.10 for ten percent, and 1.15 for 15 percent.)

What I like about these adjustments is that they seem consistent with Steps Three and Four in terms of the percentages. In other words, Steps Three and Four seem to adjust the R values in the range of five to fifteen percent. Since Step Five is no more or less important than Steps Three and Four, this range of percentages works magic.

I also like the idea of increasing the R value more in larger leagues. Shallow positions tend to be extremely shallow in larger leagues, as indicated by the deficits in Figure 44, so increasing the R value applies an appropriate amount of additional pressure to draft from positions that really need it.

CASE A.NALYSIS CONT'D

Before: R(QB) = 13.40, R(RB) = 35.24, (WR) = 43.66, R(TE) = 12.78, R(K) = 10.96,
R(D/ST) = 9.72.
Implementing the guidelines gives us a new set of customized R values. Notice that only the RB position is adjusted for a 12-team league.

After:
R(QB) = 13.40
R(RB) = 35.24 x 1.05 = 37.00
R(WR) = 43.66
R(TE) = 12.78
R(K) = 10.96
R(D/ST) = 9.72

Step 6) Reduce the R value of deep positions.

This concept is the mirror image of Step Five because everything is essentially reversed. Here you want to reduce the R values of positions that are deep. "Deep" indicates that the position has more than enough serviceable players (surplus). The need to draft serviceable players early and often doesn't exist in deep positions because they'll be available later in the draft. In fact, one can even consider picking up serviceable players after the draft as needed in free agency. As we already know, without much pressure to draft from a position, its R value should be decreased.

The cool part about this step is that most of the work and analysis is already completed from the prior step. We already know which positions have a surplus of players and which ones don't (Figure 44). It's just a simple matter of translating the surplus levels into R value adjustments.

Basically, the more value a surplus offers, the more we should reduce a position's R value. This concept relates to Step Four where we reduced the R value based on sleepers. The premise there was to reduce the R value in order to stall ourselves from drafting a position. This method of stalling is a great strategy if there is a lot of good value, whether it's sleepers or serviceable players, waiting for us.

Measuring the value of a surplus is mostly a matter of counting the number of players in the surplus. The more players there are the more value that awaits us, and the more the R value should be reduced. **I recommend reducing a position's R value by five percent if its surplus is four to nine players, ten percent if its surplus is 10-14 players, and 15 percent if its surplus is 15 or more players.** Looking at Figure 44, for example, we would reduce the R(QB) by ten percent in a ten-team league because it has a surplus of exactly ten players.

We're not done yet. There are two additional factors that can increase the value of a surplus, inclining us to reduce a position's R value even more, the first factor being match up analysis. Match up analysis is where a fantasy manager analyzes NFL teams and starts certain players based on favorable NFL match ups. There are only two positions that constantly offer an advantage in match up analysis: the QB and D/ST positions. Take the QB position, for example. Suppose there are seven serviceable QBs in the free agent pool from which to choose. A fantasy manager can choose the QB who has the best upcoming NFL match up. One can usually find a particular QB who's playing some very weak passing defense, bolstering his chances of scoring more fantasy points than usual. This selective process maximizes the value of a group of players. Therefore, I recommend reducing the QB and D/ST positions an additional five percent, but only if the position shows a surplus of four or more players, otherwise the factor itself is nullified.

The second factor is the likelihood a fantasy player will be a top scorer on any given week. I've found that the QB, K, and D/ST positions make it very possible for even the lowest ranked serviceable players to rise to the occasion on any given week. Consider the kicker position. Even the worst starting kicker in the NFL has a realistic chance to boot a bunch of field goals and score a lot of fantasy points on any given week in a given game. Same goes with quarterbacks. Any NFL starting QB can turn a huge game of three or more TDs. This huge potential alone adds tremendous value to a position's surplus because you know anyone you pick up can have a great game. Thus, I recommend reducing the QB, K, and D/ST positions by another five percent, again, only if the position's surplus is four or more players.

In helping you correctly reduce R values, to reduce a number by five percent, multiply it by 0.95; to reduce a number by ten percent, multiply it by 0.90; to reduce a number by 15 percent, multiply it by 0.85; to reduce a number by twenty percent, multiply it by 0.80; and, finally, to reduce a number by 25 percent, multiply it by 0.75.

CASE ANALYSIS CONT'D

Before: R(QB) = 13.40, R(RB) = 37.00, (WR) = 43.66, R(TE) = 12.78, R(K) = 10.96, R(D/ST) = 9.72
Using the above guidelines and data in Figure 44 for a 12-team league, we should reduce the QB position by a total of 15 percent, the TE position by ten percent, the K position by 20 percent, and the D/ST by 25 percent.

After:
$R(QB) = 13.40 \times 0.85 = 11.39$
$R(RB) = 37.00$
$R(WR) = 43.66$
$R(TE) = 12.78 \times 0.90 = 11.50$
$R(K) = 10.96 \times 0.80 = 8.77$
$R(D/ST) = 9.72 \times 0.75 = 7.29.$

Step 7) Round R values to nearest whole numbers

Congratulations! You've finished tweaking, adjusting, and customizing the R values. The last step is to round the R values to the nearest whole number, allowing you to determine exactly who the baseline player is for each position. Round up if the fraction is 0.5 or greater, otherwise round down.

CASE ANALYSIS CONT'D

Before: $R(QB) = 11.39$, $R(RB) = 37.00$, $R(WR) = 43.66$, $R(TE)$
$= 11.50$, $R(K) = 8.77$, $R(D/ST) = 7.29$.
After: $R(QB) = 11$, $R(RB) = 37$, $R(WR) = 44$, $R(TE) = 12$, $R(K)$
$= 9$, $R(D/ST) = 7$.

This indicates our set of baseline players to include the 11th ranked QB, 37th ranked RB, 44th ranked WR, 12th ranked TE, ninth ranked K,and seventh ranked D/ST.

APPLIED RESULTS

It's only fitting to apply this set of baseline players to the rankings and projections in Figure 27 (Chapter Six) since this was also done with the Worst Starter, Average Starter, and 100 Pick Methods in the previous two chapters. This way we can objectively analyze the results of the RV Method in the previously controlled environment.

The calculated X values are listed here in Figure 48 along with the overall rankings in Figure 49. (Two notes on Figure 48: **1.**

Baseline players are listed in bold. **2.** The WR position does not show a baseline player because the table only ranks up to 40 players while the WR baseline player is the 44th ranked WR.)

QB	X#	RB	X#	WR	X#	TE	X#	K	X#	D/ST	X#
QB1	115	RB1	322	WR1	204	TE1	119	K1	24	D/ST1	28
QB2	96	RB2	255	WR2	178	TE2	73	K2	20	D/ST2	22
QB3	73	RB3	227	WR3	167	TE3	70	K3	16	D/ST3	17
QB4	61	RB4	206	WR4	151	TE4	52	K4	14	D/ST4	7
QB5	56	RB5	196	WR5	139	TE5	47	K5	8	D/ST5	3
QB6	50	RB6	186	WR6	123	TE6	39	K6	6	D/ST6	1
QB7	31	RB7	181	WR7	118	TE7	23	K7	3	**D/ST7**	**0**
QB8	23	RB8	173	WR8	117	TE8	14	K8	2	D/ST8	-10
QB9	15	RB9	156	WR9	113	TE9	11	**K9**	**0**	D/ST9	-11
QB10	9	RB10	148	WR10	112	TE10	7	K10	-3	D/ST10	-13
QB11	**0**	RB11	142	WR11	105	TE11	4	K11	-4	D/ST11	-17
QB12	-9	RB12	134	WR12	101	**TE12**	**0**	K12	-6	D/ST12	-19
QB13	-18	RB13	130	WR13	98	TE13	-7	K13	-7	D/ST13	-23
QB14	-21	RB14	126	WR14	92	TE14	-10	K14	-10	D/ST14	-25
QB15	-28	RB15	118	WR15	88	TE15	-11	K15	-11	D/ST15	-25
QB16	-38	RB16	111	WR16	85	TE16	-17	K16	-13	D/ST16	-26
QB17	-40	RB17	107	WR17	78	TE17	-19	K17	-14	D/ST17	-28
QB18	-43	RB18	102	WR18	69	TE18	-20	K18	-16	D/ST18	-29
QB19	-52	RB19	97	WR19	66	TE19	-23	K19	-17	D/ST19	-30
QB20	-59	RB20	93	WR20	64	TE20	-23	K20	-21	D/ST20	-31
QB21	-63	RB21	85	WR21	60	TE21	-26	K21	-25	D/ST21	-33
QB22	-70	RB22	82	WR22	58	TE22	-33	K22	-28	D/ST22	-35
QB23	-76	RB23	79	WR23	53	TE23	-36	K23	-29	D/ST23	-37
QB24	-80	RB24	70	WR24	45	TE24	-40	K24	-32	D/ST24	-38
		RB25	58	WR25	41						
		RB26	53	WR26	38						
		RB27	49	WR27	36						
		RB28	39	WR28	32						
		RB29	31	WR29	29						
		RB30	29	WR30	27						
		RB31	25	WR31	24						
		RB32	19	WR32	21						
		RB33	17	WR33	18						
		RB34	14	WR34	16						
		RB35	5	WR35	15						
		RB36	1	WR36	13						
		RB37	**0**	WR37	9						
		RB38	-5	WR38	6						
		RB39	-9	WR39	5						
		RB40	-11	WR40	4						

FIGURE 48:
X VALUES
(RV METHOD)

FIGURE 49: OVERALL RANKINGS (RV METHOD)

RANK	PLAYER	X#
1	RB1	322
2	RB2	255
3	RB3	227
4	RB4	206
5	WR1	204
6	RB5	196
7	RB6	186
8	RB7	181
9	WR2	178
10	RB8	173
11	WR3	167
12	RB9	156
13	WR4	151
14	RB10	148
15	RB11	142
16	WR5	139
17	RB12	134
18	RB13	130
19	RB14	126
20	WR6	123
21	TE1	119
22	RB15	118
23	WR7	118
24	WR8	117
25	QB1	115

BRIEF ANALYSIS AND CONCLUSION

Whether or not it has sunk it yet, absorbing the content involved in the RV Method will pay dividends on draft day. A personalized set of R values (and baseline players) increases the chances for an optimal draft, providing a significant edge over league opponents. You'll find the RV Method to offer all the advantages of the top competing VBD apps, such as the 100 Pick Method, and then some.

Take a look at the overall rankings in Figure 49, for example. This looks like a terrific set of rankings, for many reasons including, but not limited to, the following five:

First, there are no TEs or QBs ranked in the top 20. Second, we now understand why there are no TEs or QBs ranked in the top 20 (as every adjustment to an R value is justified with a purpose and a reason). Third, Ks and D/STs do not find their way in the top 25 overall. In fact, these positions don't even compete for the top 50 which is great since we already knew them to be of very little value. Fourth, flex players are taken into account. Lastly, there are 120 players that do not have negative X values. This allows us to apply the RV Method well into the draft without worrying about dipping into negative X values.

Note there's a WR ranked in the top five overall. This probably seems crazy to most folks, considering I've witnessed every competing WCOFF manager draft a RB in the first six picks each season. However, the RV Method tells me to strongly look at the WR position in the middle of the first round. It says that a WR should be considered with the fifth pick of the draft assuming the top four RBs are already taken, and that's exactly what I did in the 2002 WCOFF; I drafted Randy Moss with the fifth overall pick. I remember the managers smiling behind me when I passed up on RBs Priest Holmes, Edgerrin James, LaDainian Tomlinson, and Deuce McCallister, all taken by those same managers in the next four picks. Of course, I had the last laugh after reaching my league's championship game and taking 2nd place overall among all 46 WCOFF leagues, a nice $22,000 payday.

But again, if you play in fantasy league that is much different than the WCOFF, which is expected and perfectly fine, make sure you use the RV Method and case analysis only as a tool and guide in customizing your own unique set of R values. I invite you to visit **DraftingToWin.com** for the latest in drafting software developments including a programmable RV Method tool. This tool would do all the calculations for you, essentially customizing your own unique set of R values in just seconds! In any case, following each step of the RV Method carefully is a recipe for fantasy football stardom!

CHAPTER 8 –
DYNAMIC DRAFTING –
INTRODUCING THE ZVBD

I once was putting the finishing touches on planning a vacation: my bags were packed, my hotel room was booked, and all that was left to do was schedule my flight. I performed the typical due diligence, eventually succumbing to a great deal on Travelocity. Before I could book my flight, however, that little voice in my head persistently nudged at me: "Go for it," the voice insisted, and soon I found myself upgraded from coach to first class.

Granted, even with coach tickets, I had guaranteed myself an amazing stay at sunny South Beach: but a first-class ride really upgraded my chances for a once-in-a-lifetime escapade.

So what?

Well, if we liken the RV Method to a trip to Miami, then *dynamic value-based drafting,* or simply *dynamic drafting,* should be considered a first-class upgrade. Without it, you'll be fine on draft day; with it, you'll be living large over your opponents. Mastering this methodology will catapult you to the front of any draft day class.

Dynamic drafting involves baselines (or baseline players) that actually change as the draft proceeds, known as *dynamic baselines*. For example, the 22nd ranked RB might be the baseline player in the first round, then the baseline player could shift up to be the 18th RB in the second round, and by the third round it could be bounced down to the 35th RB. Later in the chapter I'll provide a system to determine a new set of baseline players for each round of drafting, known as the ZVBD. For now, understand that changing baselines also creates a new and improved list of X values and optimal overall rankings list *each round.*

Obviously, this dynamic concept is different from the VBD apps detailed in the previous chapters such as the Worst Starter Method and the RV Method, which use *static baselines*. These are baselines that do not alter. For example, the case analysis in Chapter Seven resulted in the 11th QB being the baseline player after implementing the RV Method. So no matter which round you were drafting in, the 11th ranked QB would always be the baseline player. The same goes for the other positions in the case analysis. The 44th ranked WR will always be the baseline reference point whether it's the first round of the draft or the tenth. Thus, the overall rankings list, which is the list we draft players off of, remains locked in place when using a static system like the RV Method.

So what makes dynamic drafting and dynamic baselines advantageous?

As the draft progresses, several variables affect the optimal set of baselines at any given instant. These variables affect the amounts of pressure you, as well as your opponents, face in drafting each of the various positions. For example, it is likely you may face the most pressure to draft a RB in the first round but then in the seventh round you may face more pressure to draft a WR. Thinking back to the pressure gauge analogy from Chapter Seven, a position's X values should go up when you face more pressure to draft that position and go down when you face less pressure to draft that position. Well, dynamic drafting adjusts for these varying pressures. It recalculates X values of the players as the pressures to draft from the various positions fluctuate, resulting in an optimal set of overall player rankings each round, and truly maximizing value over several rounds.

So why did we just tackle the RV Method if dynamic drafting is that much better? Well, think "Miami:" If that first-class ticket was sending you to, say, Akron, its luster is suddenly not quite as shiny, right? The ZVBD is only good in conjunction with the RV Method.

Or, in realistic terms, the knowledge you have gained in the prior chapters is not only a prerequisite for understanding dynamic drafting, but it is also needed for implementing it. Specifically, the RV Method is used as part of the dynamic drafting system detailed later in this chapter, known as the ZVBD.

Moreover, the RV Method makes a great alternative to dynamic drafting, if changing baselines is not your cup of tea. Dynamic systems require a lot of work and hand calculations *during the draft,* making draft day more of a "work day" than a "party." Of course, for many of us, we anticipate and savor the party aspect of the draft.

Therefore, I've found myself following this general rule of approach:

If I'm drafting against my friends I will use the RV Method, simply drafting players off of a permanent, static overall rankings list. This allows me to enjoy the socializing part of the event a lot more while still sporting a huge drafting advantage over them. However, if I'm drafting against mostly strangers or if the stakes are very high, such as the WCOFF, then I will definitely opt for a dynamic drafting system, even though I'm going to have to do a little bit of legwork during the draft. This will give me the absolute best chance of winning.

Let's examine my four main variables that affect the varying pressures to draft from positions and the X values that follow. These variables should be associated with any dynamic drafting system. Learning and understanding them will improve your understanding of a dynamic VBD, particularly the ZVBD.

Variable No. 1) Your position needs

Your position needs refer to the number of players that you should draft from a position while implementing value-based drafting. Naturally, the more players you should draft in a position, the more pressure you face to draft them. This makes common sense; the more you need of something, the more pressure you face in getting it. Thus, it's important to keep an eye on your position needs as the draft proceeds because any changes will have a direct affect on the pressure you face to draft from a position as well as that position's X values.

This concept also works vice versa: the more pressure you face to draft in a position, the more players you should draft. So, at the start of the draft, your position needs can be found by determining the exact amounts of pressure you face to draft from the various positions. These amounts of pressure generally depend on a lot of factors, such as starting line-up requirements, backup needs, et cetera, all of which were covered in Chapter Seven regarding the RV Method.

Therefore, the set of R values as determined from the RV Method can be used to determine your initial position needs. The set tells you the exact pressures you face in drafting each position, and with the help of a mathematical formula (revealed in the ZVBD), these pressures can easily be translated into how many players you should draft from a position – defining your initial position needs.

Of course, what the RV Method doesn't take into account is the fact that you reduce the pressure after each time you draft from a position. If you draft, say, a RB in the first round – a common occurrence in fantasy football – then you no longer have as great a pressure to draft from the RB position in the second round because you essentially reduced your position needs by one player. Indeed, it's not only important to correctly determine your initial position needs (RV Method) but it's equally important to properly reduce these needs as you draft players (dynamic drafting).

Variable No. 2) Opponents' position needs

Your *opponents' position needs* refer to the positions they are most likely to draft from in the next two rounds. Such needs significantly affect the pressure you face to draft from a position. If your opponents, specifically those who pick after you, need to draft a certain position, then it is likely they'll draft many players from that position before it's your turn to pick again (assuming that draft adheres to a serpentine format). Expect to see a big drop off in that position's value by the next round, so it might be wise to put pressure on yourself to draft from the position now (increase X values).

Conversely, if your opponents are collectively sufficient in a position, then it is likely they won't draft many players, if any at all, from that position before it's your turn to pick again. In this case, the value within the position should remain available to you in the next round, and you probably shouldn't feel much pressure to draft a player in that position at the moment (decrease X values).

This strategy can be frequently applied to positions that have only one starter such as the QB, TE, K, and D/ST positions. Take a look at the QB position, for example. Fantasy managers tend to feel very sufficient in the QB position after drafting just one QB in the first half of the draft. You can take advantage of this knowledge by reducing the X values of QBs when most or all opposing managers draft their starting QBs during the first half of the draft. You know there's an excellent chance these managers will not draft their second QB until later in the draft. In other words, you know the best available QB is not likely to be drafted by the next round because the opposing managers aren't looking to draft another QB yet. Then why draft a QB now if you can snag him later? This is exactly why it is wise to reduce the X values of the QBs – so you don't make the mistake of taking one too early.

Over the years I've noticed many managers applying this strategy, purposely waiting to draft a QB because managers behind them already have a QB. Whether these managers know it or not, they are utilizing dynamic drafting.

Of course, such implementation of dynamic drafting will not come to fruition if you're one of the first to draft a stud QB (or TE, K, D/ST). Drafting a QB early triggers your own sufficiency in that position. Now the role has reversed: your opponents can counter attack with dynamic drafting. This is just another reason I prefer to wait on drafting a QB, TE, K, & D/ST – it allows me to be the one implementing all the tricks in the book. As the saying goes in fantasy football, "Good things come to those who wait, especially when drafting QBs, TEs, Ks, and D/STs."

In the 2002 World Championship of Fantasy Football, I waited on drafting a QB, as I always do, and the perfect opportunity came upon me to implement dynamic drafting. Unfortunately I blew the opportunity! Let me show you what happened and what I should have done differently.

Figure 50 illustrates the draft tracker which lists the picks made by each team (positions only). The draft started with Tm1 (short for Team One) picking a RB with the first overall pick, then Tm2 picking a QB, etc. Since the draft is serpentine style, the picks went from left-to-right in the odd rounds and right-to-left in the even rounds.

Rd	Tm1	Tm2	Tm3	Tm4	RZ	Tm6	Tm7	Tm8	Tm9	Tm10	Tm11	Tm12
1	RB	QB	RB	RB	WR	RB	RB	RB	RB	QB	WR	RB
2	QB	TE	WR	RB	WR	RB	WR	RB	WR	RB	RB	RB
3	WR	WR	QB	RB	RB	QB	WR	WR	WR	WR	WR	WR
4	RB	WR	RB	WR	RB	WR	RB	WR	RB	WR	RB	RB
5	WR	WR	WR	QB	RB	WR	WR	RB	TE	RB	QB	WR
6	?	?	?	?	???	RB	WR	WR	RB	WR	RB	RB
7	?	?	?	?								

FIGURE 50: 2002 DRAFT TRACKER (WCOFF LEAGUE #17)

The column labeled "RZ" is my team. You can see I focused on drafting the most needy positions in the first five rounds: WR and RB. In the sixth round Tm6 had just taken a RB, and I was on the clock indicated by the "**???**." The block of eight picks that were going to be made by my opponents after my pick is indicated with eight individual question marks.

Looking down at my ZVBD calculations I saw the top overall player to be QB Rich Gannon who offered the highest X value among all remaining players. The second best pick was WR Muhsin Muhammad, but since I already had two top WRs, Gannon was a no brainer, or so it seemed.

Within seconds of taking Gannon my face turned red and I became furious at myself: I realized I didn't take into account my opponents' position needs! Specifically, I failed to notice that Tm1, Tm2, Tm3, and Tm4 all had a QB, indicating that they weren't likely to draft another QB for at least a couple more rounds. In other words, those eight question marks listed in Figure 50 weren't likely to turn into a QB.

This also meant that there was very little pressure to draft Gannon in the sixth round. I should have snagged the next highest player on the overall list, Muhammad, so Gannon could slide down to me in the seventh. I would have taken Gannon in the seventh round because a bunch of teams drafting after me at that point, specifically Tm7, Tm8, Tm9 and Tm12, had yet to draft their first QB. So there was a good chance one of the teams could very well pick up Gannon if I didn't do it by then.

After realizing my mistake I begged the fantasy gods to let Muhammad fall to me in the seventh. I knew it wasn't going to be easy, though, because all four teams drafting behind me could easily snag a WR with any of their picks. This was especially true for Tm4 who only drafted one WR so far, hence my begging for mercy from the almighty FF lords.

So here's how things shook out. Tm4 took a WR immediately after my mental lapse, but fortunately he wasn't Muhammad. The next three picks went TE, RB, RB. Sixth round of drafting was over. So far, so good, and my fingers were still crossed. The first two picks in the seventh round went TE and RB, made by Tm1 and Tm2, respectively. There were only two more picks left before it wrapped back to me. Tm3 then went on to pick a WR. Uhhhhh-ohhhhh. It was Peter Warrick of the Cincinnati Bengals. Whew, close one. Just one more pick and Muhammad is mine. Tm4 announces. ... Muhammad! Like a punch in the gut, the RZ camp was left gasping for air and scrambling for a comparable WR option. The gods have cursed me.

At this point I was definitely on tilt, as they say in the poker world. Without doing much analysis I simply took the next guy with the highest available X value from the overall list, Peerless Price. I wasn't happy about it, though. Price was ranked far below Muhammad, and since several of the receivers ranked just below Muhammad were already drafted by my opponents, I had no choice other than to accept my loss.

But wait, maybe I wasn't cursed. In fact, maybe the gods were looking down upon me all along. Fast forward four months, and Price goes on to be the sleeper pick of the year! He finished the season as a top ten fantasy WR, while Muhammad suffered an injury and didn't even finish in the top 40. I guess it goes to show you sometimes it's better to be lucky than skillful.

Nevertheless, this was a hole I never want to have to dig myself out of again.

Variable No. 3) Your solid players

The concept here is to reduce the pressure to draft from a position after selecting "solid players." A player can qualify as being solid in two ways. The first is his likelihood of being a top fantasy scorer. The second is his likelihood to stay healthy for an entire season (durability). In either case, a solid player reduces the need for back up players which, in turn, reduces the overall pressure to draft from a position (as explained in Step Three of RV Method, Chapter Seven).

For instance, if you draft a player who is likely to play very well (think Marvin Harrison), then you don't have to worry about sitting him due to bad performances. Or, if you draft a player who's not likely to get injured (think Brett Favre), then you don't have to worry about sitting him due to injury. Bottom line: the need for drafting backups greatly lessens when you draft solid players. Therefore, after you draft one or more solid players in a position, you should start to think about lowering the X values of the remaining players in that position.

Under what criteria are solid players determined?

It's important to be very strict in ultimately determining who is solid, otherwise you may find yourself reducing X values more than normal on every pick, especially since we all have a tendency to think every player we select is solid. As far as top fantasy producers, only give credit to players worthy of being drafted in the first two rounds of the draft. Most of the other players should probably not be considered solid in terms of productivity, even if they are projected to score a lot of fantasy points, due to the inconsistencies I've found in player scoring over the years.

Drafting solid fantasy producers was the underlying variable that influenced my sixth round pick of Gannon in the 2002

WCOFF draft. When I drafted Gannon, I had already taken two stud WRs with my first two picks in Randy Moss and Torry Holt. Aware that such solid players reduced the pressure to draft another WR, I opted to pick Gannon over Muhammad in the sixth. Unfortunately, as you very well know, I failed to realize that there was even less pressure to draft a QB because all the managers behind me already drafted a QB!

As far as determining solid players based on durability, these types also tend to be few and far between. I can only name a handful of players who I would deem solid due to durability. Guys like Peyton Manning and Brett Favre quickly come to mind. Take a look at Manning, for example. He has never missed an NFL start from 1998-2004. That's a streak of 112 games and counting. What's Manning's profile to be so durable? He is a big, strong QB who can take a pounding. Moreover, his quick release makes it so he doesn't get hit that often. So not only can he withstand some punishment, he doesn't really endure that much of it in the first place. What makes Manning extremely solid is his ability to also be a top fantasy player. He's got the complete package when it comes to being a solid player.

But even guys who seem to never get injured can still get bit by the bug. Take a look at Randy Moss, for instance. Here's a guy who played every game in his first six seasons in the NFL. Durable, right? That's what I thought until 2004 when he missed three straight games due to a partially torn right hamstring. Even worse, for fantasy managers, a couple of the games he did play after the tear "healed" were for decoy purposes only. In other words, he was still injured and only on the field to fool the opposing team (and his fantasy owners into starting him). My point is that you should be very careful before labeling someone as durable.

Knowing how solid a player is can have a severe affect on draft strategy. Suppose I were to draft Manning in the second round of the WCOFF. At that point I would significantly reduce the X values on the remaining QBs because there is not really any pressure to draft another QB. In fact, I probably wouldn't draft another QB for the rest of the draft. While this might seem a surprising move, there are three reasons that justify it: first, Manning is a great fantasy QB who has produced top stats every year, so the risk of bad play is minimal; second, his injury risk is minimal; third, I should be able to pick up a serviceable QB from free agency when I do need a backup, such as the bye week.

Unfortunately, I have never had the pleasure of drafting Manning's "complete package" because the RV Method tells me not to take a QB in the first three rounds, which is when one must draft Manning; otherwise, someone else will.

Variable No. 4) Your questionable players

The strategy here is to continue to apply pressure to draft from a position after selecting "questionable players." A questionable player is a high-ranked player who is prone to injury. In such a case there's a better-than-average chance you'll need to rely on back up support, and you'll need to draft extra players. Consequently, you should maintain relatively high X values in that position. Just like the previous variable, this systematic approach is justified in Step Three of the RV Method, Chapter Seven.

Let me offer an example. Suppose my draft choice boils down to QBs Peyton Manning or Michael Vick, both high-ranking fantasy QBs. We already know my drafting Manning will assure me the likelihood of not needing much back up support, hence my consideration to reduce, even likely remove, all the X values from the remaining QBs. On the other hand, if I drafted Vick I would certainly maintain high X values on the QBs in order to preserve the need to draft a back up. While Vick is projected to score a lot of fantasy points, he is a big injury risk. Vick is a relatively small and fragile QB who likes to run a lot. Consequently, he endures a large number of hits throughout the course of a season, making him a huge risk to injury (exemplified by his broken leg in 2003). Indeed, there's some value in drafting a qualified backup behind Vick.

In the 2003 WCOFF, I found myself drafting a questionable player too early and had to adjust accordingly. I selected RBs Deuce McAllister and Fred Taylor in the first and second rounds, respectively. McAllister was a solid player for his ability to be a top scorer. On the contrary, Taylor was very questionable. He had a reputation as a "soft" player susceptible to injuries. In fact, several managers who dealt with Taylor's injuries in past seasons advised me to prepare for the worst. You know what? I listened to their advice. I dubbed Taylor as a very questionable player, and continued to apply a lot of pressure in drafting more RBs. In other words, I didn't reduce the X values of the remaining RBs. If Taylor was going down, I wasn't going to be left holding the bag!

I insured myself by taking two more RBs in the next three picks. In other words, I drafted a total of four RBs with my first five picks!

After looking around I knew full well that many of the present WCOFF managers scoffed at my latest stunt. When the draft finished, one of them asked me if I made the mistake of thinking we were allowed to start four RBs. We both laughed, but to be perfectly honest with you, I started to question whether this was the right play. *Maybe I was nuts* for taking four RBs so early. Whatever the case, I needed the backup support so I went with it. Had I drafted a solid RB with my second pick, I would not have gone crazy in drafting so many RBs so early.

This goes to show you the importance of drafting solid players early, so there's no worry about covering oneself for potentially bad picks. I guess you're probably wondering then, why did I draft Taylor? The truth is, I had no intention of drafting him in the second round. It's actually a bit comical how he landed on my team. Here's what happened.

After I drafted McAllister with the seventh overall pick of the draft, I set my eyes on the best available WR with my next pick, the 18th overall pick. Specifically, I was targeting Torry Holt. When it wrapped back around to me something happened that I thought would never happen in my wildest dreams: Not only was Torry Holt available, but more significantly, so was WR Terrell Owens. This was extraordinary because I had Owens ranked higher than Holt. In fact, I had Owens ranked as a top-three WR just as I assumed everyone else would. I was ecstatic that Owens, a stud WR, fell this far. He was the clear and obvious choice for me. ... until my instinctive paranoia set in.

As I was on the clock, and everyone was waiting for me to make the pick, this crazed animal came to life inside of me. I started thinking, "Why the heck is Terrell Owens still available?" I started to wonder if I had missed something in the latest injury report which, unfortunately, I didn't have handy. After much deliberation my paranoia got the best of me, and I concluded that something must be wrong with Owens for him to fall this far. I decided I didn't want to risk taking Owens. Now the choice was back to Torry Holt, right? Well, my inner demons did it to me again. I started thinking, "If I take Holt and Owens is healthy, then I will look and feel pretty stupid." So, not only did I pass on Owens, but now I decided to pass on Holt.

There I was in the heat of the moment, where experts tend to flourish, yet I completely cracked. If I wasn't going to take a WR, the only remaining option was to take the best available RB. As the time to make a pick dwindled down I dug real deep in a last effort to take one of those golden WRs, but could only muster the words "Fred Taylor."

The next pick, within seconds, was resoundingly announced: "Terrell Owens is mine!" When this fortunate owner leaned over and whispered to me, "Wow, I'm surprised you didn't take him," my pride – and my goal of drafting only solid players early – took a hit.

Somehow, someway, this story has a happy ending. Taylor emerged with a monster season, surpassing the production from Owens by a large margin. Taylor ironically remained healthy the entire year while Owens cracked his left collarbone late in the season. Oh yeah, did I mention that Holt fell to me in the third round? This was another of those situations where it was better to be lucky – or shall I say instinctively paranoid – than skillful.

To reiterate the main point of this section, if you draft questionable players - especially early in the draft – it is wise to continue to apply pressure on yourself to draft more players from the same position (keep X values high). This strategy will ensure you go after sufficient back up support where it is likely to be needed.

What you have just read teaches you the underlying concepts of dynamic drafting. If you want to learn how to implement dynamic drafting READ ON.

Introducing ZVBD

The ZVBD system is the most powerful tool I have ever used in fantasy football. I almost hate to disclose this prized possession to the public. But, that's why I wrote, and why you purchased, this book – so you can dominate fantasy football. But, first. ...

IMPORTANT NOTICE!!! Please read and accept the following before using the ZVBD: Any monies won using the ZVBD system shall require the user to render 8% royalty payment or $200, whichever is greater, to the creator of said licensed property, Robert Zarzycki the First, within thirty (30) days of winning such monies. Read on. ...

Okay, that was obviously a silly little joke. Have no fear: you'll owe me no money when you win using this system. If you send me anything, I hope it's a testimonial of how much money you've won or pride and glory you've obtained.

The ZVBD provides a systematic way for determining a new set of baseline players each round, taking into account all four variables previously described. I developed this dynamic system before entering my first World Championship of Fantasy Football back in 2002. Not having any kind of a name, I originally dubbed it the "$22,000 Draft System" after winning that amount in its inaugural year. But then I won another $15,000 the following year, plus some smaller change in the next, and so on, so now I simply refer to the system as Zarzycki's Value-Based Drafting System, or ZVBD in short.

ZVBD App

PRE-DRAFT

Step 1) Determine the number of players to draft in each position (N Values).

This step determines *your initial position needs* (Variable No. 1). Each position is given an N value, which refers to the ideal number of players to draft in a position using the ZVBD.

I've created a formula that says a position's starting N Value is equal to its R Value (as determined from the RV Method) divided by the number of teams in the league. So we have N = R / # teams.

Like R values from the RV Method, N values will be denoted with the respective position written in parentheses such as N(QB) or N(WR).

To see how this formula works, consider what happens when R(QB) = 12 in a 12-team league. This R value tells us that there are 12 eligible QBs to draft from (players that don't have negative X values). Considering there are 12 teams, it's logical to assume each manager will take one QB each, thus our need ends up being one QB. This fits the formula because R divided by the number of teams equals one.

Now, suppose we set R(QB) = 24. This creates 24 eligible QBs to draft from. Here, we can safely assume we'll end up drafting two QBs under value-based drafting, and most importantly it becomes apparent our need is two QBs. Again, this fits the formula because now R divided by the number of teams equals two.

Of course, there are going to be many instances where the formula results in a fraction. Therefore, finish this step by rounding the N values to the nearest whole number. Let's look at an example illustrating how this is done.

Using the results of the case analysis in Chapter Seven, we have the following set of R values: R(QB) = 11, R(RB) = 37, R(WR) = 44, R(TE) = 12, R(K) = 9, R(D/ST) = 7. Because the analysis applied itself to a 12-team league, we divide each R value by 12, then we round to the nearest whole number:

N(QB) = 9 / 12 ≈ 1.
N(RB) = 37 / 12 ≈ 3.
N(WR) = 44 / 12 ≈ 4.
N(TE) = 10 / 12 ≈ 1.
N(K) = 8 / 12 ≈ 1.
N(D/ST) = 7 / 12 ≈ 1.

This set of N values indicates we want to draft 1 QB, 3 RBs, 4 WRs, 1 TE, 1 K, and 1 D/ST while using the ZVBD system. Note these numbers only total 11 players even though a complete roster takes many more. The WCOFF roster, for example, allows 20 players. This is perfectly fine. I remind you, value-based drafting, whether it's static or dynamic, is only meant to be implemented in approximately the first half of the draft. Other needs and strategies eventually become more important than X values such as handcuffing and sleeper picks. This was explained in Chapter Six regarding the 100 Pick Method. Bottom line: you should never draft your entire roster using a value-based drafting system. Drafting approximately one-third to one-half the maximum roster is the way to go.

Step 2) Transfer N values of K & D/ST positions.

Note $N(K) = 1$ and $N(D/ST) = 1$. This should be the case in most fantasy leagues. I recommend transferring each of these N values to the two positions that have the highest N value as determined in Step One. In our example it would be $N(RB)$ and $N(WR)$ which have values of 3 and 4, respectively. Thus, we would end up with the following new set of N values: $N(QB) = 1$, $N(RB) = 4$, $N(WR) = 5$, $N(TE) = 1$.

Obviously, this maneuver eliminates the N values of the K and D/ST positions completely, and at the same time it increases the N values of the two most important positions each by one. This results in three advantages:

First, it prevents you from drafting a K and D/ST in the first half of the draft because, as you'll soon learn, the ZVBD has you drafting only from positions that have positive N values. This is advantageous since the K and D/ST positions offer very good value in the second half of the draft, and the expert fantasy footballer knows to wait in order to obtain this value.

The second advantage is that by ignoring the K and D/ST positions, you will reduce the amount of work that has to be done each round. I remind you, dynamic drafting requires work and calculations. We'll touch more upon this later, but for now, understand that if you ignore the K and D/ST positions then you don't have to worry about doing any work and calculations for these positions. This takes a bit of work load off your shoulders each round.

The third advantage is that you get to focus solely on the core positions (QB, RB, WR, TE). These positions, especially the RB and WR positions, are the ones that make or break your fantasy squad. Because you don't have to worry about Ks and D/STs, you can now concentrate your efforts on drafting the best players among the positions that truly make a difference in fantasy leagues – the core positions.

Step 3) Predict opponents' picks (P Values).

There's a group of players collectively drafted by your opponents after each time you pick. As a dynamic drafter it's important to try and predict how many players of each position will be drafted in each of these groups. This step relates to knowing your *opponents' position needs* (Variable No. 2). The number of players you estimate being drafted in a position is known a P value, and you'll have a set of P values for each round (representing each group of players to be drafted after each of your picks).

To give you an example let's go back to Figure 50. There was a group of eight players drafted after my sixth round pick, each pick labeled with a "?." I had to predict how many of each position would likely be drafted in the group of eight players following my selection. Based on research prior to the draft, I anticipated 3 WRs, 3 RBs, 1 QB, and 1 TE to be drafted within this group. This resulted in the following set of P values for the sixth round: $P(QB) = 1$, $P(RB) = 3$, $P(WR) = 3$, and $P(QB) = 1$.

To fully prepare for draft day, it is essential to determine a set of P values for as many rounds as there are N values. For example, you'd need eleven sets of P values to satisfy a set of N values such as $N(QB) = 1$, $N(RB) = 4$, $N(WR) = 5$, and $N(TE) = 1$.

Since most drafts are fast paced, with the exception of online drafts that allow one or more days to make a selection, all sets of P values must be determined prior to the big day. Predetermining P values is not an exact science, as there's obviously no way to know for sure who your opponents are going to take, especially before the draft even starts. I once saw an owner select Jim Miller before Pro-Bowlers Steve McNair and Aaron Brooks, so always keep in mind that anything can and will happen. We can still make an educated guess based on research and observation, nonetheless.

For starters, knowing your draft slot is needed before determining P values. Whether you pick first, fifth, last doesn't matter; you need to know which spot you will be drafting from in order to know how large the P values need to be. For example, if you are picking from the fifth slot in a 12-team league, like that shown in Figure 50, then you know there will be a group of 14 players drafted after each pick in an odd round and a group of eight players drafted after each pick in an even round. Therefore, the sets of P values should add up to 14 in the odd rounds and eight in the even rounds.

Now let's delve into how to predetermine a set of P values for any round in the draft.

My favorite method is to simply observe the results of a mock draft. Make sure the mock draft is of similar size and scoring to the fantasy league at hand. Simply observe the number of players that were drafted in each position within the groups of players that were drafted between your slots. Each group's observation will result in a set of P values for a particular round.

For example, let's say you observed the first three rounds of a ten-team mock draft to look like that in Figure 51.

Rd	Tm1	Tm2	Tm3	Tm4	Tm5	**YOU**	Tm7	Tm8	Tm9	Tm1 0
1	RB	RB	RB	RB	RB	**QB**	WR	RB	WR	RB
2	WR	WR	WR	RB	RB	**TE**	RB	WR	WR	RB
3	RB	QB	RB	WR	WR	**RB**	WR	RB	TE	QB

FIGURE 51: SAMPLE MOCK DRAFT (POSITION ONLY)

Let's also say you are drafting out of the sixth position. This means you should be observing results around that column, labeled "YOU". Assuming the draft is a serpentine style draft, there will be a group of eight players drafted by your opponents after each time you pick in an odd round and ten players drafted after each time you pick in an even round.

The group of eight players drafted after your first pick consist of four RBs and four WRs were drafted. Consequently, the first set of P values should be P(RB) = 4 and P(WR) = 4. The next group of ten players after your second pick consists of four RBs, five WRs, and a QB. Thus, you'll end up with the following second set of P values: P(RB) = 4, P(WR) = 5, P(QB) = 1.

This process should be followed until you have a sufficient number of sets of P values, which is based on the total number of N values.

However, I must point out a potential flaw in the above application. While the data in Figure 51 shows four RBs and four WRs drafted after your first pick, and four RBs, five WRs and a QB drafted after your second pick, it is still missing a vital piece of the draft. *Specifically, it is missing the picks that were made in your drafting slots.*

These picks have an indirect affect on what the P values should be or could have been. For example, notice that a QB was taken in the first round. Well, if this QB had not been taken in this slot, then there's a good chance that *that* QB would be drafted in the group of eight players that followed. Likewise, if you had passed on drafting a TE in the second round, the same logic applies, and it's wise to assume a TE will be drafted soon afterwards.

Therefore, when observing mock drafts, it's best to include your draft slot's pick in the group of players that follow. Therefore, P(QB) = 1 should be included in the first set of P values, and P(TE) =1 should be included in the second set, and so on.

Figure 52 shows what the new set of P values should look like based on this approach.

	P(QB)	P(RB)	P(WR)	P(TE)
First Set	1	4	4	0
Second Set	1	4	5	1

FIGURE 52: P VALUES REGARDING FIGURE 51

Here's another example that provides enough data for eleven rounds' worth of P values – the exact number we would need to satisfy our current set of N values.

Again, the example has you drafting out of the sixth slot of a ten-team fantasy league. Let's say you observe the results of an online mock as shown in Figure 53. Note that the slot you would be drafting out of is listed in bold under "Tm6."

Rd	Tm1	Tm2	Tm3	Tm4	Tm5	**Tm6**	Tm7	Tm8	Tm9	Tm10
1	RB	RB	RB	RB	RB	**RB**	RB	WR	RB	RB
2	RB	RB	WR	QB	RB	**RB**	WR	RB	WR	RB
3	QB	RB	WR	RB	WR	**QB**	TE	RB	RB	WR
4	RB	QB	QB	WR	RB	**WR**	WR	WR	WR	QB
5	WR	TE	RB	RB	WR	**RB**	QB	WR	RB	WR
6	WR	WR	RB	WR	WR	**WR**	RB	WR	WR	WR
7	TE	WR	D/ST	WR	WR	**WR**	RB	RB	D/ST	RB
8	WR	WR	WR	K	RB	**TE**	WR	QB	QB	QB
9	QB	WR	K	TE	QB	**D/ST**	RB	K	TE	RB
10	RB	D/ST	QB	RB	RB	**RB**	WR	RB	K	K
11	K	K	TE	WR	WR	**K**	RB	D/ST	RB	D/ST
12	D/ST	QB	WR	RB	QB	**QB**	K	RB	WR	TE

FIGURE 53: SAMPLE 10-TEAM MOCK DRAFT (POSITION ONLY)

Observing the data in Figure 53 allows you to predetermine sets of P values for each round. The sets should be logged in a chart, and it should look similar to that shown in Figure 54.

Round	P(QB)	P(RB)	P(WR)	P(TE)
1	0	6	3	0
2	2	6	3	0
3	2	2	4	1
4	2	4	4	1
5	1	3	5	0
6	0	1	8	0
7	3	2	2	1
8	2	1	4	2
9	0	3	1	1
10	1	4	2	1
11	0	3	1	1

FIGURE 54: ROUND-BY-ROUND LOG OF P VALUES REGARDING FIGURE 53

Notice that the P values of the K and D/ST positions are excluded in Figure 54. This is a direct consequence of Step Two – which has us ignoring these positions. Also, make note that the positions drafted by Tm6, which is the slot you will be drafting from, are included in the P values. For instance, the first set of P values includes the RB drafted by Tm 6 in the first round, second set includes the RB drafted in the second round, the third set of P values includes the QB, et cetera.

ALTERNATIVE METHODS FOR PREDETERMINING P VALUES

While the previous example observed a single mock draft to predetermine P values, there are two other methods that can be used. The first is to observe the average results of multiple mock drafts. For example, Antsports.com and MockDraftCentral.com allows its visitors to observe the average results of 100 compiled mock drafts if they wanted to. These results can be observed and used as you would observe and use the results of any singular mock draft to predetermine P values.

The second method is to observe the overall rankings from an expert source. Following this premise, assume that players will be drafted in the *exact order* as the overall rankings. Assuming this, you can deduce which groups of players will be drafted before and after each of your picks in the draft. This is a great alternative for predetermining P values, as the general public tends to draft according to what the experts say.

Step 4) Understand proper usage of cheat sheet and draft tracker.

ZVBD requires proper usage of the cheat sheet and draft tracker. The cheat sheet is used to keep track of player rankings and projections (as determined from Chapters Three and Four) and should look something like Figure 55, except the generic names such as QB1 and RB23 will be actual NFL players such as Peyton Manning and Corey Dillon. For the purpose of this example, the generic names will continue to be used to maintain the illustration's conciseness.

Rank	QB	Pts	RB	Pts	WR	Pts	TE	Pts	K	Pts	D/ST	Pts
1	QB1	400	RB1	441	WR1	357	TE1	222	K1	148	D/ST1	162
2	QB2	381	RB2	375	WR2	331	TE2	176	K2	144	D/ST2	156
3	QB3	358	RB3	347	WR3	320	TE3	173	K3	140	D/ST3	151
4	QB4	346	RB4	326	WR4	304	TE4	155	K4	138	D/ST4	141
5	QB5	341	RB5	316	WR5	292	TE5	150	K5	132	D/ST5	137
6	QB6	335	RB6	306	WR6	276	TE6	142	K6	130	D/ST6	135
7	QB7	316	RB7	301	WR7	271	TE7	126	K7	127	D/ST7	134
8	QB8	308	RB8	293	WR8	270	TE8	117	K8	126	D/ST8	124
9	QB9	300	RB9	276	WR9	266	TE9	114	K9	124	D/ST9	123
10	QB10	294	RB10	268	WR10	265	TE10	110	K10	121	D/ST10	121
11	QB11	285	RB11	262	WR11	258	TE11	107	K11	120	D/ST11	117
12	QB12	276	RB12	254	WR12	254	TE12	103	K12	118	D/ST12	115
13	QB13	267	RB13	250	WR13	251	TE13	96	K13	117	D/ST13	111
14	QB14	264	RB14	246	WR14	245	TE14	93	K14	114	D/ST14	109
15	QB15	257	RB15	238	WR15	241	TE15	92	K15	113	D/ST15	109
16	QB16	247	RB16	231	WR16	238	TE16	86	K16	111	D/ST16	108
17	QB17	245	RB17	227	WR17	231	TE17	84	K17	110	D/ST17	106
18	QB18	242	RB18	222	WR18	222	TE18	83	K18	108	D/ST18	105
19	QB19	233	RB19	217	WR19	219	TE19	80	K19	107	D/ST19	104
20	QB20	226	RB20	213	WR20	217	TE20	80	K20	103	D/ST20	103

FIGURE 55: SAMPLE CHEAT SHEET

The cheat sheet is also used to keep track of every player drafted. As the draft proceeds, simply cross out players as they are drafted by your opponents and circle or highlight the players you select. This will allow you to quickly analyze the cheat sheet to see who's taken already and who's on your team. Some people also like to cross out (or circle/highlight) the projections of the players as they are drafted.

I should point out that while the K and D/ST positions are ignored while utilizing the ZVBD (Step Two) *they should still be kept track of on the cheat sheet,* for after you are finished utilizing the ZVBD, you will need to draft from these positions, and the cheat sheet will help you do that in the latter rounds.

While the cheat sheet keeps track of the exact players drafted, a second sheet, called the draft tracker, is also needed to keep track of the positions as they are drafted by each fantasy team. Simply log the positions as they are drafted with each pick of the draft, specifically keeping track of each fantasy team separately. It should end up looking something like Figure 53.

DRAFT-DAY

On draft day you'll need to do some quick and efficient work in order to make dynamic drafting come to life. The work mostly involves determining a baseline player in each position and calculating the best available player's X value in each position. The following steps teach you how to do this, but you'll need to practice them before entering the draft. I recommend practicing in one or more mock drafts.

Step 5) Determine Baseline Rankings (R Values).

Due to the nature of dynamic drafting, you'll need to determine a new set of baselines each round, specifically a new set of baseline rankings. As we know from the RV Method, the baseline ranking is also known as the "R value" or simply "R," and it refers to the number of players to count down on the cheat sheet in order to find the baseline player.

Under the ZVBD system, R can be determined for each position by adding up its P values in the next "X-number" of rounds, where " X-number" is equal to the position's N value. Okay, I know what you are thinking right about now. *What the $#@! does that mean???* Sure it sounds confusing, but I assure you it's an easy step.

To show you the gist of things, let's determine R values in the first round using our set of N values as determined after Step Two where N(QB) = 1, N(RB) = 4, N(WR) = 5, N(TE) = 1, as well as using the P values given in Figure 54.

Since N(QB) equals one, we only need to add up one round's worth of P values. Since P(QB) equals zero, for the first round the QB's R value becomes zero.

For the RB position we have N = 4. Therefore, we add up the next four rounds' worth of P values. Using Figure 54, that gives us 6 + 6 + 2 + 4 = 18, which make R(RB) = 18.

Similarly, the WR position shows N being equal to five. Adding up the first five rounds' worth of P values gives us R(WR) = 19.

Finally, we have the TE position which has N equal to one. Like the QB position, you should find its R value to be zero because the P value in the first round is zero.

It's important to make sure that when you add up the rounds of P values, you begin in the round you are drafting out of. For example, if it was the third round, and you see that N(RB) = 4 then you add up the next four rounds' worth of P values starting in round three. Looking back at Figure 54, the result would be 2 + 4 + 3 + 1 = 10.

These are just a few examples of how to determine the baseline ranking for a position in a given round. It took me a little practice to get used to the methodology but after a few tries it becomes natural. *Fortunately, this step can be implemented before you're on the clock.* To be more specific, you can start to calculate the next set of R values immediately after you make each draft pick. For instance, as soon as you draft a player in the first round, you can start to work on the set of R values for the second round. So, as long as it takes for your opponents to pick their players before it's your turn to pick again is as long as you have to calculate the next set of R values. Sometimes this could be as long as 20 minutes, other times it could be just a few seconds. It all depends on which slot you are drafting out of and how long your opponents take to make their picks.

Note: If you draft first or last in the first round see Appendix F on how to deal with this unique situation.

Step 6) Adjust R Values in sufficient positions (if necessary)

After you've made your pick, and you've finished calculating the upcoming set of R values in Step Five, you should hopefully still have some time remaining as your opponents are still picking players. Even if you're on the clock already, you should be allotted enough seconds to finish implementing the remaining steps of the ZVBD, all of which can be done fairly quickly. (This is why it's important to practice all these steps, so you don't find yourself short of time!)

The next step is to briefly analyze the group of managers who'll be picking after you. You may find certain circumstances that require an adjustment in the predetermined set of R values, specifically in positions that require just one starter. These situations arise when the group of teams picking behind you is collectively sufficient in a position (Variable No. 2). In other words, the teams behind you should all pretty much seem satisfied in a position.

This strategy can best be exemplified by the situation faced in the sixth round of the 2002 WCOFF (Figure 50). Notice that the group of four teams drafting behind me all had a QB. Since they were collectively sufficient in the QB position, none of them still needed to draft from the position, and the R value should have been reduced to zero.

The general rule is to reduce a position's R value to the number of teams that still need to draft from this position. Again, this is only looking at the group of teams to pick after your next draft selection, and not the teams picking at the moment.

Suppose there was one team that had yet to draft a QB in the group of four teams in the prior example. Well, in this case, I would reduce R(QB) to one. Again, the rule is to reduce the R value to the number of teams that have yet to draft from that position. Of course, the R value will usually be equal to or lower than the number of teams, in which case no adjustment needs to be made.

I don't recommend implementing this step for positions that start more than one player, such as RB and WR. I've found that most fantasy managers, including myself, never feel sufficient in these positions during the first half of the draft, even if they already stockpiled players. This sense of insufficiency stems from these positions requiring many starters and a multitude of back up support. As a result, just about any manager is liable to snag a RB or WR at any instant regardless of the situation. Therefore, it's a little too risky to adjust the position's R value based on the potentially wrong assumption that opposing teams might be sufficient in a position.

Step 7) Find the baseline players.

At this point you've finalized the set of R values, and just like the RV Method, you can determine the baseline players by counting down the appropriate number of players in each position. For instance, if R(QB) = 11 simply count down eleven QBs on the cheat sheet and you've found the baseline player.

The one very important difference in the ZVBD system, as compared to a static system such as the RV method, is that you'll eventually be counting down a list that has players already drafted from it. *It's important not to include those players already drafted when counting down.* In other words, you should only count down those players that you can still draft, known as "live players."

Let's say you enter draft day with the cheat sheet previously shown in Figure 55. As the draft proceeds you'll be crossing out players as they are drafted. You will also be circling or highlighting the players you select. Now suppose it's your turn to pick in the third round and the cheat sheet resembles Figure 56:

Rank	QB	Pts	RB	Pts	WR	Pts	TE	Pts	K	Pts	D/ST	Pts
1	QB1	400	RB1	441	WR1	357	TE1	222	K1	148	D/ST1	162
2	QB2	381	RB2	375	WR2	331	TE2	176	K2	144	D/ST2	156
3	QB3	358	*RB3*	*347*	WR3	320	TE3	173	K3	140	D/ST3	151
4	QB4	346	RB4	326	WR4	304	TE4	155	K4	138	D/ST4	141
5	QB5	341	RB5	316	WR5	293	TE5	150	K5	132	D/ST5	137
6	QB6	335	RB6	306	WR6	276	TE6	142	K6	130	D/ST6	135
7	QB7	316	RB7	301	WR7	271	TE7	126	K7	127	D/ST7	134
8	QB8	308	RB8	293	*WR8*	*270*	TE8	117	K8	126	D/ST8	124
9	QB9	300	RB9	276	WR9	266	TE9	114	K9	124	D/ST9	123
10	QB10	294	RB10	268	WR10	265	TE10	110	K10	121	D/ST10	121
11	QB11	285	RB11	262	WR11	258	TE11	107	K11	120	D/ST11	117
12	QB12	276	RB12	254	WR12	254	TE12	103	K12	118	D/ST12	115
13	QB13	267	RB13	250	WR13	251	TE13	96	K13	117	D/ST13	111
14	QB14	264	RB14	246	WR14	245	TE14	93	K14	114	D/ST14	109
15	QB15	257	RB15	238	WR15	241	TE15	92	K15	113	D/ST15	109
16	QB16	247	RB16	231	WR16	238	TE16	86	K16	111	D/ST16	108
17	QB17	245	RB17	227	WR17	231	TE17	84	K17	110	D/ST17	106
18	QB18	242	RB18	222	WR18	222	TE18	83	K18	108	D/ST18	105
19	QB19	233	RB19	217	WR19	219	TE19	80	K19	107	D/ST19	104
20	QB20	226	RB20	213	WR20	217	TE20	80	K20	103	D/ST20	103

FIGURE 56: SAMPLE OF CHEAT SHEET MID-DRAFT

Those players who are crossed out are those drafted by your opponents. The two players you drafted, RB3 and WR8, are labeled with asterisks.

Suppose that you determined the following set of R Values: $R(QB) = 3$, $R(RB) = 7$, $R(WR) = 5$, and $R(TE) = 2$. Using these R Values you would count down players on the cheat sheet in Figure 56 in order to determine the baseline players. Again, you would only count those players who are still available to be drafted. Let's take a look at the results you would find.

For the QB position you would count down three live players. You would start counting down from the highest-ranked live player, QB2. Counting down one player brings you to the next live player, QB3. Counting down another player brings you to QB4. Counting down a third player brings you to QB6. (QB5 was skipped because he was already drafted). So, counting down three live players results in QB6 being the baseline player for the QB position.

Now let's take a look at the RB position. With R(RB) = 7 you need to count down seven live players. The counting starts at RB9 who's the highest-ranked RB player still available. After counting down seven players, while skipping those RBs who are already drafted, you will end up at RB19, who becomes the baseline player for this round.

The WR and TE baseline players can be quickly found in a similar fashion. Counting down five live WRs would result in WR17 being the baseline player. Likewise, counting down two live TEs you'll find TE4 to be the baseline player.

Step 8) Determine the X Value for each position's best available player.

Now that you have the baseline players for the various positions, this step consists of determining the X value of the best available player in each position. There's no need to determine the X values of all the players, as you would in a static value-based drafting app, because the current baselines will become obsolete by the next round. So, for this round, the goal is to simply determine the X values of only the best players in each position, and then to pick the player with the highest value.

Continuing with the example from Step Seven, we know the best available player in each position is QB2, RB9, WR9, and TE1, and we also know the baseline players for each position is QB6, RB19, WR17, and TE4. Looking at the projections in Figure 56 we can determine the difference between each position's best live player and the baseline player, giving us the players' X values:

QB: 381 − 335 = **46.**
RB: 276 − 217 = **59**
WR: 266 − 231 = **35**
TE: 222 − 155 = **67**

Step 9) Draft the player with the highest value.

It's time to reap the reward from all the legwork: drafting the best available player as determined by the ZVBD. The calculations from the last step's example show TE1 as having the highest X value, so that's the best guy to take. Whoever you ultimately pick at your draft, don't forget to circle him on the cheat sheet.

Step 10) Subtract one unit from the N value of the position you just drafted.

In a static system you'd just sit back, relax, have a drink, or two, or three depending on how long your fellow compadres mull over their choices, and keep track of who gets drafted until it's your turn to pick again. However, in a dynamic system the work continues, namely adjusting the N value of the position you just drafted from. Each time you draft from a position, your need for that position has just been reduced by one player. Therefore, one unit should be subtracted from its N value.

Note three exceptions to this rule:

First, for core positions that allow more than one starter (usually RB and WR), reduce the N value by one additional unit, making the reduction a total of two units, if you draft two solid players from the same position in the first two rounds (Variable No. 3).

Secondly, for core positions that allow just one starter (usually QB and TE), reduce the N value by one additional unit, making the reduction a total of two units, whenever you draft a solid player in the first four rounds (Variable No. 3). If this reduction puts the N value below zero, and you are playing in a league of 14 or fewer teams, then I recommend not drafting another player in this position for the remainder of the draft. In other words, if N is minus one then not only should you not draft from this position anymore under the ZVBD but all the rounds thereafter as well. The reasoning is that you have a solid player (thus, no need for backup) and, when the occasion arises where you would need a backup, such as a bye week, there should be plenty of serviceable free agents to pickup for the short term.

Thirdly, do not reduce a position's N value whenever you draft a questionable player in the first three rounds (Variable No. 4). The ZVBD app defines a questionable player as a player who has missed two more games per season on average in his NFL career than his position's MG value as determined in step three of the RV method. For example, in the 2003 WCOFF draft I didn't reduce the R value of the RB position after drafting Fred Taylor because his career stats indicated an average of 5.8 missed games per season (29 missed games over his first five seasons), which was at least two more than the MG value calculated from Step Three of the RV Method.

The three aforementioned exceptions indicate you need to do a little background research on the higher-ranked players before the draft starts. Basically, analyze those players you might draft in the early rounds and determine if any of them are solid or questionable. This will allow you to properly and quickly adjust the N values if and when you draft any of them.

Step 11) Repeat steps 5 through 11 until all N values are depleted.

Again, dynamic drafting is a continuous and repetitive process. After you've adjusted the N Value in Step Ten, go back to Step Five and start working on your next set of R values. Continue to repeat steps 5-11 each round until there are no more N values left. At that point you can abandon the ZVBD, since all position needs have been satisfied, and start drafting players using different manners, those of which you'll learn in the chapters to follow.

CLOSING THOUGHTS

Ever since the dawn of fantasy football, league champions have followed a unanimous mantra: *those involved have evolved*. In other words, the people who participate in fantasy sports keep getting smarter, better, faster and stronger, so to speak. Just take a look at this book, for example, as you can see the evolution within. The book introduced value-based drafting with the Worst Starter Method. After that new-and-improved VBD apps were introduced such as the 100 Pick and RV Methods.

This chapter has introduced the most recent development, and improvement, in fantasy sports – dynamic drafting. In addition, now you have the ZVBD at your fingertips in a step-by-step format. Remember, this is the exact system that has helped me win thousands upon thousands of dollars. It is the most powerful – and reliable – system I've ever known, let alone developed. As you begin to review and analyze the system, you'll begin to appreciate its beauty in design. It is well-schemed to take advantage of the four variables discussed earlier in this chapter.

Nonetheless, we are just at the tip of the iceberg, and there is so much more to learn in this *moving* science. Hopefully, this book - and this chapter in particular - will help stimulate your mind and creativity so we can all quickly advance to whatever the next late-breaking methodology be. It will be very interesting to see what new and creative dynamic systems are developed in the years to come. I believe the future of fantasy football, and all fantasy sports, will rely heavily on dynamic drafting because of the tremendous power and advantage it gives one manager over another.

Even more interesting might be how dynamic drafting promotes itself in the advent of laptop computers. I foresee every owner sitting at a table with some sort of dynamic drafting software spitting out picks each round. Imagine bringing a computer to the draft to do all the on-the-spot calculations for you. Mind boggling? Not really: I've already competed against some people in the WCOFF using laptops and some sort of drafting tool and software, although I don't fully trust the validity of those tools. Either way, when push came to shove, I beat them doing my hand calculations via the ZVBD.

This brings us to the next stage of the ZVBD, and that is for it to be developed into software just as so many other drafting systems have. This would put a stop to all the manual labor involved with calculating things like P and N values. With manual labor a thing of the past, we would all be able to enjoy the socializing aspect of any draft while implementing the power of dynamic drafting, particularly the ZVBD. I invite you to visit DraftingToWin.com for the latest news, software tools and drafting strategies. An active message forum with various subjects and FAQ will also be made available to assist you in your endeavor to win!

Robert points to his newly drafted team after
the 2004 WCOFF draft

CHAPTER 9 – STOCKPILE THEORY

Professional poker player and millionaire Doyle Brunson wrote in his book *Super System* "everyone gets lucky once in a while but no one is consistently lucky." Doyle goes on to explain that his style of poker play makes it seem like he is consistently lucky, but it's his skillful approach that gives him many winning hands.

I like to think the stockpile theory is *my* skillful way of consistently "getting lucky" in fantasy football. It has given me that luck factor needed to consistently finish with the best of the best and amazingly above the best. Take a look at my first two entries in the World Championship of Fantasy Football, for example. Both years I consistently outperformed every single opponent in league competition, scoring the most overall fantasy points. Moreover, I scored in the overall top three teams during the WCOFF playoffs, which pits more than fifty league winners against each other. Bottom line, I finished second out of 552 participants the first year and third place out of 600 participants the second year. The odds of accomplishing this feat are 1 out of 55,200 – assuming all participants are on an equal playing field (the exact calculation is 1 / (2/552 x 3/600) = 55,200).

So was I lucky or skillful?

Many fellow WCOFF members seem to be debating that question. For example, one WCOFF'er who refers to himself as LegendSSS on the message boards, wrote this about me, "he's either the best player in the world, or the luckiest." While I'll be the first to admit luck played its usual, fortuitous part, I can guarantee you, and LegendSSS, that skill played a greater role in my winning, and much of which is owed to the stockpile theory.

I feel that crediting my performances with luck is similar to attributing the dynasty New England Patriots success with luck—it just doesn't properly explain their outline for success. Like the New England Patriots who stockpiled players to fit their individual team's game plan for winning, stockpile theory focuses on drafting players that can *win you a championship*. The downfall to so many fantasy managers is that they know how to draft a solid team, but they don't know how to draft a championship team. After years and years of playing fantasy football, I've found that a "solid draft" usually ends up being second or third best. I know because I've had my fair share of solid drafts only to see some lucky-duck owner win the championship with a plethora of sleepers who came out of nowhere. That's going to happen almost every year – that is, there will be some random owner that gets lucky in some way or another. Think about it. Whether your league has 10 teams or 16 teams, there are so many fantasy managers trying to draft a stellar team that chances are at least one of them is going to hit the lottery by accident. And chances are this is the team that will take down the trophy and the prize money in the end. This re-enforces my previous mantra – sometimes it's better to be lucky than skillful.

This got me thinking, "if someone is going to get lucky then why not me?" Therefore, after much deliberation I thought of a technique that would substantially improve my chances of getting lucky – a stockpiling technique. This technique is based on a theory which suggests that loading up on high-potential players, especially players in positions that allow you to start more than one player (usually RB & WR), will give you a great chance to get "lucky." The premise of this strategy is to 1) maximize your chances of hitting one or more sleepers and 2) start all of them at once. This second point is very critical. It hints that it doesn't make much sense to go for a sleeper if you cannot start him or, equally bad, you have to sit another great player if you decide to start the sleeper.

Of course, if you end up with extra talent sitting on the bench, you can always trade it away in order to improve the starting team (assuming your league allows trading), but this is a risky move. Too many times trade offers fall through the cracks, and too many times owners are forced to sit their extra talent on the bench.

This is a disaster because talent on the bench gives no points in return. Having talent on your bench is similar to you filling up the gas tank in your car and then riding your bike to work everyday. What good does all that gas sitting in your tank do? Well, having a talented QB on your bench is like not using your gas. Nevertheless, this wasted talent situation is commonly problematic in the QB position. Each year I find a handful of owners spending two relatively high draft picks on QBs. Their hope is to get at least one good QB – a good idea. The downfall to this otherwise good idea is that if they land two good QBs, they won't be fully rewarded since most fantasy leagues only allow one starting QB. The second QB must sit on the bench regardless of how great he is.

On the other hand, take a look at positions that allow managers to start multiple players at the same time, such as the RB and WR positions. These positions allow fantasy owners the opportunity to strike it rich because two or more sleepers and studs can be inserted into the starting lineup each week.

There's also an added bonus to stockpiling in positions that allow two or more starters: additional backup support is drafted. Let me explain. Positions that require a lot of starters tend to require more backup. For example, suppose your starting lineup involves one QB and three WRs. By having three times more starters in the WR position, there's about a three times greater probability that backup duty will be called upon. In addition, there are three bye weeks to deal with among the starting WRs while there's just one bye week for the solo QB. Similarly, there is a three times greater chance one of the starting WRs will get hurt, et cetera. Additionally, it's quite possible two or three of your starting WRs will get hurt at the same time, in which case multiple backup players will be needed simultaneously. This puts even more pressure on the fantasy manager to make sure there is enough backup support just in case this un-fortuitous situation arises. By stockpiling extra WRs, you are likely to have the backup support needed to last the season.

The QB position, on the other hand, doesn't induce as much pressure to draft backups. Only one starting QB can get injured at a time, so only one backup QB is really needed. Therefore, stockpiling doesn't do much justice in this department.

To reiterate: the stockpile theory is all about drafting many potential sleepers in positions that allow several of them to start simultaneously. I have struck it rich ever since I discovered this theory. It has no doubt helped me reach fantasy stardom, as I'm sure it will help you.

Stockpile theory specifically supports the following two concepts: 1) it's better to draft a high-potential player or sleeper over a proven, mediocre veteran and 2) it's okay to draft as many of these potential sleepers as you possibly can. Let me elaborate on each of these concepts.

The first concept exploits a weakness found when strictly following math and statistics. Let's say you have to rank two WRs. The first is a proven veteran who consistently scores around 150 fantasy points each year – a solid but close-to-average score. The second WR is a young player who's yet to prove himself. The last two years he has averaged only 100 fantasy points, but this year he could burst out into stardom. Suppose you put him at a 3-1 shot to score 200 fantasy points otherwise he'll finish around 100 points again. This means he has a 1 out of 4 chance to score 200 fantasy points. Which wide receiver should you rank higher?

The young WR is 75 percent likely to score 100 points and 25 percent likely to score 200 points. According to math and statistics, his projected value is (.75 x 100) + (.25 x 200) = 125 fantasy points. Obviously, this is less than the veteran's projected value of 150 fantasy points. Therefore, the veteran should be ranked higher and valued more, right?

The answer is surprisingly N-O. The better pick is actually the young WR. Mark these words: *Don't always follow the math.*

While the math per se in the above example is correct it sends you in the wrong direction. The direction you want to go is towards winning the league championship. The veteran will provide a solid 150 fantasy points. While he's minimal risk to score less than that he's also unlikely to score more which is where the elite WRs finish. In other words, he's not going to be powerful enough to help you outperform those lucky fantasy teams that end up with several of the elite WRs. The bottom line with the veteran is he probably won't carry your team to the fantasy championship, nor will he win it for you should you get lucky enough to make it there.

The young WR, however, is likely to be a bust, and a 75 percent chance at that. That's an acceptable risk because he has a 25 percent chance to turn into a real difference-maker. If he explodes into a stud then your fantasy team will turn into a powerful force. This is the type of player that can give you enough of an edge to reach and win the championship. The bottom line with the sleeper is you are taking a chance, but if you hit it correctly, then you can win the whole damn thing.

As you can see, the first concept of the stockpile theory looks beyond numbers. It indicates the young WR is much more valuable than the veteran because your goal is to win the league championship – which is where most of the prize money is as well as all the prestige! Unfortunately, most owners don't see it this way and end up drafting the solid veteran. Actually, consider this a fortunate situation because it's to your advantage when your opponents make this mistake.

The second concept of stockpile theory suggests drafting as many sleeper candidates as possible, specifically in those positions that start two or more players such as the RB and WR positions. The benefits are two-fold. The first being that each candidate you draft gives you a chance to win the championship, as described in the first concept. The second benefit deals with improving your chances of hitting one or more sleepers. If you draft just one sleeper candidate offering 3-1 odds, then you only have a 25 percent chance of landing a sleeper. When you draft two guys each offering 3-1 odds, your chances jump to 44 percent. If you drafted three potential sleepers, each offering 3-1 odds, then the chances are actually in your favor of landing at least one stud at 58 percent. *Now hitting a sleeper becomes more a result of skill rather than luck.* Not only that, you've opened the door to the possibility of landing two or more sleepers. If you really get lucky, then you could end up with a dream team filled with studs and sleepers giving you an enormous advantage over your opponents.

Now, don't misinterpret what I just said. Don't think you have to determine exactly what the odds are for various potential sleepers before drafting them – although, in general, you should have an idea of who's in the vicinity of 3-1 odds and who's more like 30-1 odds. The point is: if you draft a bunch of guys who have a half-decent chance to turn into something good then, all of a sudden, the odds can turn in your favor.

Of course, there is a sacrifice to be made with stockpiling: you can't pick potential sleeper after sleeper without passing up on players you would normally draft. Fortunately, there are several "insignificant sacrifices" that can be made in order to stockpile. For instance, if it's a 14-team league or smaller, then you don't have to draft a back up K, TE or D/ST. You can simply wait for the regular season before picking up one of these back ups, such as a bye week, and scoop him up in the free agent market. This methodology alone opens up three draft picks to be used for stockpiling. Another example of an insignificant sacrifice that anyone can make is to pass on drafting those "solid" veterans as described earlier. Again, solid veterans usually do not win fantasy championships so you shouldn't miss them. So, next time you find yourself looking at Wayne Chrebet for your roster try taking a chance on a potential sleeper instead.

One more insignificant sacrifice presents itself to owners who like to draft three QBs. If you are this type of owner, then you can free up another draft pick by only drafting two QBs. You might even get away in drafting just one QB if you select someone like Peyton Manning as explained in Chapter Eight. In either case, you free up at least one more pick to be used on stockpiling.

FINDING POTENTIAL IN THE
WR & RB POSITIONS

I'm not Nostradamus and won't ever claim to be. Therefore, I won't spend too much time researching players trying to figure out exactly who will be this year's group of best players and sleepers. Although I do offer a few hints on finding sleepers in Chapter Four, my process mostly involves watching the TV, listening to the radio, and reading newspapers, magazines and the Web. Anytime I see, hear, or read the slightest hint that someone can turn into a sleeper or be a huge player – assuming the source is credible – I will put an asterisk next to his name on the cheat sheet. I'll put two asterisks if I find two or more credible sources supporting the same player. This way, when I'm drafting, I know all players who have potential to be on the top and which ones have the best potential.

One type of player I don't need a source telling me he's sleeper-worthy is a young WR, particularly a guy who was drafted in the early rounds of the NFL draft and is now in his second or third season in the NFL. Like a teenager who is eager to lose his virginity on prom nite, these players are eager to plant their seed in the NFL. For instance, in the last three years I observed 39 2nd/3rd year WRs who were not ranked in Fantasy Football Pro Forecast's top 30. Of these players, twelve of them finished the season in the top 25 (WCOFF scoring). Based on this evidence there's about a 31 percent chance to land a sleeper in this group of receivers, offering approximately 2-1 odds. Therefore, I will put an asterisk next to just about every such 2nd and 3rd year receiver on my cheat sheet.

Sleepers in the running back position are generally very tough to find. To give you an idea, in the three year period of 2001-2003 I did not find one expert in the Fantasy Football Pro Forecast Magazine to successfully predict a RB sleeper. In this particular instance I defined "sleeper" as a RB who wasn't ranked in the magazine's pre-season top 20, yet finished the season in the top 15. This is not to say those experts aren't good. In fact, the experts in the Pro Forecast are some of the savviest and most well-respected experts in the industry. I'm just making a point that a group of today's best experts even have difficulty in finding RB sleepers.

Why is this?

I do have a theory behind this "difficulty." I found that potential RB sleepers often do not get the opportunity soon enough to make a seasonal impact. Their opportunities arise after a starter either gets injured or performs badly, and this usually doesn't occur until several weeks into the season if not in the second half. In the end, it's usually too late to accumulate enough points to finish in the top 15 for the season. Hence, it's difficult for anyone to predict a sleeper RB because, quite frankly, there just aren't many of them with the seasonal stats to fit the bill.

This is not to say you shouldn't look for RB sleepers. In fact, you want to keep an eye out for RB sleepers just as much as you would WRs. While RB sleeper candidates may not finish with extraordinary seasonal stats, they can still flourish in the later part of the season – which turns out to be very significant as it involves the fantasy playoffs! The truth is, I've seen many mediocre fantasy squads kill their opponents in the second half of the season because some back up scrub turned into a late-breaking RB stud. If the timing is right these teams usually have a cakewalk through the playoffs. So I must emphasize that when searching for and drafting RB sleeper candidates you are really looking for those players that can flourish in the latter part of the season especially during the fantasy playoffs.

This begs the question: Which running backs are best to target as sleepers?

A lot of fantasy managers will draft a talented No. 2 sitting behind a stud RB hoping that the stud will get injured so the back up RB takes over with as the new No. 1 stud. This I don't like, as it's akin to marrying your high school sweetheart with every intention to divorce her as soon as Heidi Klum comes calling; although this plan sounds enticing, unfortunately, it is a big mistake. While starting RBs suffer more injury time than any other position (Figure 35 in Chapter Seven) it's still a long shot for the starter to get hit with a very serious injury.

In general, the odds are as high as 15-1 and sometimes 20-1 for such an injury occurring. Like the odds of Heidi coming along, this certainly isn't that good of odds for a sleeper pick especially when you consider there are other potential sleepers available in the WR position offering 2-1 odds.

This strategy becomes even less attractive when you consider that even if the starter gets injured and the No. 2 finally gets his shot at stardom, there still is no guarantee he'll rise and shine. He could turn out to be a bust, and nothing is seen in return after all. Yikes!

With this in mind, I'd much rather take a shot at drafting a running back who's either part of a RBBC or a very questionable No. 1 himself. In either case, he's likely to see playing time that could eventually give him the opportunity to get a stronghold on the No. 1 spot. I've seen NFL backups play sparingly, but then produce, and then all of the sudden the coach has him playing a ton. A perfect example was rookie Dominick Davis with the Houston Texans in 2003. He turned a little bit of playing time into a starting role and finished runner up in rookie of the year voting.

There's yet another advantage with this draft strategy. Even if the RB sleeper pick never takes over as the No. 1 guy, he may still end up garnering enough playing time each week to serve as a decent fill in player. He might serve useful for those times your fantasy squad needs to endure bye weeks and short-term injuries.

PLUS, let's not forget that any such RB sleeper pick still has a chance to turn into an instant stud should one of the other leading RBs gets seriously injured and the sleeper pick instantly takes over as the main ball carrier. This is the sole hope of those managers who draft a No. 2 behind a stud RB. At least now this hope is not the bread and butter; rather, it's icing on the cake.

Of course, I'm not entirely against drafting a No. 2 RB who's waiting behind a stud. There are situations that arise in which case you should go ahead and take your shot on such a player. For instance, if the No. 2 will serve as a handcuffer to one of your starting RBs, then go for it. Should your starter get injured you'll have yourself an excellent insurance policy. Another situation arises when a decent No. 2 RB is available so late in the draft that it doesn't cost you much to draft him. I'll keep my eyes open for just about any No. 2 RB if it's the last three or so rounds of the draft and I've satisfied all my other drafting needs.

DRAFTING POTENTIAL SLEEPERS

Surprisingly, the rankings of potential sleepers aren't really that important. Once a guy gets an asterisk next to his name it doesn't matter as much where he's ranked on the cheat sheet. That's because I tend to draft potential sleepers according to their *average draft position* (ADP).

ADP is where a player has been drafted, on average, in recent mock drafts. For example, if you find that Julius Jones' ADP is 3.12, then that means he's being drafted in the 3rd round with the 12th pick, on average, among those mock drafts observed. ADP data is a great indicator for when players are likely to be drafted in your upcoming draft. Dot coms like Antsports and MockDraftCentral provide all the ADP data you can eat.

Here's how my strategy works. I'll use the ADP as a reference point. I know that this is the point in the draft at which opposing managers are likely to draft a player. My goal, as the savvy fantasy manager that I am, is to draft a potential sleeper as close to his ADP without significantly risking someone else drafting him first. Obviously, waiting until the ADP or after is a significant risk because he's expected to be drafted by that time. Thus, I try to draft a potential sleeper at or before his ADP.

Exactly how far ahead of the ADP to draft a potential sleeper depends on three factors: 1) the number of asterisks next to his name, 2) the amount of hype he received in the media, and 3) the stage of the draft. Let me elaborate on each of these factors.

If a guy has one asterisk, then he's considered to be a mediocre prospect. I probably won't try to draft him until he's at or near his ADP. However, if a guy has two asterisks, then he has much more potential for turning into a sleeper. So, if I see a player with two asterisks – meaning he is a highly touted sleeper – then I'll be more willing to draft him way ahead of his ADP. Chances seem pretty good that this guy can turn into something lucrative, hence my aggression in drafting him.

Regarding the second factor, when the media hypes or praises a player, there are one or more suckers in the draft who end up drafting him much too early. They heard the good news and now they "gotta have him." Unfortunately, if I'm very interested in the same player, then I have to be even more aggressive if I hope to get him. If it's a player who has two asterisks and I really like him a lot, sometimes I force myself to go ahead and draft him extremely early just so the suckers don't get to him first. It's a comical approach – to draft earlier than the suckers who are already drafting too early. I start wondering if I'm the one who's the sucker. As they say in poker, if you can't find the sucker at the table in the first fifteen minutes then...

The stage of the draft, which is the last factor to consider in determining how early you should draft a sleeper candidate, may be the most important of all. The earlier the draft, the more reluctant you should be in using one of your picks to snag a sleeper. Why? Because the pick you sacrifice is more valuable the earlier the draft.

To give you an idea of how much value is afforded with each pick, check out Figure 57. The data comes from a *Trade*

FIGURE 57: TRADE ANAYLYZER			
Pick #	Value	Pick #	Value
1	292	36	65
2	226	37	65
3	197	38	64
4	177	39	62
5	169	40	59
6	166	41	57
7	156	42	56
8	152	43	53
9	144	44	52
10	143	45	50
11	132	46	49
12	126	47	43
13	124	48	41
14	119	49	40
15	116	50	33
16	113	51	32
17	105	52	32
18	105	53	30
19	103	54	28
20	101	55	28
21	97	56	27
22	89	57	25
23	88	58	24
24	82	59	23
25	82	60	23
26	81	61	20
27	81	62	18
28	80	63	17
29	77	64	10
30	77	65	9
31	76	66	9
32	72	67	6
33	70	68	5
34	70	69	3
35	67	70	2

Analyzer developed by Footballdiehards.com's Emil Kadlec.

Do you remember as a kid when you traded your Barry Sanders rookie card away because you thought he was going to be a bust? Even though you got those "Sportsflix" pro-bowl cards, I'll bet that you wish you had the Trade Analyzer during that transaction. Well, the Trade Analyzer gives you an absolute measure of how much each pick is worth. Basically, it was created to help managers in trading draft picks. For instance, if someone offered you their 19th and 37th overall picks for your 12th overall pick you can use the Trade Analyzer to find that the 12th overall pick has a value of 126 units while the other two picks have a combined value of 168 units. So you should probably opt to go ahead and make the trade.

Of course, my use of the *Analyzer* is different. I'm using its data to show you how much value is likely to be obtained with each draft pick, and this value is basically how much you sacrifice when opting to draft a potential sleeper. For instance, if you took a sleeper with the 35th overall pick then, according to Figure 57, you figured to have given up on another player worth 67 units. Compare this to picking a sleeper in the later rounds such as with the 68th overall pick where you would be sacrificing the chance of getting someone else worth five units. The point is you should be more willing to draft potential sleepers in the later rounds because the sacrifice is much smaller.

Owing to the above analysis, I recommend "tightening up" early in the draft and "loosening up" later in the draft. In other words, be more conservative with the early picks while getting a bit more liberal in the later rounds. I follow certain guidelines that tell me exactly when it's time to snag a sleeper. For example, I'll go ahead and draft a one-asterisk sleeper up to five picks before his ADP in the first third of the draft. In the middle rounds, or middle third of the draft, I'll be willing to draft a one-asterisk player within ten picks of his ADP. And in the bottom third, or very late stages of the draft, I'll be willing to draft such a player up to 20 picks prior to his ADP.

I will draft even looser when I'm dealing with two-asterisk players. Again, this is because two-asterisk players show more potential than one-asterisk guys, and the extra risk in taking a guy earlier than usual is worth it. My recommended guidelines are as follows: You should look to draft a two-asterisk player up to ten picks prior to his ADP in the first third of the draft, 20 picks in the second third, and 40 picks in the last third.

The above drafting guidelines have served me well over the years. They seem to help me stockpile the right number of sleeper candidates in the WR and RB positions. For quick reference, I listed them here in Figure 58:

FIGURE 58: No. PICKS A PLAYER CAN BE DRAFTED BEFORE HIS ADP			
No. Asterisks / Stage	Early (first third)	Middle (second third)	Late (last third)
*	5	10	20
* *	10	20	40

Let me give you an example to make sure this figure is used properly. Suppose you are drafting in a 20 round draft. So, the first seven rounds could be considered the early stages. The next six rounds could be treated as the middle stages. The last seven rounds serve as the late stages, or "last third," of the draft. Let's say you have RB Kevan Barlow listed on the cheat sheet with two asterisks. His ADP is 10.05, meaning his average draft position is the fifth pick in the tenth round. Since this falls in the middle rounds, then you should be willing to draft Barlow as early as 20 picks prior to the fifth pick in the tenth round. If he's available in this range of opportunity you should go ahead and snag him, even though it might seem a bit premature.

Two Cases in Point

I stockpiled in both the 2002 and 2003 World Championships of Fantasy Football. The following will show you some of the things I did, why I did them, and how they panned out.

My fantasy teams are shown in Figure 59 in the order I drafted them (by position only). Those positions listed in **BOLD** signal those players who I drafted via stockpiling technique according to the guidelines listed in Figure 58.

FIGURE 59: STOCKPILE TECHNIQUE PROVES ITSELF IN WCOFF DRAFTS		
Round	2002 WCOFF Draft	2003 WCOFF Draft
1	WR	RB
2	WR	RB
3	RB	WR
4	RB	**RB**
5	RB	**RB**
6	QB	WR
7	**WR**	**WR**
8	RB	**WR**
9	TE	QB
10	**WR**	TE
11	**WR**	RB
12	K	**WR**
13	RB	QB
14	**WR**	**WR**
15	**WR**	**WR**
16	**WR**	**WR**
17	**WR**	**WR**
18	**WR**	K
19	QB	**WR**
20	D/ST	D/ST

There are three things to take notice of in Figure 59. First, I drafted more sleepers in the later rounds. This is the result of my tightening in the early rounds and loosening in the middle and later rounds. Second, notice how all the players stockpiled are RBs and WRs. This goes back to my comments earlier on stockpiling in positions that allow more than one starter. The last thing to notice is that I stockpiled far more WRs than RBs. This is justified by the fact that there are many more sleeper candidates in the WR position. In addition, fantasy managers seem to be equally or more aggressive in snagging RBs. This makes it that much more difficult for potential RB sleepers to fall far enough in order to snag them.

So what were my results?

Let's start with wide receivers. I obviously drafted a ton of WRs both years. In fact, you'll see that half my 2002 roster was players from the WR position! This is because I stockpiled eight receivers after already drafting two via ZVBD in the first two rounds. It turns out that I landed only one successful WR sleeper each year. But trust me when I tell you – that's all I needed to win. In 2002, it was my seventh pick, receiver Peerless Price, who finished the season ranked sixth among all WRs and helped my squad score the most total fantasy points in the entire league. (If you remember from Chapter Eight, I ended up with Price because I had missed out on drafting Muhammad via ZVBD. Price was the next best available WR who also happened to be listed on my cheat sheet with an asterisk.) In 2003, it was my fourteenth pick, Panthers receiver Steve Smith, who finished the season ranked tenth among all WRs. Once again, this was enough to help my fantasy team score more points than everyone else in the league, and it led me to a league championship. Without these guys I would not have qualified for the playoffs in either year, nor would I have won so much money!

Let's talk about running backs. In 2002, not one single drafting opportunity for a potential RB sleeper presented itself. Weird but true. Fortunately, the solid corps of RBs I drafted with my third, fourth, and fifth picks in Tiki Barber, Duce Staley and Charlie Garner, respectively, served me very well all season, so I didn't have to rely on a sleeper.

The situation was quite different in 2003 where I stockpiled two potential RB sleepers. They were taken in the early rounds, nonetheless. This was one of the underlying reasons why I ended up drafting four RBs with my first five picks, as previously elaborated in Chapter Eight when discussing my situation after drafting the questionable Fred Taylor. My fourth round pick was San Francisco's Kevan Barlow. I saw Barlow sitting on the cheat sheet with two asterisks next to his name. If he only had one asterisk, then I probably wouldn't have used such an early pick on him. One of the sources promoting Barlow as a potential sleeper, Fantasy Football Pro Forecast Magazine, had this to say, "While team officials believe that Barlow is physically the superior talent to 32-year-old teammate Garrison Hearst, some reportedly wonder privately if Barlow has matured sufficiently to realize the opportunity he has and then seize it. We believe he will."

For most of the season Barlow played in the shadows of Hearst, getting less than half the team's carries. It wasn't until the fantasy playoffs where Barlow finally paid off. RB Hearst injured himself in Week 12 and Barlow turned into a stud in Weeks 13-16. It was perfect timing. While Barlow was seizing the moment in San Fran, I was seizing the moment during the WCOFF fantasy playoffs. Barlow gave me that extra push I needed to finish in third place overall out of 600 WCOFF participants, good for an additional $10,000 in prize money. This is a prime example of how a RB sleeper pick can work out, even though he doesn't necessarily have complete seasonal statistics.

In the fifth round of my 2003 WCOFF draft I was staring at another high-upside RB in Minnesota's Onterrio Smith — again listed with two asterisks. Before the season began Smith was a third stringer "waiting in the wings." But then starter Michael Bennett broke a bone in his left foot in the preseason, and speculation on Smith's new role spread throughout the media. There was serious talk about Smith taking over the starting job by the time the season started. I decided to take a chance on this very talented and young rookie. Unfortunately another RB in Minnesota, Moe Williams, filled in admirably for Bennett and kept Smith on the back burner. It wasn't until Week 15 when Smith starting getting most of the carries. By that time I had already dropped him from my roster.

As you can see, it's either boom or bust when snagging a potential sleeper. Barlow went boom, while Smith went bust. The risk is worth it, however, when you consider those who go boom can lift you to the playoffs and beyond.

CLOSING THOUGHTS

When stockpiling, you'll often find your fantasy roster filled with a bunch of high risk, high potential players. Naturally, many of them will turn into clear-cut busts just a few weeks into the season. This isn't such bad news. First, it allows you to open up your roster for some free agent pick ups early in the season. You may want to pick up that back up QB, TE, K or D/ST at this point. Second, you may see several other potential sleepers lurking in free agency. In any case, you will have the freedom to drop players without worrying about releasing significant value for your opponents to scoop up. You can pick up players with that peace of mind. The key here is that you must be patient. After all, patience is a virtue as your grandma used to say. Hopefully, your patience will be rewarded as your stockpiled roster starts to pan out for you.

Chapter 10 -- Putting it All Together-- A Durable Draft System

Draft day for guys is similar to an all day shopping spree for girls at the mall. Has your girlfriend ever dragged you out to one of those? At first she'll take you to Macy's or Nordstrom's and buy exactly what she intended to get. However, just when you think it is time to go home, she then drags you to innumerable boutiques or thrift shops and browses around looking for any minor items or accessories. Well, this is what draft day is like for guys.

Face it fellas: we are just like the chicks. On draft day, we know just what we want and then we look for other things that suit our taste. The majority of fantasy footballers seem to know exactly whom they want in the early rounds of a draft, picking players almost instantaneously. Then, as the draft moves into the later rounds, this same group of managers inevitably starts to scramble around, needing more and more time as the difficulty in picking someone increases with each passing round. Eventually, they are forced to make quick gut-based decisions, not having any theory or strategy in mind, that usually turn into mistakes.

The truth is I have never seen a fantasy owner who was cool, calm, and collected through every single round of a draft. Even I have difficulty moving through an entire draft without hitting any speed bumps.

Several things could be the cause of this. Sometimes distractions play a part such as a six pack of Heinies, twins on a commercial, or that last slice of pizza up for grabs. The biggest culprit, however, is a failure to devise a strategy or drafting tool for each and every round. The majority of people I've observed over the years spend most of their time preparing for the early rounds, which clearly explains why they handle these rounds so smoothly. But the problem occurs when they neglect the middle and late rounds which, ironically, require more attention than the earlier rounds.

There are three reasons why preparing for the latter rounds is so important. First, there's no telling who will be available thus making it very difficult to plan a specific pick in advance. This means you better be prepared to have some kind of tool or strategy to determine a pick on short notice. At least in the early rounds you have a good idea of which handful of players will be available each round, so even without a drafting tool, you still get to think in advance about which of these players you like the most. In essence, you are predetermining your picks in the early rounds. This can't be done in the middle and late rounds.

Second, you don't know what your roster needs will be in the middle and the late rounds which greatly affects the specific strategy you should be using. For instance, you might find yourself with an abundance of RBs but few or no WRs. In this case, it would be wise to start strategizing a way to draft additional WRs. At the same time, you might begin to feel a need for a K or D/ST since you don't have one yet even though the draft is more than halfway complete. To make things even more ticklish, suppose your starting QB isn't all that superb, and you notice a couple of high-quality backups available. So I ask, do you take a WR, K, D/ST, or QB? Decisions...Decisions... but, you may only have a minute to decide.

Compare that difficult decision to one you are likely to encounter in the early on-goings. Early on, you don't have to worry about drafting a K and D/ST. Even the TE position can be ignored with the exception of a few outstanding players. And, if you're like me, the QB position can be pretty much ignored too, at least for the first five rounds or so. This means you only have to contemplate two positions: WR and RB. I cannot emphasize enough how much this simplifies things in the early rounds, which is all the more reason why it's important to spend more time preparing for the middle and late rounds.

Third, value-based drafting can only be used in the early rounds. It's eventually phased out because X values lose their importance the further you move into the draft. To put it differently, you can no longer rely on a VBD app telling you who to pick in the second half of the draft. You'll need to develop other tools and draft strategies to make it through those latter rounds. If you don't have these tools available, then you might as well get ready to accept the last alternative: gulping the rest of your warm beer, letting out a huge belch so as to announce you'll be making your pick, then looking down and choosing the first player your woozy eyes can decipher on the cheat sheet.

It's obviously clear that it's important to prepare for every round, especially the middle and late rounds. Now let's get into how this is done. The idea is to create what I like to call a "durable draft system." This is a complete system that offers enough drafting applications and strategies so players can properly be selected in every round of the draft. This way you won't have to rely on that good 'ole gut of yours for anything other than digesting that last slice of Dominos.

Developing a durable draft system involves ten steps:

Step One) Choose VBD app.

The first step is to decide which value-based drafting app you are going to implement. The VBD app acts as a strong foundation for any durable draft system.

Of course, I recommend the RV method if you prefer something static-based and the ZVBD if you prefer something dynamic-based.

Step Two) Determine how many rounds the VBD app can be applied.

Every VBD app has a limited number of rounds it can be applied. Now is the time to determine exactly how many rounds you can apply yours. For instance, the ZVBD as exemplified in Chapter Eight can be applied for approximately the first eleven rounds because that's how many units of N values were determined (ZVBD lasts until all N values are depleted, and approximately one unit is depleted per round).

If you are using a static VBD app, you can determine how many rounds it can be applied by counting all the players on the cheat sheet that don't have negative X values. Using this number, divide by the number of teams that are playing in the fantasy league, and round it to the nearest whole number. This is how many rounds you could apply the static VBD app for. For instance, the 100 Pick Method results in exactly 100 players that don't have negative X values. If you were playing in a ten-team fantasy league, then the 100 Pick Method could be applied for ten rounds (100 divided by ten equals ten).

Step Three) List additional drafting applications.

In addition to value-based drafting, now is the time to list any and all other apps, concepts, strategies, and methods you plan on using to draft players. The durable draft system is ultimately going to be comprised of all the strategies and drafting concepts added to this list. These additional strategies will be especially important when drafting players after the VBD expires, but they can also assist in drafting players early on as well.

Of all the strategies and apps previously described in this book, the only one you should add to the durable draft system is the stockpile theory. If you are wondering about strategies such as AVT and rankings players, these concepts cannot be considered here because, again, we're only looking for concepts that are to be applied *at the draft,* not before it.

Step Four) Sort apps in order of importance on a round-by-round basis.

If you are like me, you'll really only have two apps on the list at this point: ZVBD (or some other VBD app) and stockpile theory. Back in '02 when I was creating a durable draft system for the WCOFF, I noticed that these two apps were at my disposal in each of the early rounds. If both revealed the same player then my pick was golden. But what about those times, which was more often than not, when each app suggested I draft a different player? Then what?

This brings us to one of the main reasons for doing a durable draft system. That is to avoid as much confusion and internal debate as possible during the draft. Thus, I decided it was best to predetermine which app was more important to use each round. This would help avoid any serious decision making, especially under the pressure of a ticking clock.

Getting back to the WCOFF, I decided that the ZVBD was the preferred method in the first two rounds. I felt there wasn't any need to stockpile when the best overall players were up for grabs. This coincides with the idea that it's ill-advised to take a chance on sleepers when there's so much value afforded with each of the two first picks as indicated by the Trade Analyzer in Figure 57 (Chapter Nine). However, I decided that it would be a good, calculated risk to start looking for high-potential sleepers in the third round and thereafter. So, from the third round and thereafter, I preferred to use the stockpile theory before ZVBD.

Now, some of you may not agree with this "risky" approach, and that's fine. If you prefer to utilize value-based drafting as the primary tool further into the draft, then go ahead and maintain it that way for as many rounds as you see fit.

FIGURE 60: DRAFTING MAP		
Round	Primary Tool	Secondary Tool
1	ZVBD	Stockpile
2	ZVBD	Stockpile
3	Stockpile	ZVBD
4	Stockpile	ZVBD
5	Stockpile	ZVBD
6	Stockpile	ZVBD
7	Stockpile	ZVBD
8	Stockpile	ZVBD
9	Stockpile	ZVBD
10	Stockpile	ZVBD
11	Stockpile	ZVBD
12	Stockpile	
13	Stockpile	
14	Stockpile	
15	Stockpile	
16	Stockpile	
17	Stockpile	
18	Stockpile	
19	Stockpile	
20	Stockpile	

Step Five) Create a map.

We've reached the fifth step which is to list the results thus far in an easy-to-view chart such as that shown in Figure 60. I like to call the chart a "map" because you'll use it to ultimately guide you through every twist and turn of the draft, and hopefully it'll keep you from getting lost or hitting any dead ends, so to speak.

As you can see in Figure 60, I have ZVBD listed as the primary drafting tool in the first two rounds, and stockpile theory takes over thereafter. Again, that's simply my aggressive style for drafting players. If you prefer a different approach, by all means create your own unique map to guide you through your draft. For instance, you may prefer the RV Method in the first five rounds and then stockpiling, or any other drafting tool you may have developed, to be the primary drafting tool thereafter.

Also, notice that ZVBD isn't listed in rounds 12 through 20. That's due to the results found from Step Two, determining how many rounds VBD can be applied.

In any case, you want to create a map so you can clearly see which tools you have available and what their order of preference is on a round-by-round basis. From this point forward, you'll concentrate on fine tuning this map to ensure a complete and optimal draft. This type of preparation goes a long way in making sure you move through all the rounds with as little friction as possible.

Step Six) Determine which apps on the map guarantee a player.

While a map such as that in Figure 60 may provide a drafting strategy in every round, that doesn't necessarily guarantee you'll have a player to draft in each of those rounds. This is because some apps aren't devised to recommend a player 100 percent of the time.

Take the stockpile theory, for example. There are likely to be numerous rounds throughout the draft where no viable, potential sleeper pick is available. This is due to the nature of the stockpile methodology itself which is limited by certain constraints. For instance, stockpile theory says to draft a potential sleeper when he's within a certain range of his average draft position (ADP). Well, what if, among all the potential sleepers listed on the cheat sheet, there isn't anyone yet is in range of his ADP? Or, equally realistic, what if your opponents draft all the potential sleepers before they get in range? The point is that there is no guarantee that a potential sleeper will be available in any given round; therefore, you cannot rely solely on the stockpile, as is shown in the latter rounds of Figure 60.

What about ZVBD?

Well, fortunately, all VBD apps, not just the ZVBD, guarantee someone to draft in each round, at least for as many rounds as it can be applied as determined from Step Two. That's because a VBD app continuously offers someone to draft as long as there are enough players available with positive X values. You need not to worry about the depletion of such players because Step Two already determined how many rounds a healthy dose of players with positive X values would remain available.

This also explains exactly why value-based drafting acts as a strong foundation for any durable draft system. Not only does it provide an excellent drafting technique in the early rounds of the draft but it also guarantees someone to draft each and every round in these stages.

Of course, the fate of any VBD app is to eventually expire in the middle rounds. It's at that point you'll need to primarily rely on other strategies, such as stockpile theory. However, since stockpile theory doesn't guarantee you'll have someone to draft, it's vital to devise a map that offers exactly one drafting application per round that guarantees a player, which brings us to our next step.

Step Seven) Make sure each round guarantees a pick.

Again, the purpose of the map is to ultimately lead you through every twist and turn of the draft without getting lost. But what good is that if the map leads you to a dead end? This, we now know, could easily happen with a map like Figure 60 in the event the stockpile theory doesn't offer someone to draft in, say, the fifteenth round. Without a backup strategy in a situation like this, well, you're at a dead end. This step analyzes the map for such dead ends and forces you to insert the necessary back up drafting systems so you can make it to the finish line without having to make some quick pick with your eyes closed.

Enter ingenuity and creativity. You'll need to devise a new strategy or two in order to ensure you'll definitely have someone to draft each round. Start by determining which rounds you need to insert a backup strategy. This is the easy part. A backup plan is needed for any round that doesn't already have a strategy that guarantees a player. For instance, if I were to analyze Figure 60, I'd see that a backup plan is needed for rounds 12 through 20, specifically one that guarantees a player in case the stockpile theory were to falter.

The next part is to determine what kind of backup strategy to insert in each of those rounds. Fortunately, I have found a single application that can be used any round, and it practically guarantees a player. It's an aggressive version of the stockpile theory I like to call "forced stockpiling."

Forced Stockpiling

Whenever I'm in need of a drafting tool that guarantees a player, I resort back to the stockpile theory, only this time I force myself to draft high-upside players (those listed with asterisks according to stockpile theory) even if the guidelines set forth in Figure 58 of Chapter Nine tell me not to. I call this technique "forced stockpiling."

Here's exactly how this strategy is implemented. I'll take either the highest ranked RB or WR listed on the cheat sheet with an asterisk, regardless of his ADP. Which position I draft from ultimately depends on my own needs. For example, if I see that I'm stronger in the RB position (say my first two picks were solid RBs), then I'll opt to take a shot at the weaker WR position. On the other hand, let's say I notice I've drafted twice as many WRs as RBs (a good indication that I need more help in the RB position), then I'd probably take a shot at a high-upside RB. There's no hard and fast rule here. You just have to analyze your team and make a guess as to which position you need more help in. Fortunately, more times than not, you'll find a clear cut choice.

This forced approach all but guarantees someone to draft in every round because, if you are like me, the cheat sheet will be filled with players who have asterisks. There should almost always be at least one player with an asterisk available for most of the draft. However, once in a blue moon you may find yourself in a situation where every single player with an asterisk has been drafted. This could occur in the very late stages of the draft, particularly the last few rounds. In such a scenario, I would then look to scoop up any remaining young talent at the WR position even if they are rookies who are otherwise not expected to play much. I'll even consider some fourth or fifth-year receivers even if they haven't done much in their NFL careers (which is probably why they are still available). I'm basically looking for anyone, regardless of his position on the depth chart, who has raw talent and is on a team that doesn't have a solid corps of starting WRs. This type of guy fits the mold of stockpile theory because he has a shot, albeit a long one, to move up the ranks and become an impact player. Even if he is a 40-1 shot to turn into a top fantasy producer, I won't mind taking a chance on him because he costs only a late draft pick. Worst-case scenario: he fails, I drop him a couple weeks into the season, and I pick up someone else.

I see two advantages to forced stockpiling. The first is the fact that I am getting a player who has the chance to turn into a difference-maker and win me the fantasy championship. To me, this is an invaluable quality in a fantasy player, as was explained in Chapter Nine.

The second advantage is that by drafting potential sleepers "ahead of schedule," the chances of two or more sleeper candidates being available in the same round are minimized. Why is this good? We are only allowed to draft one player per round so it does us no good if the stockpile theory recommends multiple players in a given round. For instance, you may find a one-asterisk player with an ADP of 10.07 and a two-asterisk player with an ADP of 11.08 available in the tenth round. The stockpile theory, according to the guidelines set forth in Figure 58, would recommend that both these players be drafted in the ninth round. The only problem is that we can only draft one of them in the ninth. However, if you had forced yourself to draft one of these players in a prior round, then this situation would be avoided.

I am aware that forced stockpiling is a bit of a radical approach to drafting players. If this extremely aggressive style isn't your cup of tea, then you'll have to think of some other drafting strategy to guarantee yourself a draft pick in each and every round. One idea to consider is something I like to call the "replenished VBD."

Replenished VBD

It's already established that value-based drafting can guarantee several rounds of players as long as there are plenty of them available with positive X values. Well, what if I told you it's quite possible to utilize a second VBD app once the original expires? Actually, there are countless varieties and ideas one can come up with regarding a second VBD approach. The second app would establish a new set of baselines, essentially replenishing a list of players with positive X values and guaranteeing you more players to pick.

For instance, here's my idea on how one could re-establish the ZVBD in the middle and late rounds:

Say it's the twelfth round of a 20-round draft, and the ZVBD just expired. At this point, one could choose to implement a second ZVBD based on a new set of N values. This set of N values can be customized according to one's current team needs. In other words, when it's time to switch over from the first ZVBD to the second ZVBD, you could look at your roster and guesstimate how many more of each position you still need to draft. Suppose, with nine rounds left in the draft, you conclude that you need to draft another QB, two RBs, four WRs, one K and one D/ST. Well, you can essentially re-establish a new set of N values as follows: $N(QB) = 1$, $N(RB) = 2$, $N(WR) = 4$, $N(K) = 1$, and $N(D/ST) = 1$. With a replenished set of N values, the second ZVBD would offer a whole new list of players with positive X values, and you'd be good to go as if the draft just started.

Round	Primary Tool	Secondary Tool
1	ZVBD	
2	ZVBD	
3	Stockpile	ZVBD
4	Stockpile	ZVBD
5	Stockpile	ZVBD
6	Stockpile	ZVBD
7	Stockpile	ZVBD
8	Stockpile	ZVBD
9	Stockpile	ZVBD
10	Stockpile	ZVBD
11	Stockpile	ZVBD
12	Stockpile	Forced Stockpiling
13	Stockpile	Forced Stockpiling
14	Stockpile	Forced Stockpiling
15	Stockpile	Forced Stockpiling
16	Stockpile	Forced Stockpiling
17	Stockpile	Forced Stockpiling
18	Stockpile	Forced Stockpiling
19	Stockpile	Forced Stockpiling
20	Stockpile	Forced Stockpiling

FIGURE 61: GUARANTEED DRAFTING MAP

As intriguing as a second ZVBD sounds, or any VBD app for that matter, I still prefer to focus on forced stockpiling. I'll say it many times over: I like to take as many chances as possible on high-upside players. Again, this is just my aggressive way of trying to win a championship.

Here's what my map would look like at this point, which now guarantees a player in each and every round:

There are two quick observations to make regarding Figure 61. First, notice that each round in the map has one, and only one, application that guarantees a draft pick (guaranteed apps listed in **bold lettering**). Second, notice that such guaranteed apps act as the final drafting strategy in every round. This makes sense. There's no need to list a backup plan to one that already guarantees a player. For example, the only app listed in the first two rounds is the ZVBD because that drafting application guarantees you'll have someone to pick up.

Step Eight) Make sure every position is taken into account.

We now have a map that guarantees someone in each and every round. However, we've yet to make sure it'll provide us with a complete roster taking into account every position. For example, if you were to actually follow the map in Figure 61, you'd eventually start to wonder, *When and how the heck am I going to draft a kicker and D/ST?*

The fact is, up to this point we haven't delved into any specific strategies for drafting the K and D/ST positions; neither the ZVBD nor stockpile theory suggest these positions. Consequently, if you were to strictly follow the map in Figure 61 then you'd end up never drafting a K and D/ST, an obvious downfall.

Additionally, there's nothing in Figure 61 that guarantees you'll draft a QB, let alone a backup QB. That being said, here are my systems for drafting the QB, K and D/ST positions:

QUARTERBACKING

Quarterbacking is a series of drafting rules, or guidelines, that I follow to ensure myself a starting and backup QB. The first guideline is to follow the ZVBD, overriding all other drafting strategies including the stockpile theory, if the ZVBD suggests a QB in the ninth round or thereafter. The fact is, the ZVBD *will* suggest a QB in one of these middle rounds if a starting QB hasn't already been drafted. So this first guideline all but forces me to draft a starting QB.

The second guideline of the quarterbacking methodology is very general. It allows me to draft a backup QB in any round at my own discretion. This might be the one guideline/rule among all my systems that encourages making a gut decision. Basically, I'll keep my eyes peeled for a backup QB and if one tickles my fancy at any instant then I'll snag him. I'll generally look to pick up a backup QB in the middle rounds (9-13 range) if I'm not very confident in my starter. Otherwise I'll probably defer to the third and last guideline.

The last guideline, which is more of a hard rule, is to draft a backup QB in the 17th round (assuming a 20-round draft) if I had not drafted one yet. This guarantees that I won't be left without a backup QB. It also assumes I haven't drafted someone like Peyton Manning who doesn't need a backup (as explained in Chapter Eight). Why the 17th round? Well, I like to use the remaining three rounds for implementing MUD, handcuffing, and drafting deep sleepers. Plus, I figure if there's any decent QB still available this late in the draft I might as well take him sooner than later so as not to risk losing him to someone else.

Mop Up Duty (MUD)

Mop Up Duty, or MUD for short, is a system used to draft a K and D/ST. The acronym MUD is fitting because, well, let's face it, fantasy Ks and D/STs are practically worthless like mud in the house. Don't get me wrong, I have nothing personal against kickers or defensive players, and I'll be the first to admit these guys play an important role for their respective NFL teams, but from a fantasy perspective I've yet to see a manager win the championship because he drafted a stud K or D/ST. Yet, managers still tend to pick them up early in the draft only to be left walking through the remaining rounds with "mud on their feet." I, on the other hand, try to keep my "house" as neat as possible for as long as possible by not picking up the mud early, unless a superb opportunity presents itself. Hence the title: Mop Up Duty.

MUD operates in a straight forward, goal-oriented manner. The first goal is to draft a top three K and D/ST at least two full rounds *after* their ADPs. So, if you have Adam Vinatieri ranked No. 1 and his ADP is 9.02, then your goal is to draft him as soon as the draft reaches 11.02. If none of the top three players in either position fall far enough for you to accomplish this goal (a likely occurrence since there's almost always a good handful of fantasy football managers who have that tendency to draft the top Ks and D/STs early – which, by the way, is a good thing because their mistakes are to your advantage), then the next goal is to draft a top ten player five full rounds *after* the ADP.

If, once again, all the eligible Ks and D/STs are taken before you can accomplish the second goal, then the last alternative is to take the best available K and D/ST in the last two or three rounds of the draft. This isn't such a bad last resort since any K and D/ST, including those "scraps" left for grabs in the very last rounds, can easily turn into a valuable asset within the position. That's the nature of these positions. Most Ks and D/STs tend to score in close proximity to one another giving any one of them a decent chance to finish the season at or near the top.

Keep in mind the ultimate goal in MUD is to draft just one K and one D/ST. So, once you draft a K or D/ST, then you no longer need to consider the position. The only exception to this rule is if you play in a league that has 16 teams, in which case you probably want to devise a strategy that has you snagging two players from each of these positions.

In the end, you'll find that MUD offers two advantages. First, it forces you to get good value for your draft pick. The only time you would spend a middle round pick on a K or D/ST is if the value presents itself – that is, a top player falls far enough where he becomes worthy enough to draft. Otherwise, you'll take the best of what's available in the last few rounds. This offers good value because you can still end up with a decent player at minimum cost: a late draft pick.

Second, by not taking a K or D/ST in the middle rounds, which happens more often than not when applying MUD, you open up more possibilities for drafting from the other, more-important fantasy positions.

Step Nine) Handcuffing.

Sometimes you need a backup date to the prom if Brittany all of a sudden has to go on tour and can't make it. Therefore, Suzi Creamcheese must be waiting in the wings if this disaster should happen. This is similar to what is known as "handcuffing" in fantasy football. Handcuffing involves drafting the NFL backup to your fantasy starter. The idea is that if and when your fantasy starter isn't going to play, you won't lose because your fantasy "handcuff" – the NFL backup – now moves into the starting position. It's like having an insurance policy on your fantasy starter.

Handcuffing lies in the realm of dynamic drafting because values of certain players change as the draft proceeds. Specifically, the No. 2 player on the depth chart increases in value once you draft the No. 1 player on the depth chart as your fantasy starter. A good analogy is the properties Boardwalk and Park Place from Parker Brother's popular board game *Monopoly*. At the start of the game the value and cost of Park Place is $350. However, the moment you buy Boardwalk, then the value of Park Place moves way up. Even though it still costs $350 you would probably be willing to pay an exorbitant amount above $350 for the rights to get Park Place before your opponents.

That's because both properties become very valuable when together. Of course your opponents would hate to see you get strong so they will be very happy to get Park Place before you. This psychology also happens in fantasy football when an opponent goes out of his or her way to obtain your handcuff so you don't reap the benefits. Unfortunately, that strategy hurts both parties since the handcuff is not nearly as valuable for the manager that doesn't have the starting counterpart.

You should be aware that handcuffing doesn't work in every position. Receivers aren't feasible for handcuffing because NFL teams play so many of them. There's no guarantee one particular WR is going to get more playing time (and fantasy points) if a starting WR gets injured. So, no one WR really makes a good insurance policy for another WR. Tight ends don't work because most backup tight ends aren't used much in the passing game. Therefore if anyone gets thrown into the starting role it'll be mostly for blocking, and no fantasy points are awarded for that. Kickers don't work because NFL teams only carry one (not to mention you probably don't want to draft two kickers). D/STs are not applicable.

The two positions where handcuffing is feasible are QB and RB. When a starter in one of these positions gets injured, or sits out for any reason, there's usually just one other player that picks up most or all of the slack. Even then, you still need to analyze the situation because handcuffing may not be the best choice of action.

Let's start with the QB position. You should only consider handcuffing your starting QB if he's in a great offense and his backup is considered to be one of the best in the league. The offensive system is critical. It must be a high-powered machine including super-talented wide receivers. The coach and/or offensive coordinator must show a propensity to call a lot of passing plays, especially the deep ball. Otherwise, the backup-turned-starter is likely fall into the lower echelon of point-scoring fantasy QBs, making him worthless to draft in the first place. Oh yeah, one more thing, the starting QB must also be somewhat injury prone for handcuffing to pay off. I always think it's a waste when I see my opponents draft a second QB to the likes of Peyton Manning and Brett Favre. These guys never get hurt! (Knock on wood for the superstitious.)

Nonetheless, just when conditions seem right to handcuff a QB, it still may be wise to pass on the opportunity (no pun intended). The point of handcuffing is for an insurance policy, right? So why not shop around for the best insurance policy. In fact, most NFL-starting QBs probably serve as a better backup to your starting fantasy QB than the actual handcuffer. For one thing, if you draft another starting QB as a fantasy backup you get to see how he fares during the first few weeks of the NFL season. If he's a bust then you can drop him and pick up someone else. If he turns out to be a stud, terrific! This you can't do with the handcuffer because he's always on the bench. So you really have no idea how good (or bad) a handcuffer will be for your fantasy squad until the actual moment you are forced to start him. Another reason not to handcuff the QB position is the bye week. Realize that a QB and his handcuff will have the same bye week. Therefore, one would have to draft, or pick up at some time during the season, a third QB to fill in for the bye week. Having three QBs on a fantasy roster is like keeping your high school jeans in the drawer just in case you get back in shape: you're wasting space. This is especially true if your roster is limited to 20 players or less. That's the equivalent to holding on to that pair of old jeans when you only have one drawer for clothes.

Turning our attention to the RB position, this is where the best opportunities arise when it comes to handcuffing. This is especially true after you draft a stud RB. Studs are typically on NFL teams that are made for the run game (big offensive line, good coaching). This is a great situation for the backup RB to step into if the starter gets injured because he's likely to continue right where the stud left off: a perfect insurance opportunity.

However, you have to be a little bit careful about handcuffing RBs who are involved in a RBBC. The one big disadvantage here is that you may have to pay too great of a price for the insurance policy. Managers like to draft second and third string RBs in a RBBC much earlier than they would a strict backup. This is due to the simple fact that all RBs in a RBBC are expected to get some PT and score fantasy points. Consequently, you will probably have to use a relatively early draft pick, maybe somewhere in the first third of the draft, to handcuff your starter. That may be too pricy.

What round should you draft a handcuff?

In determining when you should handcuff the QB position, first understand that managers typically do not look to draft a No. 2 QB unless it's insurance for their own QB. Think about this for a second. Who the heck would draft Eagles backup QB Koy Detmer if they didn't have Donovan McNabb? The answer is no one. Using the principles of dynamic drafting, if no one really demands the guy you would need to handcuff your starting QB, then you are almost sure to get away until the very last round of the draft before taking him. In fact, you could even take this principle to an extreme by not taking him in the draft at all knowing the handcuff will still be available in free agency. Sometimes I'll do this when I notice my starting QB has an early bye week. I'll draft another NFL starting QB as my temporary backup. Once my starter's bye week passes, I'll drop the backup and pick up the handcuff. The advantage here is that I no longer have to worry about picking up a third QB because the bye week is done and over with.

For the RB position, it's good to use ADPs as a guide for determining when it's appropriate to go ahead and handcuff. To give you an example, if I'm insuring a stud RB I'll look to draft the handcuff about three rounds earlier than his ADP. The price may be steep, but I feel it's worth it.

Just remember, whenever you take a handcuff earlier than his ADP, make sure he's the undisputed backup. In some cases there are two or more guys competing to replace the starter in the event of an injury. You can usually find out this information by reading NFL team reports and preseason articles. Think about what happened when Chiefs RB Priest Holmes missed half the season in 2004. Larry Johnson and Derrick Blaylock shared backup duties, and both started a handful of games. In such a situation, I would *not draft* a handcuff ahead of his ADP since it's too risky. I would probably take the best prospect of the backups (the No. 2 guy on the depth chart) as close to his ADP as possible. If another owner snags him first, then it's not a huge loss since there's certainly no guarantee the No. 2 guy would replace my stud in the first place. It could end up being the No. 3 guy, as we saw with Johnson and Blaylock. Assuming someone else drafts the No. 2 guy, I would probably look to get the No. 3 guy but only if he falls about two or three rounds after his ADP. Again, with so much potential downfall, I want to make sure I'm not overpaying for him.

When dealing with RBBCs I'll take one of the backups – who, by the way, really isn't a "backup" because he's already sharing time with the starter – as close to his ADP as possible. I probably won't draft him much earlier because I feel he's just too much baggage. This is another one of those situations where if another owner takes him first, I don't consider it a huge loss because of the risk involved.

I remind you, the purpose of handcuffing is to draft a guy who's going to take over most of your starter's carries in the event of an injury or missed game. If there isn't a clear cut backup, or if there are two or more guys who might share the backup duty, then the insurance policy may not be worth picking up.

For those of you who really want to get scientific, there's a way you can determine an exact round you should draft a player if you want to base it on the amount of risk you are willing to take in losing that player to someone else. This method not only works for handcuffs but for any player. Let's say you figure you want at least an 80 percent chance of drafting player A. In other words, you are willing to risk a 20 percent chance of someone else drafting player A before you. To determine the round you should draft Player A you need to analyze many mock drafts. I'd say to observe at least 20 mock drafts (the more the better). Determine the round player A is drafted by at least 20 percent of the time. For example, say you observe 20 mock drafts, and in these drafts you observe that player A is drafted in the seventh round once, the eight round three times, the ninth round five times, the tenth round ten times, and the eleventh round once. You can see that player A is drafted 20 percent of the time by the eighth round (4 times in 20 drafts). So, you should set yourself to draft him in the eighth round.

Step Ten) Finalize the map.

With all these new drafting tools and concepts in mind we can finalize the map. It's like putting all the pieces of a jigsaw puzzle together. Once you are finished, you should be able to see a complete, full picture. This finalized map is going to be the blueprint to creating a superb fantasy team from top to bottom. Here's the actual, finalized map that I used to lead myself through the treacherous grounds of the World Championship of Fantasy Football:

FIGURE 62: FINALIZED MAP

Round	Primary Tool	2nd Tool	3rd Tool	4th Tool	5th Tool
1	ZVBD				
2	ZVBD				
3	Stockpile	ZVBD			
4	Stockpile	ZVBD			
5	Stockpile	ZVBD			
6	Stockpile	ZVBD			
7	Handcuffing	Stockpile	ZVBD		
8	Handcuffing	Stockpile	ZVBD		
9	Quarterbacking	Handcuffing	Stockpile	ZVBD	
10	Quarterbacking	Handcuffing	Stockpile	ZVBD	
11	Quarterbacking	Handcuffing	Stockpile	ZVBD	
12	Quarterbacking	Handcuffing	Stockpile	MUD	**Forced Stockpiling**
13	Quarterbacking	Handcuffing	Stockpile	MUD	**Forced Stockpiling**
14	Handcuffing	Stockpile	MUD	**Forced Stockpiling**	
15	Handcuffing	Stockpile	MUD	**Forced Stockpiling**	
16	Handcuffing	Stockpile	MUD	**Forced Stockpiling**	
17	Quarterbacking	Handcuffing	Stockpile	MUD	**Forced Stockpiling**
18	MUD	Handcuffing	Stockpile	**Forced Stockpiling**	
19	MUD	Handcuffing	Stockpile	**Forced Stockpiling**	
20	MUD	Handcuffing	Stockpile	**Forced Stockpiling**	

Figure 62 has been a terrific map for me to follow for several reasons. First, it takes advantage of dynamic value-based drafting. It also takes an aggressive approach as stockpiling seems to be a major theme throughout. Stockpiling is basically my fingerprint that says, "I'm *Drafting To Win,* not to come in second place." Another excellent aspect of this map is that it guarantees I'll have someone to draft each and every round. You'll notice tools in **bold lettering** are those that guarantee a pick, and each round has one as its last resort. Finally, the map in Figure 62 ensures that I'll draft every position including the K and D/ST positions. By the way, I listed MUD as the primary tool in the final several rounds just in case I haven't drafted a K or D/ST by then. However, if I did draft a K and D/ST in the earlier rounds, then I'd ignore MUD at that point.

A note for ZVBD users:

Whenever you use a tool instead of ZVBD, it's important to still adjust the N values after each pick. There may be several instances where you'll opt to use another drafting approach instead of the ZVBD. For example, in the 2004 WCOFF I drafted two RBs in the fourth and fifth rounds using the stockpile theory as my primary tool. So, even though I didn't exactly use the ZVBD in those rounds, I still reduced the N value of the RB position by two units.

CONCLUSION

The point of this chapter was to show you the importance of creating a durable draft system. Along the way I presented my style for mapping which included all my latest developments in drafting tools and strategies. Sure these methods have worked great for me but that doesn't mean you have to follow them exactly as I laid them out, especially if you have a different opinion. I must stress how it's okay, and encouraged, for everyone in fantasy football to exercise their own freedom to create and choose whatever drafting strategies they like, ultimately devising their own unique map and durable draft system. You may just find something else that works better for you! Like they say in the poker world, what works for one player may not work for another. I believe this to also be true in fantasy football. Managers can succeed using different strategies.

Take a look at experts John Hansen of Fantasyguru.com and Jon and Ian Millman of FFChamps.com, for example. They are tremendous managers when it comes to consistently drafting a winning team of fantasy football players. Yet, these guys take a very different approach to drafting players as I do. When I was featured in Comcast Cable's *Spotlight: Fantasy Football* for my groundbreaking ZVBD methodology, Hansen noted he's been playing fantasy football for over ten years without ever knowing or using any form of value-based drafting. He went on to say how that hasn't stopped him from dominating the hobby. I obtained a similar nugget of knowledge regarding the Millmans in that they expressed to me their drafting style was very different from mine. In fact, at the WCOFF's first annual Hall of Fame draft at the Hilton Las Vegas, Jon Millman, who was sitting to my left, leaned over and whispered how he would have never drafted a team the way I did. Well, that didn't stop me from making the playoffs and competing for the Hall of Fame title. During the playoffs, Jon graciously sent me an e-mail giving me credit for knowing how to draft a pretty damn good team. Thank you, Jon!

The point is this: by all means, go ahead and create your own approach and methodology for drafting players if you feel uncomfortable with my recommendations in this chapter. The beauty of creating a durable draft system, and the map that comes with it, is that you can easily mix and match drafting tools in any manner you like. If you like to stockpile, as I obviously do, then use it. If you don't like MUD, then get rid of it. Of course, I imagine many of you won't want to change anything because my methods are already proven. In that case, don't change a thing! Just remember that the main goal with any map is to make sure you 1) have a guaranteed player each round and 2) draft enough players in all the positions. (Both are accomplished with the finalized map in Figure 62, at least according to WCOFF rules.) After that, you are free to form your own path to success. Good luck!

CHAPTER 11 – DRAFT DAY PROPS

Donald Trump has stated many times on his hit show *The Apprentice* that a golf course is a place for both business and pleasure. It is a place where associates can strike up a deal while having fun and enjoying the outdoors. However, the astute businessman knows that either the success or the failure of his golf game should not affect his ability to make the proper business decision. In other words, the pleasure should not rationally influence the business. Draft day is no different. It is traditionally and undeniably a mix of business and pleasure. This can have positive or negative results depending on how you handle the situation. You need to ensure your "business side" is keeping track of the draft, analyzing your opponents' rosters, analyzing players still available, and determining the best possible pick for your fantasy team. With the exception of entering a professional draft such as the World Championship of Fantasy Football, the "pleasure side" will naturally be socializing with friends, making fun of their picks, drinking beer, eating pizza, and watching TV in the background. The real genius is the one who is able to have fun without detracting from the business side of things. Hopefully that's you. The fantasy football fool (say that five times fast) is the one who gets carried away by talking too much, laughing too much, drinking too much, and drafting players already taken. Hopefully, most of your opponents will be doing such foolish things. As fun as draft day can be, you must remember this: you can have all the pleasure you want *during the draft,* but if you make a mistake you damn well won't be able to re-pick your team *after the draft.* So, make "The Donald" proud and enjoy yourself, but don't lose focus on what you set out to accomplish.

This begs the question: how can we successfully mix business with pleasure?

Obviously, the first thing is to make sure you are strategically prepared for the draft; that we already covered in the prior chapters. Once you have an idea of what you want to do at the draft, the next thing is to make sure you bring everything you need to implement such tactics. You wouldn't dare approach the 492 yard Par Five without your golf glove and favorite Big Dog, would you? Fantasy football is no different. You need to make sure you bring all the right "equipment" or props, if you will, to do the best you can. Here's basically what you'll need to bring to the draft:

1) Cheat sheet

2) Draft tracker

3) Blank piece of paper

4) Fantasy magazine

5) Injury/suspension sheet

6) Depth charts

7) Pens, pencils, highlighters

8) Calculator (optional)

9) Drafting map

10) Tylenol

12) Alka-Seltzer

13) Valium

Okay, last three are a joke, at least for most of us. These "props" will allow you to move through the draft on cruise control. In other words, it'll make it so you can easily accomplish all the things you set forth prior to the big day. Let's take a look at each of these items separately.

1) Cheat sheet

The cheat sheet is the hub of every draft day manager. It is the constant center of attention and holds all the player rankings and projections that managers scrutinize before making a pick. I also like to list teams, bye weeks, sleeper potential (denoted by asterisks), average draft position (ADP), and overall rankings on the cheat sheet. That's a lot of information to put on one sheet, for sure, but I find it very convenient to have all this info handy on one sheet. It makes my section of the table neater, cleaner, and easier to deal with. It also helps minimize time to analyze things, rather than fumbling around multiple papers.

To give you an idea of how I can cram all this info on one sheet, here's what the first twenty ranked RBs might look like on my cheat sheet:

Rk	RB Name	ADP	Team/Bye	Pts
1	Edgerrin James		Ind/7	441
2	Onterrio Smith		Min/6	375
3	Kevan Barlow		SF/10	347
4	*Willis McGahee	1.06	Buf/9	326
5	Deuce McAllister		NO/10	316
6	Marshall Faulk		StL/5	306
7	Duce Staley		Pit/7	301
8	Tiki Barber		NYG/4	293
9	*Thomas Jones	1.11	Chi/3	276
10	**Stephen Davis	2.04	Was/8	268
11	Shaun Alexander		Sea/4	262
12	*Chris Brown	2.09	Ten/9	254
13	Corey Dillon		NE/10	250
14	*Rudi Johnson	3.02	Cin/6	246
15	Michael Pittman		TB/4	238
16	*Amos Zereoue	4.11	Oak/8	231
17	Ahman Green		GB/8	227
18	Curtis Martin		NYJ/3	222
19	**Warrick Dunn	3.05	Atl/8	217
20	*Ricky Williams	6.08	Mia/8	213

FIGURE 63: CHEAT SHEET (RB POSITION ONLY)

Keep in mind this only shows the first twenty ranked RBs, whereas the complete cheat sheet will contain many more ranked RBs in addition to all the other fantasy positions that need to be drafted from. Chapter Four determines exactly how many players in each position should be ranked.

Each position should have five columns of information. The first column simply shows the number of rank. The second column lists the actual player names and which of them have high upside potential (denoted by an asterisk according to Chapter Nine's stockpile theory).

The third column displays average draft positions (ADPs). ADP is an important stat on draft day. You'll find many types of drafting strategies rely on the ADPs of the various players including MUD, handcuffing, and stockpiling. I will only list the ADPs for certain players on the cheat sheet including all QBs, and the top ten TEs, Ks, and D/STs. I will also list the ADPs for any player with an asterisk as well as RB handcuffers. This covers basically all those strategies that use ADPs such as MUD, stockpile theory, and handcuffing strategy. I do not care to list the ADP for anyone else because I don't want it to alter my thinking or trap me into making a wrong move during the draft. Basically, I like to draft the best player available regardless of his ADP. I've been burnt too many times waiting on a player because his ADP indicates he shouldn't get drafted, only to watch someone else happily pick him up first.

The fourth column shows the teams that the players play for and what their respective bye weeks are. I'll have bye weeks on my cheat sheet, even though I believe them to be one of the most overrated categories on draft day. We have been conditioned by the industry's experts to believe that we should pay close attention to bye weeks in order to prevent ourselves from getting in trouble. What trouble? Well, the experts say you could get stuck with a bunch of guys who all have the same bye week leaving you in a big hole. The truth of the matter is there isn't much trouble you can get into in a league that has twelve or fewer fantasy teams. The free agent pool in these leagues is so large that, should you accidentally draft too many players with the same bye week, there are plenty of decent players available to pick up for a quick, short-term fix. Sure, your team may be a little weak for that one week, but at least you'll have your big guns ready to go for the rest of the season.

However, in larger leagues of 14 or more teams, the experts may be right. The free agent pool is likely to be dried out for a quick fix. In such leagues, you will want to make sure you don't overstock on players having the same bye week in the same position. I've found that most people play in leagues of 12 teams or less, so there should not be so much hype on bye weeks.

The fifth and last column will list the projected fantasy points scored. The projections should be the result of the Average Value Theory (AVT) as described in Chapter Three.

2) Draft tracker

The draft tracker keeps track of what positions have been drafted by you and your opponents. This helps determine each team's positional needs. In Chapter Eight, you learned why it's important to keep track of everyone's positional needs. See Figure 50 (Chapter Eight) for an example of what a draft tracker should look like. Obviously, you'll be bringing a completely blank draft tracker with the blanks being filled in as the draft proceeds.

I found that some managers like to record the players' names in the boxes as they are drafted, essentially keeping an exact record of the draft. Personally, I prefer to just keep track of positions because it's easier to analyze. If I want an actual record of the draft, I'll obtain it after the draft when there's no hurry to do things. Sometimes I'll bring my digital camera if I know the commissioner will be keeping track of the draft on a master board. This way I can take a few snap shots of the draft board afterwards for my own complete record of what went down.

3) Blank piece of paper

There are times during the draft where I may want to jot down notes or do some hand calculations. Here, a blank piece of paper will suffice. This way I don't have to scribble the same stuff down on important papers like the cheat sheet.

4) Fantasy Football magazine

Bring a magazine that provides credible profiles for most of the players listed on your cheat sheet. This allows for quick and easy reference should you need to garner that little bit of extra information before making a draft decision. The magazine should also have an easy-to-read NFL schedule just in case you need to see certain match ups. I recommend *Fantasy Football Pro Forecast Magazine*.

5) Injury/Suspension sheet

The NFL provides several injury reports each week detailing the official injury status of its players. It's vital that you bring the most recent report to the draft. Sometimes injuries happen so often that even the latest NFL report doesn't keep you fully abreast. To compensate, I recommend visiting TFLreport.com as well as Footballdiehards.com right before the draft, and even during if you have internet access, so you know you have the latest developments.

6) Depth charts

Depth charts will always play a significant role on draft day. I remember my college roommate, Neh, didn't use a cheat sheet but rather picked his fantasy players right off the depth chart. I don't recommend using depth charts to that extreme, but they are still useful on draft day.

Depth charts rank players per position per NFL team. This list typically reveals who's starting in the NFL and who would be next to start should a starter get injured. Obviously, depth charts are important for strategies such as handcuffing.

Just like injury reports, you'll want to print out the most recent depth chart heading into the draft as things can change on a daily, sometimes hourly, basis. NFL.com is the obvious choice for official depth charts. Footballdiehards.com provides even more accurate and up-to-date depth charts once training camp opens.

7) Pens/pencils/highlighters

These writing utensils are brought for obvious reasons. I like to use highlighters or colored pens to keep track of my own players on the cheat sheet. This way I can quickly see what my own positional needs are first.

8) Calculator (optional)

Depending on your drafting methodologies, you may want to bring a calculator if you'll be doing some quick calculations, like you would when using the ZVBD. Some people prefer to do such calculations by hand, so the calculator is optional.

9) Drafting map

Finally, you'll need to bring the drafting map as created from Chapter Ten. This is the sheet of paper that will guide you through every round of the draft, telling you what strategies and drafting tools to implement.

Conclusion

A fantasy football draft is such a big event it can sometimes be very long and a little bit stressful. Just like when an athlete prepares for a big event, it might be wise to eat proper the day before and of the draft. This should include eating meals with a proper mix of carbs, proteins, and fats to ensure energy levels are high and consistent. This chapter listed all the things you should bring to the draft. You might want to include bringing an energy bar or some sort of snack to make sure you retain enough energy from start to finish. The bottom line is that you want to win your league. Therefore, be sure to have fun as if you were playing golf while negotiating a million dollar business deal, but remember to not lose focus on what is truly important—becoming a fantasy football champion!

Chapter 12 – Clock Management

There are two major tasks throughout the draft: keeping track of the draft and picking players. How you approach these tasks and how much time it takes is what I call *clock management*.

Of course, keeping track of the draft is pretty simple. You cross out the players your opponents choose, circle or highlight the players you pick, and log the players and/or positions via the draft tracker. The challenging, as well as exciting, part is picking the players. Naturally then, this requires a bit of time. The key is how you utilize and manage this time.

Do you ever notice the numerous NFL war rooms on draft day? Do you notice that there is not just one executive in the room making the decisions, but a whole team full of number crunchers advising the GM on which player to choose? This is where having a co-manager can be an advantage because one person can keep track of the draft while the other plans the next pick. I have never had this luxury since I like to play fantasy football solo. This makes me a minority, especially in big money leagues. For instance, in three years of competing in the WCOFF over 95 percent of the teams were co-managed. In some aspects this puts me at a disadvantage. To compensate for this lack of support I had to find a unique drafting methodology to stay one step ahead. I call it clock management. Over the years I have learned two extremely valuable lessons in clock management. I strongly believe them to be the keys to out-drafting and out-thinking my "two-headed" opponents.

LESSON 1: BE PROACTIVE.

Being proactive means to start determining your next pick well before it's your turn to make that pick. In fact, it's always good to determine several candidates just in case one or more of them get drafted right before you. This gives you a back door. You're doing this because you don't want to have to worry about determining who to draft under the pressure of a ticking clock. When things are done correctly, you should be able to make your pick efficiently and quickly once it's your turn. If you ever have a chance to watch me in a draft, you would notice my consistency to call the player I want within just a few seconds of being on the clock. This comes from being proactive.

An added bonus for drafting so quickly is that it immediately puts the spotlight on those who draft behind you. Some managers rely on the time you take to draft a player in preparing for their own pick, and if you don't take any time at all, then it throws them off kilter. This is all the more reason why everyone should be more proactive, because the draft can move quickly.

So, how does one determine a pick in advance?

The trick is to start analyzing the next pick immediately after making the last pick. If you just made your third round draft pick, then you'd immediately begin analyzing who you should draft in the fourth round. You can do this by looking at the drafting map, as created using the durable drafting system in Chapter Ten, and implementing all the drafting tools and strategies listed for the next round. You'll end up with a list of top players to draft. Let's revert back to Figure 62 in Chapter Ten, for example. You'll notice quarterbacking, handcuffing, stockpiling, MUD, and forced stockpiling listed for the twelfth round, in that order. So, if you were to make your eleventh-round pick, you'd start implementing each of these strategies immediately thereafter to see, in advance, what players you'll be looking to get in the twelfth. In this particular case you might end up with a list of five players. Then again, you might end up with a list of fewer than five players because, if you remember from Chapter Ten, not every drafting tool guarantees a player.

Let's just assume, for example, that you determine a list consisting of Najeh Davenport (handcuffing), Kevin Jones (stockpiling), and Jeff Wilkins (MUD). In fact, you determined this list so fast that there's still four more draft picks to be made before it's your turn to pick again. You're feeling good and looking golden as you just sit and wait to make your next pick. Then, all of a sudden, the next two players off the board are Davenport and Wilkins. Now what? Well, whenever a player from your list gets drafted, which will occur plenty, simply re-implement the drafting tool that just lost its player. In this case that would mean re-implementing the handcuff and MUD systems. Keep in mind, re-implementing a strategy doesn't necessarily guarantee a replacement player, unless of course, it's a guaranteed system such as forced stockpiling or ZVBD.

Nonetheless, even a proactive effort as just described will sometimes fall short. You may still find yourself at some point in the draft, on the clock, not knowing exactly who to pick because there's still work and analysis left to do. Even crazier, you might find yourself not knowing who to pick as the time winds down to zero. This brings us to the second valuable lesson in clock management.

LESSON 2: DO NOT FORCE YOUR PICK.

When it's your turn to pick, if you hear the draft facilitator shout something like *three seconds left!*, puhhhlease, I urge you, do not panic and pick some random player just to keep time from running out. For one reason or another I've noticed fantasy footballers feel they must make their pick in the time allotted otherwise the world is going to come crashing to an end. In fact, I've seen this in the WCOFF on numerous occasions. I'll hear the draft facilitator give a warning shout, and all of a sudden the manager on the clock immediately spits out a player's name as if a gun was held to his head. In all fairness, though, I have to admit my Fred Taylor draft pick in the 2003 WCOFF was a forced pick in the waning seconds of my own clock. Remember that story from Chapter Eight? I guarantee you that'll never happen again.

Another situation that often puts managers in a situation of panic is when they draft a player already taken. When this happens managers are instantly forced back into the spotlight to pick someone else. Worst of all, they may not have a backup player in mind. Tick tock... tick tock. So what do you do on such short notice? You should certainly not panic and pick some player just to keep time from running out. While most managers will frantically make their quick-pick, I recommend taking your time until you regroup, even if that means letting your time run out.

The fact is that it is okay, and many times advantageous, to pass on a pick. Yet, in three of the years I played in the WCOFF (2002-04) I did not witness one opposing manager let his or her time run out. They all succumbed to the pressure of the ticking clock. In the same span yours truly passed on a total of three draft picks (coincidentally one per WCOFF season). In each of those instances I wasn't ready to make a decision in the time I was allotted. Therefore, I just let my time run out.

Here's what happens when you pass on a pick:

According to the drafting rules of most leagues, including the WCOFF, when a manager passes on a pick all that happens is the next manager waiting in the drafting line gets to choose first. After that, the person who passed gets a second chance to pick, usually in a short time frame such as five seconds. Here's the exact WCOFF ruling:

Time limit per pick: Each participant will have one minute and thirty-five seconds to make a player selection. He will be notified of the time at 1:15 and again at 1:30. If a participant does not make a selection in the allotted time, he is passed over until the next participant makes a player selection. The passed-over participant then has five seconds to make a player selection before he is again passed over.

This process would repeat until the passed-over participant makes his pick. That's not such a bad punishment for passing on a pick, especially if you need a little more time to evaluate things. It's not as if you lose your pick indefinitely. So, don't be afraid to take the extra time you need if the situation arises.

There are two divergent situations you should find yourself in when passing on a pick. The first is when you find yourself without anyone to draft. I found myself in such a situation in the 2004 WCOFF draft. Ironically, it came during the very last round of the draft. The even more ironic point is that someone at the draft had mentioned prior to it happening that this draft was going to be the first time I made all my picks in time at the WCOFF (each of the previous WCOFF drafts I had passed on a pick). As fate would have it, I wasn't going to let the streak end of letting time run out on picking a player. Here's how the situation unfolded:

I drafted Aaron Stecker in the 19th and next-to-last round to handcuff my No. 1 pick Deuce McCallister. Nice pickup, indeed. After that, it was easy sailing, or so I thought. The only position I had yet to draft was a D/ST so I knew I was going to implement MUD for sure. I was eyeing the Chicago Bears which happened to be my Dark Horse pick of the draft (they just acquired DE Adewale Ogunleye from the Dolphins, and between him and stud LB Brian Urlacher the Bears D should wreak havoc like it was the 80's). The Bears also happened to be a team that no one ever looked at. I know this because I had entered three previous drafts that year, and in not one of them did I witness an opponent pick up the Bears. Consequently, I let my guard down and assumed that this draft would follow suit, especially considering we were now entering the final round of the draft. Thus, I did not look to see who else I would pick up in the unlikely event someone took the Bears right from under my nose.

All I did was sit and wait. Sit and wait until it was my turn to pick in the last round so I can get the Bears and then drink it up in the Vegas atmosphere with a big smile on my face thinking about the fantasy season ahead. Little did I know that the owners of Team DJ's, the guys drafting just two slots ahead of me in the last round, were from Illinois. Ummm, isn't Chicago in Illinois?

Who did they pick? Noooooo, not the Bears!!!

I was so stunned and, quite frankly, upset at their pick that I believe I shouted at them right afterwards, mumbling something about how that was supposed to be my Dark Horse. (If you guys are reading this, sorry about that.) But still, how could they possibly steal the Bears out from under my feet!

Here was a situation where I left myself with no backup plan whatsoever, which ironically, goes completely against lesson number one! But heck, it was the last round, it was only a D/ ST, and I was looking forward to the draft finishing. The fact remained, it quickly became my turn to draft, and I had no one in mind. I needed to research all the available D/STs. Since my usual plan is to add/drop D/STs throughout the season based on match ups I figured to analyze each available team's first game to see who had the best match up. This was going to take time, however, and there certainly wasn't enough left on my clock. So, I simply let my time run out. In fact, I let the next three managers make their picks before I finally made mine: the Atlanta Falcons.

I believe most managers in my situation would have panicked and taken any D/ST in order to avoid the embarrassment of not picking in time. Again, I try my best to not succumb to such pressure. I wasn't afraid to use clock management to my advantage. I let the next few managers make their pick while I gathered my thoughts and re-evaluated my options.

The second of the divergent situations is when you find yourself debating between two or more players. Again, you don't have to force a pick in this situation, especially if you feel you need a little more time to evaluate things. The worst that could happen by waiting is the next manager takes one of the players you were mulling over in which case you simply take the other player. Granted, if you are debating between two or more players and feel that a few more minutes of thinking will probably not help you decide, then you might as well pick one. Flip a coin, throw a dart, pick out of a hat. Do whatever it takes to make a decision because, in this case, you'd rather make a pick *before* time's up. By passing, all you'd be doing is giving the next manager the pick of the litter.

I've taught myself to get very creative when having several players to choose from. A classic example occurred in the 2003 WCOFF draft. Until this book I've only told a select few about this strategic maneuver. It was my turn to pick in the eighth round, and the draft tracker looked like Figure 64.

Rd	Tm1	Tm2	Tm3	Tm4	Tm5	Tm6	ME	Tm8	Tm9	Tm10	Tm11	Tm12
1	RB	RB	RB	RB	RB	RB	RB	RB	RB	RB	WR	RB
2	RB	RB	RB	QB	RB	WR	RB	RB	RB	RB	WR	RB
3	WR	WR	WR	RB	WR	QB	WR	TE	TE	WR	QB	TE
4	WR	RB	WR	WR	QB	WR	RB	RB	WR	WR	RB	WR
5	QB	WR	RB	RB	WR	WR	RB	QB	RB	WR	WR	QB
6	RB	WR	WR	WR	WR	RB	WR	WR	WR	QB	RB	WR
7	TE	D/ST	QB	RB	RB	WR	WR	QB	WR	QB	RB	WR
8		?					???	WR	WR	WR	WR	WR
9		?					???					

FIGURE 64: 2003 WCOFF DRAFT TRACKER (LEAGUE #29)

At this point there were four, count 'em, four players I was considering drafting. Three of them were wide receivers via the stockpile theory: Joey Galloway, Chris Chambers, and Reggie Wayne. The fourth player was QB Jeff Garcia coming out of the ZVBD. I was leaning towards taking one of the receivers since I love to stockpile (what a surpise). However, Jeff Garcia was a top five QB who offered a lot of value this late in the draft. His ADP was 5.09 so I felt lucky enough he fell this far. After some thought, I decided to make it my goal to get not just Jeff Garcia but also one of the WRs with my next two picks. I quickly and creatively figured out the best way of achieving this goal. I started by analyzing what my options were – I had three of them.

First option: I could draft one of the WRs now in which case I'd have to simply hope Garcia fell to me in the ninth. However, I was really worried about Tm2 since they were the one team sitting behind me that didn't have a QB yet. I concluded it was too risky to simply take a WR now and just hope Garcia wrapped around to me.

Second Option: I could draft Garcia now and hope at least one of the three WRs falls to me in the ninth. This seemed like a better possibility than the first option because all three WRs would have to be drafted for this plan not to work. However,

I noticed a run of WRs being taken – six in a row had just been drafted! If this trend were to continue then I'd no doubt lose out on all three WRs. Consequently, I decided this second option was just as risky an endeavor as the first.

At this point you're probably asking, *What other options are there???*

Third Option: clock management. Of course! I could pass on my turn to wait and see how several of my opponents draft after me before taking any action. I was under no pressure to draft a WR now because I had several at my disposal. I also felt safe in waiting to draft Garcia, at least until it was Tm2's turn to pick.

So, my plan was to wait four picks before making any kind of decision, which was right before Tm2's pick. If, by that time, none of my WRs were drafted, then I would opt to pick up Garcia. This put me in a nice position to get one of the three WRs on the wrap-around because there would only be eight picks left before it was my turn again – a much better situation than taking Garcia now and having to wait 12 picks for one of the WRs to wrap around. Should one or more of the WRs be drafted before it was Tm2's turn, then I'd have to make a judgment call before Tm2 made its selection. I'd have the same three options: I could take a WR, choose Garcia, or continue to stall. This I needed more time to think about, time I happened to have because I'm utilizing clock management.

"Three, two, one, time's up on Z-Men!," shouted the draft facilitator.

As always, I get a few looks from fellow managers wondering why the heck I just let my time run down. It was now Tm6's turn to pick, and they took TE Bubba Franks fairly quickly. I was hoping they'd take their time so I had more time to think. The draft coordinator gave me another five seconds to make my pick, which I obviously passed on again.

Now almost everyone lifted their heads, and all eyes were definitely on me. For me to pass my pick a second time meant that I was either A) stupid, B) lost, C) unaware, or D) the general manager of the Minnesota Vikings. Little did they know that it was E) none of the above! I knew exactly what I was doing, and all the while I'm sure they thought I was daydreaming or not paying attention or being just a fool. In any case, they probably didn't want to tell me anything because it was to their advantage if I kept passing on my pick.

Tm5 drafted D/ST Miami Dolphins. So far so good; neither any of my WRs nor Garcia had been drafted. I passed on my pick for the third time in a row, and now it became obvious people were staring at me. It was equally obvious that I knew they were staring at me. So, I just flailed my arms straight up in the air to let people think I was insane or something. I am not kidding; this really happened. But I was far from insane. I actually had a plan and it was working. I was "the man with the plan" as the criminals say of Roger "Verbal" Kint in *The Usual Suspects*.

I finally hit a speed bump when Tm4 took Chris Chambers. Doh! Now I had to put my thinking cap on again. If one more of my trio of WRs were drafted, then I would have to probably make an ultimate decision in the next five seconds. After some thought I said to myself that if another WR is taken from my trio, then I'd just go ahead and take the last remaining WR hoping that Garcia would fall to me. I felt that WRs were being drafted so fast at this point of the draft that Garcia had a better chance to survive.

After opting not to select for the fourth time, I watched Tm3 then draft RB Lamar Gordon. My plan was still alive, but for how long? Now it was crunch time because Tm2 was picking next, and they still needed a QB. Meaning, now would be the time for me to take Garcia. I instinctively decided that I should stall again. I figured Tm2 is also likely to wait until the ninth round to pick a QB assuming they noticed Tm1 already had a

QB. In other words, Tm2 should have known that Tm1 wasn't likely to take a QB and so there was no need for Tm2 to take a QB now either. And you thought only poker involved this much psychology. Not so in this case!

So my newest plan was to keep an eye on my two remaining WRs with the hopes of picking up Garcia right before it was time for Tm2 to pick in the ninth round. If all went well I'd be taking Garcia with a decent chance for at least one of two remaining WRs to fall to me because, at that point, there would be only five picks remaining before it was my turn to pick again.

As the draft coordinator gave me my last second to snag Garcia, my brain flinched for a millisecond, and I almost screamed his name. But I held off the urge, and my mouth remained zipped.

"Time's up *again* for Z-men."

It was Tm2's turn...judgment day. With fingers crossed, Tm2 drafted. ... a QB!

$*#! &&&%$## #@%%!!

I knew it! I knew I should have taken Garcia when I had the chance!

What? What was that? Who did they draft? Steve McNair! Ohhh, thank you football gods! Thank you, thank you thank you!

Not only was Garcia still available, but the entire drafting scenario changed significantly, likely for the better. Now, instead of planning to take Garcia and waiting on a WR, I quickly made myself aware that the best point of action is now to take a WR and wait on Garcia. That's because every team left to pick before it was my turn had a QB, giving me a good chance of having Garcia fall in my lap. So I went ahead and snagged Joey Galloway who, for some reason in the past couple of minutes, I decided I liked a lot more than Reggie Wayne.

So, when the facilitator gave me yet another block of five seconds, I quickly pounced and took Galloway. Ironically, the co-managers of Tm1, Rich and Paula, who I happened to know very well after playing together in the same WCOFF league in 2003, told me they were planning on taking Galloway with that next pick. They felt like I was somehow playing a trick on them by waiting right before they were going to pick him! Well, at least now they know the real motive for my actions.

Now it was out of my hands and into those of my opponents – and lady luck – if I was ultimately going to get Garcia. My fingers remained crossed as the few remaining managers picked before it was my turn again. After Rich and Paula took WR Curtis Conway and RB Moe Williams, it was Tm2's turn to pick on the wrap around. Guess what? They took another QB! Just when I thought it was safe to go back in the water. But once again they were playing scare tactics against me as they didn't take Garcia but rather Tom Brady.

To make this long story, well, less long, my wish came true and Garcia fell to me as teams 3, 4, 5, and 6 took two RBs and two WRs. I achieved my goal!

CONCLUSION

The above strategic maneuvering would not be possible if I wasn't proactive. When it was my turn to pick in the eighth round of the 2003 WCOFF, I already knew the four players I was interested in drafting. This gave me enough time to think about how I wanted to proceed, and so I was able to creatively find a way to improve my chances of getting Garcia and one of the WRs.

These situations show how clock management is very important on draft day. These situations also enabled me to draft the right players and earn a great deal of money, and I am confident that situations like these can earn you a great deal of money as well. Therefore, always remember that as long as you know what you are doing, then it is definitely advantageous to bluff your opponents into thinking you are not paying attention. Moreover, sometimes it is beneficial to skip a pick knowing that your squad will be strengthened in the near future. The key here is to be aware of what your opponents are doing at all times and to be patient. Your decisions might seem risky, but keep in mind that they could pay huge dividends in the future!

Robert applies Clock Management at the 2004
WCOFF Hall of Fame draft

A Final Word...

Well, there you have it folks. This book contains all of the insight, knowledge, experiences and tips that I have to offer so you can become an astute fantasy football manager. I hope you have enjoyed reading this material half as much as I enjoyed writing it! Furthermore, I believe that writing this book has made me a better fantasy footballer because it has enabled me to organize all of my techniques and strategies into one clear and organized journal, if you will.

Not surprisingly, I couldn't help but notice how the process of writing this book made me identify with my school teachers on what it must have been like to instruct me on the finer points of things like the American Revolution, long division, and photosynthesis. I felt I had to present my theories with as much clarity as I could. As a result, I tried to explain everything to the reader in such a way that was clear and with as little confusion as possible. I also became motivated by how people can and will learn as a result of writing this book. I wanted to understand the ways people learn best so that I could write in such a way that catered to my reader's ability to understand what I wrote.

My research led me to an interesting discovery. I learned about a concept called "Habits of Mind" from a couple of teacher friends. Basically, there are certain types of habits, or learning qualities, that a learner should exhibit when confronted with a challenging problem or learning new material. In other words, learners must employ certain patterns of intellectual behavior if they plan to produce powerful results. I noticed many qualities learners should possess when tackling new material and concepts; most of which pertain directly to applying the concepts I wrote in this book.

Here are some of those habits you, the reader (as a learner), should employ while applying what you have learned in drafting your next team:

1. Precision of language and thought

2. Drawing on past knowledge

3. Checking for accuracy

4. Flexibility of thinking

5. Managing impulsivity

6. Persistence

Many of these habits are self-explanatory. For instance, as fantasy footballers, we choose our team based on the stats the players accumulate over their careers. Therefore, it is imperative that you be precise in having the correct information at your fingertips so that you can make an intelligent choice. Furthermore, you must have an accurate memory of your players' prior statistics and your own prior experiences so that you can evaluate the scenario and apply your knowledge. Also, you must have flexible thinking in choosing the right player at the right time, even though choosing him might contradict the philosophy of your original game plan. You must manage your impulses by refraining from picking that star player which common sense says is a steal, when in reality the actual data lists him as a player with little value.

Finally, and most importantly, you must continue applying my theories if you have hopes of becoming a fantasy football champion. I am confident my theories will help you do this, but you must remember that Rome wasn't built in a day. Have faith that my theories are accurate. I know they are because my own persistence has given me several trophies and a great deal of money. Nevertheless, you must be patient if your team next season doesn't totally dominate your league. What I ask of you is to notice how much you improve as a result of my theories, and then I encourage you to keep applying those theories as you gain experience as a premier fantasy football player. In time, your championships will come.

I invite you to visit **DraftingToWin.com**. Just like my teachers offered me extra assistance after school, this is my way of offering you that same benefit. You'll find a forum in which you are free to post questions and comments regarding the content in this book. As always, I welcome your input, suggestions, critique, and/or questions. In fact, I'm looking forward to hearing what other kinds of drafting strategies lurk out there, especially in the value-based arena. I, too, have much to learn in this great hobby of ours. See you on the message boards. Until then, I wish you all my best, and I hope your upcoming Sundays bring you nothing but 100 point performances from all of your players!

APPENDIX A – WCOFF
Scoring

A player may score from any position on the field in the following manner with one exception. A player returning a kickoff, unblocked field goal attempt, or punt for a TD will not be awarded an individual score. That score will only count for the Defense/Special Teams.

a. Passing:

Yards passing divided by 20 (e.g. 215 passing yards = 10.75 fantasy points).

4 points for every passing TD.
Minus one point (-1) for every interception thrown.
2 points for every 2-point conversion.

b. Rushing:

Yards rushing divided by 10 (e.g. 89 rushing yards = 8.9 fantasy points).

6 points for every rushing TD.
2 points for every 2-point conversion.

c. Receiving:

Yards receiving divided by 10 (e.g. 112 receiving yards = 11.2 fantasy points)

6 points for every receiving TD.
1 point for every catch.
2 points for every 2-point conversion.

d. Placekicking:

1 point for every Extra Point
3 points for every FG of 1 – 39 yards
4 points for every FG of 40 – 49 yards
5 points for every FG of 50+ yards

e. Team Scoring (Defense/Special Teams):

1 point for every sack
2 points for every takeaway (interception or fumble recovery)
6 points for every TD (via interception return, fumble return, punt or kickoff return, blocked FG return, missed FG return, blocked punt return)*
2 points for every safety
5 points for every shutout **
2 points for allowing between 1- 5 points **
1 point for allowing between 6 – 10 points **

* TDs scored on "fake" FGs or "fake" punts do NOT count as Defense/Special Teams scoring. TDs scored by the offensive team after a blocked FG or blocked punt does NOT count as a Defense/Special teams score.

** Any and all points scored against a team are considered points scored against the special teams and defense. For example, a turnover by the offense that is returned for a TD is considered as points scored against the special teams and defense.

APPENDIX B – STANDARD DEVIATION CALCULATIONS

Special Note: I refer to the following results as "standard deviations" even though the processes are not exactly text book. For instance, standard deviation formulas require a sample mean, or "central point," whereas I use NFL's actual results instead.

Here are the terms and formulas used:

Deviation (D) = Projection – Actual Result
Deviation Squared = D^2
Sum of Squared Deviations = $\sum (D^2)$ (i.e., you add up all the deviations squared)
Number of Observations = N (In this case, N = 69 because that the # of RBs observed)
Variance = $\sum (D^2) / (N-1)$

Standard Deviation = Square Root of Variance

Here are the calculations and results based on the data given in Figure 2 (Chapter Three):....see next page.

CALCULATIONS AND RESULTS BASED ON FIGURE 2

	DEVIATION (AVT - ACTUAL)	AVT D^2	DEVIATION (EXPERT 1 - ACTUAL)	EXPERT 1 D^2	DEVIATION (EXPERT 2 - ACTUAL)	EXPERT 2 D^2
RB1	-6	30.99	-33	1089.00	-70	4844.16
RB2	-69	4703.67	-39	1524.90	-81	6540.77
RB3	-48	2339.33	-18	324.00	-57	3271.84
RB4	-11	124.69	37	1361.61	-3	8.12
RB5	-17	293.55	31	979.69	-5	20.25
RB6	-9	79.80	40	1560.25	8	59.29
RB7	-10	104.72	39	1521.00	11	112.36
RB8	9	82.20	58	3340.84	30	906.01
RB9	-7	44.44	57	3214.89	29	822.72
RB10	-4	17.36	59	3469.21	33	1108.89
RB11	5	27.74	73	5372.89	40	1635.39
RB12	2	3.87	73	5343.61	44	1900.96
RB13	4	19.07	69	4705.96	43	1861.92
RB14	13	166.41	58	3340.84	38	1455.42
RB15	15	237.16	42	1738.89	35	1207.56
RB16	9	78.03	29	852.64	29	864.36
RB17	5	22.09	27	739.84	14	199.09
RB18	11	113.07	37	1369.00	23	515.29
RB19	7	42.25	28	778.41	23	549.90
RB20	16	253.87	39	1482.25	32	992.88
RB21	20	389.40	47	2180.89	43	1823.29
RB22	23	510.76	53	2819.61	42	1778.73
RB23	28	770.99	57	3203.56	43	1825.00
RB24	22	488.41	43	1866.24	45	2061.16
RB25	11	120.27	36	1324.96	36	1288.81
RB26	7	43.56	36	1303.21	26	670.81
RB27	4	20.25	33	1069.29	23	549.90
RB28	-4	16.00	34	1122.25	24	591.46
RB29	-5	24.34	20	408.04	30	924.16
RB30	-5	24.01	16	252.81	30	902.40
RB31	-6	36.40	17	289.00	31	976.56
RB32	-8	68.89	11	123.21	18	322.20
RB33	-10	100.00	-6	32.49	4	18.49
RB34	2	4.69	10	90.25	-2	2.89
RB35	-7	44.67	9	73.96	-6	38.44
RB36	-6	32.11	14	187.69	-4	12.25
RB37	-3	10.24	15	234.09	-7	54.46
RB38	-3	6.59	19	368.64	-5	23.23
RB39	-4	19.65	12	148.84	-10	98.01

CALCULATIONS AND RESULTS BASED ON FIGURE 2

	DEVIATION (AVT - ACTUAL)	AVT	DEVIATION (EXPERT 1 - ACTUAL)	EXPERT 1 D^2	DEVIATION (EXPERT 2 - ACTUAL)	EXPERT 2 D^2
RB40	-6	38.03	9	82.81	-19	349.69
RB41	-3	7.47	17	275.56	-15	238.70
RB42	-3	6.76	-5	21.16	-16	254.72
RB43	-4	19.36	-4	13.69	-16	249.64
RB44	-2	4.27	-4	14.44	-13	176.89
RB45	2	4.99	3	8.41	-13	170.56
RB46	4	16.81	6	33.64	-12	155.50
RB47	5	27.74	8	70.56	-13	172.92
RB48	3	6.59	6	40.96	-11	127.69
RB49	4	19.95	6	37.21	-9	83.72
RB50	4	13.08	-2	3.61	-11	125.44
RB51	3	6.59	-2	2.89	-10	100.40
RB52	1	1.87	-8	64.00	-11	128.37
RB53	1	0.75	-10	100.00	-16	245.86
RB54	0	0.03	-15	219.04	-18	320.41
RB55	-1	1.96	-14	204.49	-18	334.89
RB56	-2	4.00	-15	231.04	-17	298.25
RB57	-3	6.85	-18	334.89	-17	286.96
RB58	-2	4.84	-18	331.24	-16	257.92
RB59	-4	15.08	-23	519.84	-17	273.90
RB60	-4	18.92	-21	443.10	-15	231.04
RB61	-6	40.96	-26	670.81	-15	222.01
RB62	-7	54.76	-25	640.09	-14	205.92
RB63	-8	66.69	-26	686.44	-14	208.51
RB64	-8	69.44	-32	1030.41	-15	223.50
RB65	-9	84.64	-34	1142.44	-15	225.00
RB66	-10	109.55	-38	1428.84	-15	231.04
RB67	-11	124.69	-38	1474.56	-15	225.00
RB68	-10	108.85	-42	1789.29	-16	252.17
RB69	-12	139.24	-43	1874.89	-16	259.21
	$\sum (D2)=$	12540.33		74999.11		49475.33
	VARIANCE=	184.42		1102.93		727.58
	STANDARD DEVIATION =	13.58 (AVT)		33.21 (Expert1)		26.97 (Expert2)

APPENDIX C - COIN FLIPPING RESULTS

APPENDIX C - COIN FLIPPING RESULTS								
FLIP #	HEADS	% HEADS						
1	Y	100%	34	Y	53%	67	Y	54%
2	N	50%	35	Y	54%	68	N	53%
3	N	33%	36	N	53%	69	N	52%
4	Y	50%	37	Y	54%	70	N	51%
5	N	40%	38	N	53%	71	N	51%
6	Y	50%	39	Y	54%	72	N	50%
7	Y	57%	40	N	53%	73	Y	51%
8	Y	63%	41	Y	54%	74	Y	51%
9	N	56%	42	N	52%	75	Y	52%
10	N	50%	43	N	51%	76	N	51%
11	N	45%	44	Y	52%	77	N	51%
12	Y	50%	45	N	51%	78	N	50%
13	N	46%	46	N	50%	79	Y	51%
14	N	43%	47	Y	51%	80	Y	51%
15	Y	47%	48	N	50%	81	N	51%
16	N	44%	49	Y	51%	82	N	50%
17	Y	47%	50	Y	52%	83	N	49%
18	N	44%	51	Y	53%	84	Y	50%
19	Y	47%	52	N	52%	85	N	49%
20	Y	50%	53	Y	53%	86	Y	50%
21	N	48%	54	Y	54%	87	Y	51%
22	N	45%	55	Y	55%	88	N	50%
23	Y	48%	56	Y	55%	89	Y	51%
24	N	46%	57	N	54%	90	N	50%
25	Y	48%	58	Y	55%	91	Y	51%
26	N	46%	59	Y	55%	92	N	50%
27	N	44%	60	N	55%	93	N	49%
28	Y	46%	61	N	54%	94	N	49%
29	Y	48%	62	Y	55%	95	N	48%
30	Y	50%	63	N	54%	96	Y	49%
31	Y	52%	64	Y	55%	97	N	48%
32	N	50%	65	N	54%	98	Y	49%
33	Y	52%	66	N	53%	99	N	48%
						100	N	48%

APPENDIX D – Zarzycki's WCOFF Player Rankings

	QB	WR	RB	TE	K	D/ST
1	K. Warner	M. Faulk	R. Moss	T. Gonzalez	M. Vanderjagt	CHI
2	D. Culpepper	A. Green	T. Owens	M. Pollard	J. Elam	PHI
3	J. Garcia	S. Alexander	M. Harrison	F. Jones	J. Wilkins	StL
4	D. McNabb	P. Holmes	D. Boston	B. Chamberlain	R. Longwell	PIT
5	P. Manning	R. Williams	T. Holt	B. Franks	M. Gramatica	GB
6	A. Brooks	L. Tomlinson	J. Horn	S. Sharpe	D. Akers	NE
7	R. Gannon	E. James	R. Smith	J. Shockey	S. Janikowski	TB
8	B. Griese	C. Martin	E. Moulds	T. Heap	A. Vinatieri	CLE
9	B. Favre	A. Thomas	T. Brown	F. Wycheck	O. Mare	MIA
10	T. Green	D. McAllister	J. Smith	C. Lewis	J. Carney	DAL
11	S. McNair	E. George	Key. Johnson	E. Johnson	T. Peterson	WAS
12	K. Stewart	C. Dillon	P. Burress	W. Walls	P. Edinger	SF
13	D. Bledsoe	T. Barber	I. Bruce	D. Sloan	M. Andersen	NYJ
14	M. Vick	S. Davis	A. Toomer	A. Becht	J. Feely	SD
15	J. Plummer	F. Taylor	D. Jackson	J. Riemersma	J. Nedney	NO
16	V. Testaverde	D. Staley	D. Mason			
17	B. Johnson	J. Lewis	L. Coles			
18	M. Brunell	C. Garner	R. Gardner			
19	J. Fiedler	M. Bennett	M. Booker			
20	K. Collins	W. Dunn	Tr. Brown			
21		T. Jones	M. Muhammad			
22		G. Hearst	C. Chambers			
23		J. Stewart	J. Morton			
24		T. Henry	Kev. Johnson			
25		A. Smith	E. McCaffrey			
26		L. Smith	P. Warrick			
27		W. Green	P. Price			
28		K. Barlow	K. Robinson			
29		M. Pittman	C. Conway			
30		J. Bettis	T. Glenn			
31		M. Alstott	J.J. Stokes			
32		J. White	K. Dyson			
33		C. Portis	T. Taylor			
34		L. Centers	J. Thrash			
35		T. Duckett	K. McCardell			
36		O. Gary	J. Galloway			
37		E. Smith	B. Finneran			
38		J. Wells	J. Rice			
39		T. Canidate	B. Shaw			
40		A. Zereoue	Q. Morgan			
41		T. Richardson	B. Stokley			
42		J. Allen	D. Alexander			

**APPENDIX D:
ZARZYCKI'S 2002 WCOFF
PLAYER RANKINGS**

	QB	WR	RB	TE	K	D/ST
1	D. Culpepper	L. Tomlinson	M. Harrison	T. Heap	D. Akers	TB
2	D. McNabb	M. Faulk	R. Moss	J. Shockey	J. Elam	PHI
3	P. Manning	P. Holmes	T. Owens	T. Gonzalez	M. Gramatica	CAR
4	R. Gannon	C. Portis	E. Moulds	R. McMichael	J. Feely	MIA
5	A. Brooks	R. Williams	J. Horn	S. Sharpe	S. Janikowski	BAL
6	K. Warner	E. James	T. Holt	F. Jones	M. Vanderjagt	ATL
7	B. Favre	T. Henry	H. Ward	B. Miller	A. Vinatieri	PIT
8	S. McNair	D. McAllister	P. Burress	A. Crumpler	J. Carney	TEN
9	M. Hasselbeck	S. Alexander	A. Toomer	B. Franks	R. Longwell	OAK
10	T. Green	A. Green	M. Booker	M. Pollard	O. Mare	NO
11	T. Brady	F. Taylor	L. Coles	D. Jolley	M. Andersen	GB
12	J. Garcia	T. Barber	K. Robinson	De. Clark	J. Wilkins	KC
13	D. Bledsoe	C. Garner	D. Mason	S. Alexander	J. Reed	SD
14	P. Ramsey	J. Lewis	T. Brown	K. Brady	J. Brown	CHI
15	J. Plummer	C. Dillon	C. Johnson	C. Lewis	J. Nedney	NE
16		C. Martin	K. Johnson			
17		W. Green	J. Rice			
18		S. Davis	D. Driver			
19		A. Zereoue	D. Boston			
20		E. George	P. Price			
21		T. Canidate	R. Gardner			
22		W. Dunn	Q. Morgan			
23		S. Mack	I. Bruce			
24		T. Hambrick	D. Stallworth			
25		K. Barlow	T. Taylor			
26		M. Alstott	R. Smith			
27		G. Hearst	T. Pinkston			
28		A. Smith	C. Conway			
29		O. Smith	J. Porter			
30		O. Gary	D. Jackson			
31		C. Buckhalter	J. Smith			
32		D. Staley	A. Lelie			
33		A. Thomas	C. Chambers			
34		E. Smith	M. Muhammad			
35		M. Williams	R. Wayne			
36		K. Faulk	J. Thrash			
37		M. Shipp	C. Rogers			
38		T.J. Duckett	I. Hilliard			
39		C. Schlesinger	A. Johnson			
40		J. Bettis	J. Morton			
41		M. Pittman	J. Galloway			
42		L. Gordon	T. Streets			

APPENDIX D:
ZARZYCKI'S 2003 WCOFF PLAYER RANKINGS

	QB	WR	RB	TE	K	D/ST
1	D. Culpepper	L. Tomlinson	M. Harrison	T. Gonzalez	M. Vanderjagt	NE
2	P. Manning	P. Holmes	R. Moss	T. Heap	J. Elam	BAL
3	D. McNabb	D. McAllister	T. Holt	K. Winslow Jr.	A. Vinatieri	CAR
4	M. Hasselbeck	A. Green	T. Owens	J. Shockey	D. Akers	TB
5	S. McNair	E. James	C. Johnson	A. Crumpler	J. Wilkins	PHI
6	T. Green	S. Alexander	H. Ward	R. McMichael	J. Brown	StL
7	T. Brady	C. Portis	D. Mason	F. Jones	M. Stover	MIA
8	A. Brooks	K. Barlow	E. Moulds	De. Clark	R. Longwell	ATL
9	M. Vick	F. Taylor	S. Smith	D. Graham	M. Andersen	KC
10	C. Pennington	D. Davis	A. Johnson	J. Witten	J. Nedney	GB
11	M. Bulger	B. Westbrook	C. Chambers	A. Gates	J. Carney	TEN
12	J. Garcia	J. Lewis	D. Jackson	B. Williams	L. Tynes	MIN
13	B. Favre	T. Jones	J. Smith	J. Kleinsasser	J. Kasay	DAL
14	J. Welcome	M. Faulk	L. Coles	Da. Clark	J. Feely	SEA
15	D. Carr	T. Barber	J. Horn	E. Kinney	S. Janikowski	PIT
16		T. Henry	S. Moss			
17		D. Staley	C. Rogers			
18		R. Johnson	K. Robinson			
19		C. Brown	J. Porter			
20		C. Dillon	P. Price			
21		C. Martin	A. Toomer			
22		M. Bennett	L. Fitzgerald			
23		Q. Griffin	R. Smith			
24		L. Gordon	J. Walker			
25		S. Davis	P. Burress			
26		W. Dunn	J. McCareins			
27		L. Suggs	I. Bruce			
28		K. Jones	D. Branch			
29		M. Williams	B. Lloyd			
30		C. Garner	K. Johnson			
31		S. Jackson	R. Wayne			
32		T. Wheatley	E. Parker			
33		J. Jones	E. Kennison			
34		R. Anderson	J. Galloway			
35		T. Duckett	D. Stallworth			
36		T. Minor	K. Johnson			
37		D. Foster	D. Driver			
38		K. Faulk	D. Bennett			
39		W. McGahee	R. Gardner			
40		G. Hearst	A. Davis			
41		S. Morris	J. Rice			
42		J. Bettis	M. Muhammad			

APPENDIX D:
ZARZYCKI'S 2004 WCOFF
PLAYER RANKINGS

APPENDIX E – WCOFF
SEASON-ENDING RANKINGS

Note: Players listed in bold are the sleepers. The number in parentheses is the total number of places that sleeper moved up within the top ranked positions.

APPENDIX E: WCOFF 2002 SEASON ENDING RANKINGS
NOTE: PLAYERS LISTED IN BOLD ARE THE SLEEPERS. THE NUMBER IN PARENTHASES IS THE TOTAL NUMBER OF PLACES THAT SLEEPER MOVED UP WITHIN THE TOP RANKED POSITIONS

	QB	RB	WR	TE	K	D/ST
1	R. Gannon	P. Holmes	M. Harrison	T. Gonzalez	D. Akers	TB
2	D. Culpepper	L. Tomlinson	T. Owens	T. Heap	J. Feely (11)	GB
3	P. Manning	R. Williams	H. Ward (40)	J. Shockey	J. Carney	Phi
4	M. Vick (9)	C. Garner	R. Moss	S. Sharpe	S. Janikowski	Atl (9)
5	A. Brooks	S. Alexander	E. Moulds	B. Franks	P. Longwell	NO (8)
6	T. Green	D. McAllister	P. Price	B. Miller (7)	M. Gramatica	Oak (7)
7	S. McNair	T. Barber	A. Toomer	M. Pollard	M. Hollis (6)	Car (6)
8	J. Garcia	T. Henry	J. Horn	K. Brady (5)	O. Mare	NE
9	D. Bledsoe (4)	C. Portis (22)	J. Rice	R. McMichael (4)	J. Elam	Pit
10	T. Brady (3)	M. Faulk	M. Booker	A. Crumpler (3)	P. Edinger	Bal (3)
11	B. Favre	A. Green	P. Burress	C. Lewis	A. Vinatieri	KC (2)
12	D. McNabb	F. Taylor	D. Driver (31)	C. Fauria (1)	M. Andersen (1)	Mia
13		J. Lewis	L. Coles			
14		D. Staley	T. Holt			
15		E. George	J. Smith			
16		C. Dillon	I. Bruce			
17		W. Dunn	F. Robinson			
18		G. Hearst	D. Mason			
19		M. Bennett	Key. Johnson			
20		C. Martin	R. Gardner			
21		J. Stewart	R. Smith			
22		M. Shipp (9)	C. Johnson (21)			
23		E. James	Q. Morgan			
24		A. Smith	J. Galloway			
25		J. White (6)	C. Conway			
26		M. Pittman	Tr. Brown			
27		S. Davis	T. Taylor			
28		M. Williams (3)	Tim Brown			
29		L. Smith	T. Pinkston (14)			
30		E. Smith (1)	J. Porter (13)			
31			J. Thrash			
32			D. Patten (11)			
33			K. McCardell			
34			B. Finneran			
35			E. Kennison (8)			
36			W. Chrebel (7)			
37			E. McCaffrey			
38			T. Streets (5)			
39			Kev. Johnson			
40			D. Thompson (3)			
41			A. Bryant (2)			
42			D. Stallworth (1)			
SMU	16	41	156	20	18	35
TRP	12	30	42	12	12	12
SMU/ TRP	1.33	1.37	3.71	1.67	1.50	2.92

APPENDIX E: WCOFF 2003 SEASON ENDING RANKINGS

	QB	RB	WR	TE	K	D/ST
1	D. Culpepper	P. Holmes	R. Moss	T. Gonzalez	J. Wilkins	NE (12)
2	P. Manning	L. Tomlinson	T. Holt	S. Sharpe	M. Vanderjagt	StL (11)
3	T. Green	A. Green	A. Boldin (40)	T. Heap	M. Stover (10)	Bal
4	S. McNair	D. McAllister	C. Johnson	F. Jones	J. Elam	KC
5	M. Hasselbeck	J. Lewis	M. Harrison	R. McMichael	J. Kasay (8)	Mia
6	M. Bulger (7)	C. Portis	H. Ward	J. Shockey	R. Longwell	TB
7	A. Brooks	S. Alexander	K. McCardell (36)	A. Crumpler	G. Anderson (6)	Ten
8	B. Johnson (5)	F. Taylor	D. Mason	I. Mili (5)	D. Akers	Min (5)
9	B. Favre	R. Williams	T. Owens	B. Williams (4)	P. Edinger (4)	SF (4)
10	J. Kitna (3)	T. Barber	S. Smith (33)	J. Kleinsasser (3)	J. Brown (3)	Atl
11	J. Garcia	M. Williams (20)	S. Moss (32)	M. Pollard	J. Hall (2)	Sea (2)
12	T. Brady	E. James	J. Horn	D. Graham (1)	S. Graham (1)	Det (1)
13		T. Henry	L. Coles			
14		S. Davis	D. Jackson			
15		M. Pittman (16)	P. Warrick (28)			
16		M. Faulk	I. Bruce			
17		D. Davis (14)	C. Chambers			
18		K. Barlow	R. Smith			
19		C. Martin	D. Boston			
20		B.Westbrook (11)	R. Wayne			
21		C. Garner	A. Toomer			
22		R. Johnson (9)	A. Johnson			
23		S. Bryson (8)	J. McCareins (20)			
24		E. George	P. burress			
25		K. Faulk (6)	E. Kennison(18)			
26		R. Anderson (5)	K. Robinson			
27		D. Staley	J. Walker (16)			
28		T. Hambrick	I. Hilliard			
29		T. Duckett (2)	J. Rice			
30		G. Hearst	R. Gardner			
31			T. Glenn (12)			
32			B. Shaw (11)			
33			J. Smith			
34			D. Northcutt (9)			
35			P. Price			
36			T. Streets (7)			
37			B. Engram (6)			
38			D. Branch (5)			
39			J. Morton			
40			M. Muhammad			
41			Kev. Johnson (2)			
42			E. Moulds			
SMU	15	91	275	13	34	35
TRP	12	30	42	12	12	12
SMU/TRP	1.25	3.03	6.55	1.08	2.83	2.92

APPENDIX E: WCOFF 2004 SEASON ENDING RANKINGS

	QB	RB	WR	TE	K	D/ST
1	P. Manning	L. Tomlinson	M. Muhammad	A. Gates	A. Vinatieri	Buf (12)
2	D. Culpepper	T. Barber	J. Horn	T. Gonzalez	D. Akers	Bal
3	D. McNabb	S. Alexander	J. Walker	J. Witten	J. Elam	Ind (10)
4	T. Green	E. James	T. Owens	R. McMichael	S. Graham (9)	NE
5	B. Favre (8)	D. Davis	M. Harrison	E. Johnson (8)	R. Longwell	Chi (8)
6	J. Plummer (7)	C. Martin	C. Johnson	J. Shockey	M. Vanderjagt	Atl
7	J. Delhomme (6)	B. Westbrook	D. Bennett	A. Crumpler	N. Kaeding (6)	TB
8	A. Brooks	C. Dillon	T. Holt	J. Wiggins (5)	M. Stover	Pit (5)
9	D. Brees (4)	C. Portis	D. Driver	D. Graham	J. Reed (4)	Car
10	T. Brady	A. Green	R. Wayne	B. Franks (3)	J. Brown	Sea (3)
11	M. Bulger	M. Pittman (20)	D. Mason	L.J. Smith (2)	S. Janikowski (2)	Det (2)
12	M. Vick	R. Droughns (19)	D. Jackson	M. Pollard (1)	R. Lindell (1)	Cin (1)
13		R. Johnson	B. Stokley (30)			
14		F. Taylor	I. Bruce			
15		T. Jones	M. Clayton (28)			
16		W. McGahee (15)	A. Johnson			
17		W. Dunn	P. Smith			
18		D. McAllister	J. Smith			
19		N. Goings (12)	N. Burleson (24)			
20		J. Bettis (11)	E. Moulds			
21		M. Faulk	J. Porter			
22		K. Jones	E. Kennison			
23		C. Brown	H. Ward			
24		E. Smith (7)	Key. Johnson			
25		K. Barlow	A. Lelie (18)			
26		D. Blaylock (5)	R. Moss			
27		O. Smith (4)	C. Chambers			
28		J. Lewis	L. Evans (15)			
29		L. Johnson (2)	L. Coles			
30		C. Taylor (1)	T.J. (13) Houshmandzadeh			
31			L. Fitzgerald			
32			R. Williams (11)			
33			D. Patten (10)			
34			D. Stallworth			
35			J. Morton (8)			
36			D. Givens (7)			
37			S. Moss			
38			K. Colbert (5)			
39			A. Bryant (4)			
40			M. Robinson (3)			
41			E. Parker			
42			R. Gardner			
SMU	25	96	176	19	22	41
TRP	12	30	42	12	12	12
SMU/ TRP	2.08	3.20	4.19	1.58	1.83	3.42

APPENDIX F – DETERMINING R VALUES WHEN YOU DRAFT FIRST OR LAST

If you are the first or last manager to draft in the first round of the draft then you'll discover a very unusual thing: every other round's worth or P values will be "zeroed out." For example, if you have the first overall pick in the draft, then you will end up logging zeros for all P values in each of the even-numbered rounds. Your log of P values would look something like this:

Round	P(QB)	P(RB)	P(WR)	P(TE)
1	2	12	5	0
2	0	0	0	0
3	4	6	8	1
4	0	0	0	0
5	2	4	12	1
6	0	0	0	0
7	5	4	6	3
8	0	0	0	0
9	3	4	4	2
10	0	0	0	0
11	2	3	3	2

As you can see, each set of P values in each even round is laden with zeros. This happens as a result of having two consecutive picks at the end of every even-numbered round, which is due to the nature of the serpentine draft. The first of the two picks doesn't have a group of players being drafted afterwards as the second pick is made immediately thereafter. As a result, there are no P values to accumulate.

If you are the last manager to pick in the first round of the draft, such as drafting 12th in a 12-team league, you'll find similar results except this time all the odd-numbered rounds will be filled with zeros for P values. Both situations, whether you have odd rounds or even rounds filled with zeros, can be treated similarly.

First, let me say that when drafting in those rounds that don't have all zeros, such as the odd rounds shown in the chart listed above, you can follow the normal formula of the R value being the sum of the position's P values in the next Nth number of rounds.

For example, in the first round of the draft you would determine the following set of R values assuming $N(QB) = 1$, $N(RB) = 4$, $N(WR) = 5$, and $N(TE) = 1$:

$R(QB) = 2$.
$R(RB) = 12 + 0 + 6 + 0 = 18$.
$R(WR) = 5 + 0 + 8 + 0 + 12 = 25$.
$R(TE) = 0$.
It's when drafting in those rounds that have all zeros for P values do I recommend a different approach. Suppose you were making your second round selection. If you followed the traditional formula you would end up with the following set of R values (assuming the same set of N values as above):

$R(QB) = 0$.
$R(RB) = 0 + 6 + 0 + 4 = 10$.
$R(WR) = 0 + 8 + 0 + 12 + 0 = 20$.
$R(TE) = 0$.
However, since the current round doesn't have any P values, I recommend treating the situation as if it's the next round. For instance, even though it's the second round I recommend you treat the situation as if it's the third round. Therefore, you would end up with the following set of R values:

$R(QB) = 4$.
$R(RB) = 6 + 0 + 4 + 0 = 10$.

R(WR) = 8 + 0 + 12 + 0 + 6 = 26.
R(TE) = 1.
An explanation why…

I'm sure many of you will be wondering why I recommend this adjustment. When you draft two consecutive times, you are essentially looking at the same situation for both picks. In other words, your opponents have done nothing after you made your first pick so you are basically in the same situation with the second pick. Owing to this, I prefer to treat both picks in the same manner. Thus, I'll determine the set of R values of the first pick the same way I would determine them for the second pick.

APPENDIX G – FANTASY FOOTBALL GLOSSARY

100 PICK METHOD

A value-based drafting application that depends on the first 100 players likely to be drafted.

ADD/DROP

To pick-up a new player for your roster and release another player to free agency.

ADP

Average Draft Position.

APP

Application, or a system to be applied.

AUCTION LEAGUE

A league in which managers acquire players by bidding on them like an auction.

AVERAGE DRAFT POSITION

Indicates when a player is likely to be drafted. For instance, 5.02 means a player is likely to be drafted in the fifth round with the second pick.

AVERAGE STARTER METHOD

A value-based drafting application that determines its baselines by taking the average projection of all the starters in the fantasy league.

AVERAGE VALUE THEORY

A statistical method that projects fantasy points solely according to historical results.

AVT

Average Value Theory

BASELINE

The reference point at which players in a position are compared in order to determine their values.

BASELINE PLAYER

Specific player chosen to determine a position's baseline. The baseline player's projection is used as the baseline.

BASELINE RANKING

Baseline ranking, also known as "R value" or simply "R," refers to the number of players to count down on the cheat sheet in order to find the baseline player.

BASIC SCORING

A scoring system that awards fantasy points solely for touchdowns.

BENCH EQUATION

Formula used to adjust R Values based on the number of games a player in a position is expected to miss each season.

BENCH PLAYER

Anyone who is not inserted in your fantasy starting line-up. Bench players do not reward your team with fantasy points no matter how well they perform in the NFL.

BLIND BIDDING

Waiver wire system that allows managers to bid for free agents. The term "blind" comes from the fact that managers must make their bids without any knowledge of what the other managers are doing.

BUST
A top-ranked fantasy player who performs significantly worse than expected.

BYE WEEK
The one week each NFL team doesn't have to play a game during the regular season.

CHEAT SHEET
Paper or spreadsheet containing at least player rankings and projections. The most important tool used on draft day.

CLOCK MANAGEMENT
The art of using time wisely during the draft.

CO-MANAGER
A second person who shares the responsibilities of managing and/or financing a fantasy team.

COMMISH
See commissioner.

COMMISSIONER
The person responsible for creating and governing the fantasy football league.

COMMISSIONER SERVICE
Online service that keeps track of all activities within a fantasy league such as team rosters, trades, add/drops, and fantasy scores to keeping track of team rosters to keeping track of each team's scores.

CONTINUOUS LEAGUE

A league that allows managers to keep players on their rosters from year to year.

CORE POSITIONS

The main fantasy positions that winning fantasy squads are built around, such as the QB, RB, WR, and TE positions.

D/ST

Defense/Special Teams. A single fantasy position that is comprised of a bunch of defensive and special teams' players on an NFL team.

DEEP

Having plenty of serviceable players.

DEFENSE/SPECIAL TEAMS

A single fantasy position that is comprised of a bunch of defensive and special teams' players on an NFL team.

DEFENSIVE BACK (DB)

A fast defensive NFL player who plays as either a cornerback or safety in what is known as the *secondary*. DB is a fantasy position in Individual Defensive Player (IDP) leagues only.

DEFENSIVE LINEMAN (DL)

A big defensive NFL player who positions himself on the line of scrimmage. DL is a fantasy position in Individual Defensive Player (IDP) leagues only.

DEPTH CHART

An official NFL chart that ranks players per position per NFL team. This list typically reveals who's starting in the NFL and who would be next to start should a starter get injured.

DRAFTING MAP

A round-by-round list of drafting tools and strategies to be followed for drafting players.

DRAFT FACILITATOR

Person(s) in charge of supervising the draft and keeping track of official team rosters.

DRAFT POSITION

The place a manager is given within a certain order to pick players during the draft.

DRAFT SLOT

See draft position.

DRAFT TRACKER

A chart that keeps a log on what positions and/or players are drafted by each team.

DURABLE DRAFT SYSTEM

A complete system that offers enough tools and strategies so players can properly be selected in every round of the draft.

DYNAMIC BASELINE

A VBD reference point that is free to move up and down as the draft proceeds.

DYNASTY LEAGUE

A continuous league that allows managers to keep all or most players from year to year.

FANTASY FOOTBALL PRO FORECAST

One of the industry's leading fantasy football magazines.

FANTASY FOOTBALLER
One who plays fantasy football.

FANTASY POINTS
The unit used to keep track of fantasy scores in order to determine who wins and loses.

FANTASY SCORING
Set of rules that determine how many fantasy points are awarded for players achieving certain NFL statistics.

FILL-IN PLAYER
Player who temporarily takes over the starting role when another fantasy player is on a bye week or is injured/suspended.

FIRST COME FIRST SERVE
Waiver wire system that allows a free agent to be picked up by the first manager who attempts to do so.

FLEX LEAGUE
League that allows managers to start one or more flex players.

FLEX POSITION
See flex player.

FLEX PLAYER
A fantasy position that allows multiple NFL positions. The most common flex player is denoted as "RB/WR/TE" which means managers can play their choice of a running back (RB), wide receiver (WR), or tight end (TE).

FLEX STARTER
See flex player.

FREE AGENT

A player who is not on a fantasy roster and is available for any manager to pick up.

FREE AGENCY

A market where managers can acquire and release players (known as free agents). Acquisitions depend on certain rules known as waiver wire systems.

FULLBACK

A running position in the NFL that is used more for blocking when compared to a running back. Fullbacks are treated as running backs in most fantasy football circles.

GENERAL MANAGER

See manager.

GOOSE EGG

Zero points.

HANDCUFF

V. To take the NFL backup to your starting fantasy player.

N. The NFL backup to your starting fantasy player.

HANDCUFFER

See handcuff (N.).

IDP

Individual Defensive Player. Positions typically include linebacker (LB), defensive lineman (DL), and defensive back (DB).

IDP LEAGUE

Fantasy league that plays individual defensive players as opposed to a Defense/Special Teams (D/ST) unit.

KEEPER

See keeper player.

KEEPER LEAGUE

A continuous league that allows managers to keep a limited number of players, usually 2-4 players.

KEEPER PLAYER

Any player that is carried over from year-to-year by a manager in a continuous league.

KICKER (K)

A common offensive fantasy position. This position garners fantasy points by successfully kicking extra point attempts (also known as a PAT, or *point after a touchdown*) and field goals.

LARGE-SCALE LEAGUE

A league that involves a large number or participants.

LEAGUE HOST

See commissioner service.

LINEBACKER (LB)

A defensive NFL player who positions himself behind the defensive lineman and in front of the secondary. Linebacker (LB) is a fantasy position in Individual Defensive Player (IDP) leagues only.

LIVE DRAFT

An event that involves managers drafting players in the presence of one another.

LIVE PLAYER

A fantasy player who is still available to be drafted.

MANAGER

Person responsible for paying team costs (entry fees), drafting players, submitting weekly starting line-ups, making trades, adding/dropping players, and much more.

MAP

See drafting map.

MG VALUE

Stands for "missed games value," which is the number of games an arbitrary player is likely to miss in the upcoming season.

MOCK DRAFT

A pretend draft managers participate in to practice drafting players. Mock draft results are also important in seeing where players are being drafted.

MONEY LEAGUE

A league that charges a monetary fee to play and awards money prizes to its top finishers.

MOP UP DUTY

System used to draft kickers and defense/special teams.

MUD

See mop up duty.

N VALUE
Number of players you want to draft from a position using Zarzycki's value-based drafting (ZVBD) system.

NEWCOMERS
New players ranked on the cheat sheet as compared to previous years' rankings.

NFL
National Football League.

NFFC
National Fantasy Football Championship.

ON THE CLOCK
When time begins for a manager to draft a player.

OVERALL RANKINGS
List of player rankings that include all fantasy positions.

OWNER
See manager.

P VALUE
Expected number of players to be drafted by your opponents as used in Zarzycki's value-based drafting (ZVBD)system.

PERFORMANCE SCORING
A scoring system that awards fantasy points for touchdowns and yardage.

PLANTING
The process of finding and inserting new players into the cheat sheet.

POSITION NEEDS
Level of demand to draft players in a certain position.

POST-INJURY PROJECTION
Prediction on the number of fantasy points a player is going to score when he comes back healthy enough to play.

PRIVATE LEAGUE
League that involves participants by invite only.

PROJECTION
Prediction on the number of fantasy points a player is going to score.

PT
Playing time.

PUBLIC LEAGUE
League that invites anyone to play, as opposed to a private league.

QUARTERBACK (QB)
The NFL player who receives the ball from the center at the start of each play. The QB is usually the highest scoring offensive fantasy position because he leads all passing plays.

QUESTIONABLE
1. Term used in NFL injury reports meaning that a player has a 50 percent chance to play in the next game.

2. A high-ranked player who is prone to injury.

R VALUE
The numerical ranking of the baseline player. Also see baseline ranking.

RBBC

Running-back-by-committee. Situation that involves two or more running backs sharing the duty of running the ball.

RB/WR/TE

Denotes that the flex player can be either a running back (RB), wide receiver (WR), or tight end (TE).

RE-DRAFT LEAGUE

League that does not allow managers to carry players over from season to season. Therefore, all managers are required to redraft an entire team of players at the start of each season.

RUNNING BACK (RB)

The NFL offensive player who primarily runs with the football. Considered by many to be the most valuable fantasy position.

RV METHOD

Zarzycki's static value-based drafting system.

SERPENTINE DRAFT

A drafting order that has managers picking from lowest-to-highest draft positions in the odd rounds and highest-to-lowest draft positions in the even rounds.

SERVICEABLE PLAYER

Someone who can consistently garner at least a few fantasy points each week.

SHALLOW

Not having enough serviceable players.

SLEEPER

A low-ranked fantasy player who performs significantly better than expected.

SLOT

1. Ranking position in a depth chart.

2. See draft slot.

SMALL-SCALE LEAGUE

A league that limits itself to 16 or fewer participants.

SNAKEBACK DRAFT

See serpentine draft.

SOLID PLAYER

Someone who isn't likely to get injured and/or is likely to be a top fantasy producer.

STANDARD DRAFT

A draft where managers pick players one at a time in a certain draft order.

STARTING LINE-UP

The group of positions and players that officially score fantasy points.

STATIC BASELINE

A value-based drafting reference point that remains constant as the draft proceeds.

STOCKPILE

To draft extra players in a position.

STRAIGHT DRAFT

A drafting style that has managers picking players in the same order every round.

STUD
A top-rated player.

TIGHT END (TE)
NFL offensive player who serves as a big receiver and also a blocker. Tight ends are sometimes treated as wide receivers depending on fantasy league rules.

TRADE
To swap players and/or draft picks with another team.

VALUE-BASED DRAFTING (VBD)
A system that places values on players according to how much they outscore other players in their respective positions.

WAIVERS
See waiver wire.

WAIVER WIRE
A system that regulates and governs how managers are able to pick up free agents.

WCOFF
World Championship of Fantasy Football.

WEEDING
The process of removing players from being ranked on the cheat sheet.

WIDE RECEIVER (WR)
An NFL offensive player who uses speed and elusiveness to move down the field and catch the ball from the quarterback. WR is one of the primary offensive fantasy positions.

WIDEOUT

See wide receiver.

WORKHORSE

A player who takes most of the load or playing time (PT) from other players. Usually refers to a stud running back.

WORST STARTER METHOD

The most basic system of value-based drafting. This system determines baselines according to those who are projected to be the worst starters in the league.

WORST TO FIRST

Waiver wire system that allows managers with worse records first dibs in picking up the best available free agents.

X Number [or X Value]

Player's value as determined from a value-based drafting system.

ZVBD

Zarzycki's Value-Based Drafting System. A complex dynamic value-based drafting system that has proven itself by winning thousands of dollars in the WCOFF.

DID YOU KNOW?

Rob hangs with Annie Duke at the
2003 Aruba Poker Classic

Did you know that Rob's second passion to fantasy football is poker? (As if you couldn't tell with all the poker references throughout the book!) He specifically loves to play No Limit Texas Hold'em, and you can find him playing mostly online and occasionally brick-n-mortar at Atlantic City, NJ. Ironically, Rob started playing just two years before the debut of the World Poker Tour® and the poker craze that immediately followed. This was good timing as it took Rob two years of many losing sessions before eventually learning how to break even. Then, it took another year of breaking even before learning how to finally win. Now, Rob has won a couple of tournaments worth over $4,000, including a first place prize of over $5,000 in the $100 buy-in at the Tropicana, Atlantic City. He has also won super satellites into two World Poker Tour® events and finished in the money in the 2003 Aruba Poker Classic (a $4,000 buy-in event). If you ever see Rob in person, feel free to strike up a conversation about both poker and fantasy football; he'll love you for it!

Printed in the United States
40262LVS00003B/181-192

9 781420 859195